Your Body's Sign Language

Clues to Nutritional Well-Being

James W. McAfee, CCN

Your Body's Sign Language
Clues to Nutritional Well-Being

Published by Image Awareness Corporation

1271 High Street, Auburn, California 95603, USA

(530) 823 - 7092

phone # on p. 281

First Edition

Printed in the United States of America

Library of Congress Control Number: 2005901689

ISBN 0-9604592-1-9

NOTE TO READERS

This publication contains the opinions and ideas of its author. It is intended to provide helpful and informative material on the subjects addressed in the publication. It is sold with the understanding that the author and publisher are not engaged in rendering medical, health, or any other kind of personal professional services in the book. The reader should consult his or her medical, health or other competent professional before adopting any of the suggestions in this book or drawing inferences from it.

The author and publisher specifically disclaim all responsibility for any liability, loss, or risk, personal or otherwise, which is incurred as a consequence, directly or indirectly, of the use and application of any of the contents of this book.

Cover Design and Illustration, Book Design,
Illustration Design, Production and Composition:
Patty Arnold, Menagerie Design and Publishing

Dedication

No work such as this can possibly be the contribution of one individual. Various people make contributions to our lives and work as we permit them and as they are willing. My mother, although she was not a Catholic, was profoundly influenced by Father Keller who founded the Christopher movement. His motto was, "It is better to light one candle than to curse the darkness." From my mother I learned that we have the choice to become part of the darkness, to curse the darkness, or to make an attempt to shed light and roll back the darkness.

My best friend, Steve Hegg, died as a young man in his early college years. His gracious parents took the money he had saved for college and bestowed it upon me as a scholarship to attend graduate school. My life would not be what it is today without their gracious gift. I have often felt as if I am living two lives rather than just one.

I was intensely lonely as a young man. Art Farstad, general editor of the New King James Bible, taught me the meaning of fellowship and communion with others. He taught me that life was not meant to be lived alone, but to be shared and experienced with others.

I struggled with communication as a young person. Wetherell Johnson, founder of Bible Study Fellowship, expressed confidence in me, took me under her wing and trained me in the art of communication after others told her such a task would be wasted time.

Five people lived before my eyes their commitment to empower others with a knowledge and understanding of nutrition: Fred Alldredge, Earl Pearson, Patty Odneal, Bob Schar, and Don Lawson. Each of these spent their lives in this endeavor and touched the lives of tens of thousands of people. The world is a poorer place because they no longer walk among us.

My close friends within the International and American Associations of Clinical Nutritionists have constantly encouraged me to grow in my understanding of the meaning of sound nutrition. Space does not permit me to list all their names.

One man has been a continual inspiration regarding the significance of sound research and the need to make a contribution to humanity. Not only I, but the world owes an immense debt of gratitude to Dr. Arthur Furst, the developer of oral chemotherapy for cancer. Dr. Furst's constant encouragement and friendship will always be a special treasure. His commitment to sound nutrition is a continual inspiration.

Linda Mailen has been a constant cheerleader and encourager not only of this present work but also of many of my other endeavors. Dr. Ron and Chris Overberg have been friends and coworkers for many years. Our family owes a great debt to the ownership and staff of Golden-Neo-Life Diamite for their commitment to improving the lives of people around the globe with good nutrition and their provision of a business opportunity in the nutrition field.

There have also been those who have been intimately involved with this project. Without their help there would have been no book. Among these were

Jill Schwinn, Anne Kemp, Sarah Paulhamus, Dorothy Harelson, Marie Sparks, and Kathy Coleman. Each played an indispensable part in making this book possible. Maywan Krach deserves a special word of recognition. Not only did she help with the manner of presentation, but also provided the necessary motivation for me to work on a project which has been sitting on the back burner for a quarter century.

Finally, there are many people who have chosen to become partners with our family in making the world more aware of the importance of sound nutrition. The past three decades have been an exciting adventure of discovery due to the friendships built in this enterprise. Literally hundreds of people have placed their confidence and trust in our work, and I would be remiss to overlook expressing gratitude to them.

Table of Contents

Index of Topics

The Journey Begins

As my car rolled to a stop at the intersection I noticed there were no road signs visible. Even though there were no signs, I thought I knew where I was as I turned right and drove. As the road began to ascend into the mountains, it dawned on me that I was headed in the wrong direction. I realized that I would have to turn around and get back to the intersection where I'd made the wrong turn.

Many of us have made the wrong turn in our lives with respect to nutrition, but fortunately there are signs to tell us how to get on the right road. An overgrown bush in front of a stop sign can result in a fatal collision. A malfunctioning signal light can create chaos at a busy intersection. Just as streets have signs to guide us, so does our body, and we must learn to read these signs.

For more than 30 years I have worked in the field of nutrition and have become increasingly alarmed. I see young people with health problems that were once limited to older people. This concern is not just mine. Last year at Stanford University I had the opportunity to attend a meeting with former U.S. Surgeon General, Jocelyn Elders. She shared the same concern as I do for the epidemic of obesity and diabetes (including the adult onset form) among young people in the United States.

Health problems are among the leading causes of financial ruin and bankruptcy. I know many people whose bank accounts have been emptied as a result of prolonged treatments for diabetes, cancer, or obesity. These diseases can be difficult to treat medically, but are oftentimes preventable with good nutritional habits. Our society has not chosen to place value on nutrition. Culturally, the subject has been neglected by both the man in the street and by our most highly regarded educational institutions. A physician friend of mine once told

Many of us have made the wrong turn in our lives with respect to nutrition, but fortunately there are signs to tell us how to get on the right road.

Health problems are among the leading causes of financial ruin and bankruptcy.

me that his only exposure to nutrition in medical school was a book by Roger Williams, entitled *Nutrition in a Nutshell*, on which he was not tested.

I see, on a daily basis, easily avoidable health problems that lead to crime and imprisonment, violence, loss of children, marital strife, and divorce. A woman, who took my suggestions on appropriate food and beverage consumption experienced elimination of her violent outbursts which she learned were caused by beer consumption. She realized that her allergic response to beer was destroying her family life.

One common denominator that I have discovered in my work is a startling lack of understanding of the relationship between food intake and the onset of physical or emotional deterioration. Today such ignorance has reached an epidemic level. Far too many people rely upon pharmaceutical companies, the insurance industry, food processors, and the government to protect them and provide for their "health care." We must each assume the responsibility for sustaining and building our own health. One fact I hope the reader will walk away with, as my clients have over the years, is that no one will ever have as much interest in your health as you do.

My Story

Let me begin with my own story. My childhood was filled with "body signs." These were indications of poor health resulting from an improper diet. My earliest memories included repeated visits to the doctor for sties and cysts. My hands became covered with warts. My feet had fungus infections. Then I developed appendicitis. (Appendicitis is one of the first diseases to appear on a low fiber diet.) One of my father's three cows was used to pay the doctor for the surgery, while a second was used to pay the hospital bill. The failure of my father's farming career was accelerated by the inadequate diet of his children.

My nickname in junior high school was "Toad" because of the excess weight I carried. I suffered with angina attacks in my early teens—shooting pains would radiate from my heart to the arm. This was a frightening and ominous sensation for a child.

Another indicator of my malnutrition was horrible muscle cramps. These would vary from twitching of the eye or the back of the hand to major cramping of the bottom of the feet or the calves. The cramping of the feet sometimes was so severe that I felt as if one of my feet would bend over double. The cramping of the calves was sometimes even worse. Riding home from

I see, on a daily basis, easily avoidable health problems that lead to crime and imprisonment, violence, loss of children, marital strife, and divorce.

One fact I hope the reader will walk away with, as my clients have over the years, is that no one will ever have as much interest in your health as you do.

school one day I was stricken by an especially painful cramp in my calf. I screamed so loud from the pain that the bus driver pulled the bus to the side of the road so he could check on me.

Only after I discovered improved nutrition did these health problems melt away like magic. My weight dropped. I went from not having enough stamina to run halfway around a track, to running and cycling for miles. There were no more chest pains or muscle cramps. It never ceases to amaze me how much abuse the body can be subjected to and then rebound to a state of restored health and a normalcy of function.

Their Stories

Not all stories like mine have a happy ending. After completing graduate school, I contacted a college classmate. He gave me an address and a time to meet him. Imagine my shock when I pulled up to the county jail. He shared with me that he had become addicted to alcohol and become involved in theft to support his drinking habit. I will never forget the parting words this young man left with me, "I realize that if I do not overcome this alcohol problem, it will destroy me." His story is not unlike many people around us whose lives have been destroyed because they cannot control their desire for alcohol, cigarettes, cookies, or soda pop.

This calls to mind another young man who came to me after a lecture. He explained that he had used heroin for almost three decades before deciding to replace it with methadone, and now he found himself unable to break the methadone habit. I shared with him the importance of good nutrition and the classic work of Dr. Alfred Libby and his colleague Irwin Stone, a well-known researcher on vitamin C. Their work proved that protein and vitamin C are helpful for heroin addicts. This young man was one of the fortunate ones who followed through and discontinued methadone with no withdrawal, and he has never looked back.

Damage from a lack of proper nutrition can become largely irreversible. In my early years of becoming aware of the importance of nutrition, I received a desperate call from a woman who was diabetic. She suffered the loss of her eyes and legs as a result of the disease. Her phone call that day was a request for vitamin C, since it stopped the bleeding of her gums. This lady continued to tell me how much she wished that she had discovered nutrition many years earlier, and that with a better understanding of nutrition she might not have

"I realize that if I do not overcome this alcohol problem, it will destroy me."

Damage from a lack of proper nutrition can become largely irreversible.

lost her eyesight or suffered the amputation of her legs. Another diabetic man facing amputation of his leg shared the same regret about not taking the disease more seriously when it was first diagnosed.

This is not to imply that all diabetic situations are hopeless. It is important to identify the problem early and take appropriate steps to control blood sugar and carbohydrate intake. I remember a man who came to me after a seminar. His eyes were deteriorating rapidly and the doctors could not seem to stop the process. I mentioned an experiment by John Douglas, M.D., which found improvements in diabetics who increased the amounts of raw foods in the diet. This diabetic took notes and made appropriate changes in his diet.

The next time I conducted a seminar in this man's hometown, I noticed him standing in the back of the lecture hall. After the meeting had begun, he strode to the front of the room and gave me a gigantic bear hug. He then turned to the audience and said, "Listen to what this man has to say. I would not have my eyesight today if it were not for him!"

Your Story

What about you?

Do you wake up refreshed in the morning or is it torture to crawl out of bed?

Are you naturally alert, or do you need to visit the coffee shop before you are ready to face a new day?

Is your thinking clear and your communication understandable to others, or do you have difficulty expressing your thoughts?

Is your mood and attitude hopeful and upbeat or are you mired in depression and hopelessness, with the feeling that the world will come to an end tomorrow if it lasts that long?

A Book Is Born

We must realize that our body does not function well without proper nutrient intake. The journey we take through life is oftentimes determined by the quality of our nutritional intake. This book was created with the hope that awareness of body signs will provide motivation to prevent the agony and suffering caused by poor nutrition. The reader is encouraged to concentrate on

The reader is encouraged to concentrate on the long-term benefits of careful and consistent maintenance of the body, and this book can get you started on the right track.

the long-term benefits of careful and consistent maintenance of the body, and this book can get you started on the right track.

The average individual spends a good deal of time maintaining an automobile, developing and managing finances, and building friendships. All of these are important; however, none is more important for our long-term welfare and the welfare of our children than sound nutrition.

We do not always make sensible food choices. Instead of nourishing our bodies, our choices are too often based upon habit and taste. We eat lowfat foods to lose weight, even though they are usually high in sugar which promotes weight gain. We give children adult size or even larger desserts despite their smaller stature. We become exhausted as a result of lack of rest and poor nutrition and then consume coffee and other stimulants to push the body even further. Coffee is a powerful nutritional antagonist. It washes B complex vitamins out of the body and causes a loss of calcium. We consume rancid fat and excessive sugar, and then seek to control heart disease with cholesterol-lowering medications and diabetes with insulin injections.

We talk about the government paying for health care when we are really talking about disease care. We spend hundreds of billions of dollars a year on disease care and virtually nothing to prevent us from becoming ill. Our approach to nutrition is inept and foolhardy. The objective of this book is to attempt to rectify this thinking and address head-on significant problems caused by poor nutrition.

This book will point out body signs associated with good as well as faulty nutrition. On the negative side, a body sign may indicate a movement in the direction of a health problem. On the positive side, a body sign may indicate proper nutritional intake due to good food choices. These body signs can be obvious and noticeable or they can go unrecognized by a trained observer. All of these body signs are closely connected to the nutrition we choose to put into our bodies.

Let's Face It

Nutrition is a very abstract concept until one finds a way to make it concrete and real. Personal body signs make nutrition come alive in meaningful ways. This book will associate body signs with medical literature supporting the reliability of the material described here.

Instead of nourishing our bodies, our choices are too often based upon habit and taste.

We spend hundreds of billions of dollars a year on disease care and virtually nothing to prevent us from becoming ill.

Nothing is more powerful in the prevention of disease than sound nutrition. Dietary and nutritional choices combined with our unique genetic makeup determine whether we will develop a health problem, delay its onset, or avoid it entirely. This book will demonstrate that nutritional choices have the ability to influence genetic predisposition to disease. In this way nutritional choices can prevent the development of health problems to which we might otherwise be predisposed.

Many of my clients at first considered nutrition a waste of time and money until they were sent costly hospital bills "or spent weeks in bed due to an illness." They failed to take into account the cost "in terms of time and money of health problems that could have been prevented by improved nutrition." Dr. Roger Williams pointed out that nutrition is rarely optimal for any plant, animal, or human. We may not have the ability to nourish ourselves optimally, but we can easily improve the quality of our nutritional intake through dietary choices.

Science has established that it is nutrition that helps us achieve total health in mind, body, and spirit. The brain is one of the most delicate and intricately balanced organs in the human body. It would be foolish for us to think that we can obtain a healthy mind by taking drugs, disregarding the nutrients and energy essential for the brain's day to day operation; or a healthy spiritual life by weighing down our body with poor nutrition.

In light of health issues caused by inadequate diet and the recent research on the landscape of nutrition, this handbook is written to help the reader identify information essential for health.

This book features body signs from top to bottom—beginning with the hair and traveling to the toes.

An "ICON LIST" comprehensively displays facts and suggestions:

Stethoscope—description of a body sign

Star—significance of the body sign

Podium—discussion of the body sign

Dinner plate and silverware—nutritional suggestions

ICON LIST

Discussions contain a list of "RELATED TOPICS" in the margin. Pay careful attention to this feature as the treatment of related subjects often provides essential insights that will clarify understanding of the topic being discussed. I have used this technique to minimize duplication of material. Each chapter ends with "Food for Thought." This section is designed to motivate you to become further involved with the material discussed in the chapter.

Unlike complicated and sometimes confusing medical journals that avoid discussion of nutritional issues, this book will boldly point out marks, signs, and symptoms caused by poor nutrition. Appropriate suggestions are made, detailed references are provided, yet this book only scratches the surface of the many ways in which malnutrition and toxic exposures can alter our lives and health.

Scientists now know that poor nutrition leaves an imprint upon our lives. It is my sincere hope that the awareness of what can happen to the quality of one's life as a result of neglecting sound nutrition will provide motivation for the reader to improve the diet and supplement where necessary or helpful.

Scientists now know that poor nutrition leaves an imprint upon our lives.

Food for Thought

How much attention do we pay to the nutrition of house pets, zoo animals, and blue-ribbon livestock compared to the attention we give to our own nutrition and that of our children? *house plants,*

In your own neighborhood do you see people happy and vibrant, or downcast and struggling? What thoughts run through your head when you glance inside someone's grocery cart or kitchen cupboards?

What price do we pay in our society for the neglect of nutrition? There is obviously a financial cost. What about the social cost? Might not faulty diet contribute to strained human relationships and a good diet promote social harmony?

Concept of Body Signs

Auburn

I live in the heart of the Gold Country only minutes from Coloma where John Marshall discovered gold in 1848. John Marshall was not sure that the yellow flakes he found in the tailrace of the saw-mill he was building for himself and John Sutter were gold. He took the flakes to Sutter, an enterprising Swiss emigrant, who owned the land under a land grant from Mexico. Sutter tested the flakes and determined that they were indeed gold.

Sutter's response was to attempt to keep the discovery a secret. He wanted to complete the saw-mill. Mrs. P. L. Wimmer, the cook at the gold discovery site, spilled the beans (to use a culinary figure of speech) regarding the gold discovery to a teamster delivering a load of provisions. This man collected some gold nuggets and used them to buy a bottle of brandy and the secret was out.

Sutter had no sense of the importance of his find, which would turn his world upside-down. Virtually all his help left to look for gold. The mill was never finished. Sutter withdrew from the gold fields and never profited from the changes taking place all around him.

A census conducted in 1847 numbered only 449 people in San Francisco. In 1850 the census bureau numbered the population of the city at almost 95,000. In May of 1850 one ship, the Panama, set sail with over $1.5 million worth of gold dust.

Body signs are like those little yellow flakes Marshall first saw in the tailrace. They are a hint that some hidden thing exists and they are a portent of things to come in the future.

Imagine two young women traveling in a station wagon. Renee, who has just attended an illustrated seminar on body signs and their significance, says to her passenger, "I'd never guess that skin tags could mean an increased risk of diabetes or blood sugar!"

Her passenger Carol replies, "I didn't know that! I go to my doctor all the time to have those ugly skin tags burned off."

Renee turns to Carol and says, "I learned that a body sign does not necessarily mean that a problem exists, but it's a warning that warrants further investigation. For example, a diabetic person is usually thirsty all the time and urinates constantly. The urine smells and actually tastes sweet."

Carol replies, "No wonder I am always thirsty and constantly urinating! I think I'd better talk about this possibility with my physician."

Incidents similar to this commonly take place as people are introduced to the messages their bodies are attempting to deliver to them. That checkup could change Carol's life. Carol could be one of millions of Americans who have signs indicating risk of diabetes that are ignored because those signs are not recognized or understood.

Virtually every health authority, including the Centers for Disease Control, has reported that the United States is experiencing an epidemic of diabetes. The number of people being treated for diabetes is only the tip of an iceberg. The number of undiagnosed cases of diabetes is about equal to the number of those who know they have the disease. A greater number of people are suffering from glucose intolerance that may lead to diabetes than the number of those who actually have the disease. [1]

Why is it so difficult, then, for the average person to realize that he or she may have or be in the process of developing a life-threatening disease? Why is it so difficult to undertake preventative measures? For many, it is easier to live in denial than to deal with the implications of a serious health problem. For others, ignorance is a result of failure to observe obvious warning indicators.

Everything has a beginning. Carol's discovery of body signs set her on a course of self-discovery. My own awareness of body signs grew out of my awareness of the importance of keen observation. When I was a graduate student, one of my professors shared the story of a young student who enrolled in a natural history course with the famous professor Louis Agassiz.

The professor pulled a haemulon, a species of fish, from a large jar, and asked the student to examine it until he returned to the classroom. In less than ten minutes, the student was done and ready to move on to the next project.

For many, it is easier to live in denial than to deal with the implications of a serious health problem.

But Agassiz had other plans. He asked the student to study the fish for eight whole months before he could move on to other studies.

At the end of eight months the student had become a trained observer who knew a great deal about fish, particularly the haemulon. This student later credited Agassiz as the source of his own ability to be a sharp-eyed scientist.[2] In the same way, this book can be used as a "Professor Agassiz" to coach the reader in the fine art of understanding his own body.

Sick People Look Sick

Many years ago I discovered Dr. Hans Selye, the famous medical doctor who developed the concept of stress. He shared an anecdote that pointed my mind toward the possibility of looking for obvious physical or behavioral clues to nutritional problems. As a second-year medical student, Hans sat in a room, watching patients being paraded in front of the class.
On the one hand, Selye was too young to be able to diagnose any patient; on the other hand, one thing did stand out to him. He couldn't help but notice that "sick people looked sick," and this observation was to change the future of his medical career.

"I cannot describe the respect and humility that I experienced in front of that great physician who could diagnose disease just by asking patients certain questions or looking for certain signs…" Selye recalled in an article published in *Human Nature*. " 'Why,' I wondered, 'did that great professor never say one word about all those manifestations of disease that even I, in my complete ignorance of medicine, could see very well?' He never mentioned that those five sick people, whatever their diseases or complaints, looked sick."

Seeing what his professor overlooked, Selye continued, "…each of these patients felt and looked ill, had a coated tongue, complained of more or less diffuse aches and pains in the joints, and of intestinal disturbances with loss of appetite. Most of them also had fever (sometimes with mental confusion), and enlarged spleen or liver, inflamed tonsils, a skin rash, and so forth. All this was quite evident, but the professor attached very little significance to any of it."[3]

Selye's remarkable perceptiveness led to the discovery of stress as a frequent precursor to and accompaniment of illness. If sickness is simply the end stage of prolonged stress, then, Selye believed, stress could be a causal factor for such conditions as arthritis, allergy, and ulcers. Selye would eventually convince the world that prolonged stress could lead to exhaustion, premature aging, and

"…each of these patients felt and looked ill, had a coated tongue, complained of more or less diffuse aches and pains in the joints, and of intestinal disturbances with loss of appetite."

undue wear and tear on the body, and that a number of different diseases would slowly but surely invade an overtaxed human body. Selye supported his observations with stunning photographs of the changes to internal organs resulting from stress.[4] It was these internal changes that cascaded into easily observable, stress-related diseases.[5]

You Are What You Eat

Some time later, I was introduced to the work of Giuseppe Arcimboldo (1530-1593), a commissioned artist for the court of Maximilian II in Prague. Arcimboldo was known for his ingenuity of forming fruits, flowers, fish, chickens and even kitchen utensils into a head-shaped painting.[6] These paintings, now permanently on display at the Palazzo Grassi in Venice, cry out to those who love fine art the powerful message that what we put into our mouth may well determine the appearance of our skin, hair or eyes. I found myself wondering, "How much can a particular kind of diet or nutritional deficiency alter how a person looks or feels?"

An illustration by Dr. Jacques May carried my thinking one step further. Dr. May likened our body's constitution to three dolls. He wrote, "It is as though I had on a table three dolls, one made of glass, another of celluloid, and a third of steel, and I chose to hit the three dolls with a hammer using equal strength. The first doll would break, the second would scar, and the third would emit a pleasant sound."[7] Our ability to cope with the stresses that come our way in life, as pictured by this hammer, is dependent upon our genetic makeup, nutritional status, and state of mind. Dr. May taught me that the ability to handle environmental assaults might reveal nutritional adequacy. Not only our appearance, but also our basic state of health when exposed to the rigors and challenges of life can be influenced by how and what we eat!

What are the components of the constitution to which Dr. May alluded? The two critical factors in the establishment of a healthy constitution are genetics and nutrition. Dr. Roger Williams, a pioneer in nutritional science, coined the phrase "genetotrophic disease" to describe the relationship between these two factors. *Genesis* is Greek for "birth" or "beginning" and *trophikos* means "feeding" or "nursing."[8] He spoke of the fact that most illnesses we see today are contributed to not only by genetics, but also by the foods we eat.

Both genetics and diet can influence how we look and how we feel. Modern man tends to emphasize genetics and minimize the role of diet when evaluating

Most illnesses we see today are contributed to not only by genetics, but also by the foods we eat.

health. This is unfortunate because we have very little control over our genetics at the present time, but a great deal of control over the food we use to nourish our bodies. As we learn more about the way in which nutrition influences genetics, the discipline of nutrition will assume increasing importance. In his book, *Genetic Nutritioneering*, Dr. Jeffrey Bland stresses that the expression of genes can be modified by what we eat.[9] This concept of "genetic expression modified by nutrition" is being increasingly accepted by the medical profession.

What's Your Body Type?

The observations of May, Williams, and Bland suggest that different groups of people might handle foods differently and be predisposed to different types of health problems. This concept has also been expressed by several individuals who have developed a concept called "body types." The term "body type" was first introduced, in the 1940s, by psychologist William H. Sheldon.[10] He was later joined by dentist Robert Peshek in similar classifications of body type.[11] Sheldon associated each body type with corresponding personality characteristics, while Robert Peshek assigned to these body types characteristics such as digestive competence and susceptibility to disease. Dr. Elliot Abravanel then attached hormonal characteristics to these body types and developed a weight loss program that attempted to address the special needs of the different body types.[12]

Different groups of people may handle foods differently and be predisposed to different types of health problems.

According to Sheldon and Peshek, there are three possible body types:

■ ENDOMORPH–They believed that these individuals with a round body and short, pudgy limbs tend to enjoy food because of a strong digestive tract. They are comfortable around others and highly interested in their lives. They tend to become ill in the fall or early in life. They can lose their hair prematurely and gain weight easily.

■ ECTOMORPH–These individuals have a lean body and frail muscle. Their brains and nervous systems are well developed. Contrary to endomorphs, these people are highly disciplined but shy. They enjoy thinking and solitude. They usually have poor health early in life and it can slowly improve as they grow older. They get sick mostly in the spring and have a hard time gaining weight.

■ MESOMORPH–Altogether different, mesomorphs have pronounced muscle and bone, especially at the shoulders. They are athletic and competitive. They focus on the present and do not withdraw from new challenges. They can gain weight easily, and lose it as rapidly.

Descriptions of these body types are only generalizations and should not be considered determinative for either personality or health. What is important is how our body can be shaped by the twin factors of genetics and the diet we consume. Body types are linked to our genetic inheritance, but diet is the primary determinant of health and longevity.

My study of body types created an awareness of the possibility that body shape could be associated with health risk factors. It also suggested that people with different types of genetic inheritance might have very different nutritional requirements. For example, we know that certain population groups (blacks and Asians) are at great risk for milk intolerance because they are much less likely than others to produce the enzyme lactase, which is necessary to digest lactose or milk sugar.

The work I have described drove me to the conclusion that people are genetically different and that these differences may result in different nutritional requirements. There was still a piece of the puzzle missing. Could dietary deficiencies be directly linked to observable changes in physical appearance and health? The classic works of dentist Weston Price and medical doctor Francis M. Pottenger, Jr., directly address this issue, suggesting that the very structure of the body can be influenced and molded prior to birth by the nutrition of a mother or after birth by the diet during early development.

Nutritional History Read in the Face

Weston A. Price, D.D.S., traveled the globe with one objective. Earnest Hooton expresses this great dentist's achievement in the foreword to his classic book, *Nutrition and Physical Degeneration*:

"Since we have known for a long time that savages have excellent teeth and that civilized men have terrible teeth, it seems to me that we have been extraordinarily stupid in concentrating all of our attention upon the task of finding out why our teeth are so poor, without ever bothering to learn why savage teeth are good....This is an exemplification of the fact that really gifted scientists are those who can appreciate the obvious."[13]

As one of the nutritional trailblazers, Price noticed a relationship between the shape of a person's face and the condition of the teeth and his nutritional behavior. He found that civilized diets resulted in terrible teeth and a

"Really gifted scientists are those who can appreciate the obvious."
Earnest A. Hooton

narrowing of the face and jaw, while primitive diets assured a wide face with ample room for teeth, and an absence of tooth decay. Tooth decay has since come to be recognized as a sign of poor nutrition. From the skeletal remains of people who lived prior to 1800 to isolated people groups of his own day who did not have access to modern foods, Price had a difficult time locating even one rotten tooth as long as he examined those who did not have access to modern foods![14] These people did not drink fluoridated water, nor did they brush their teeth. What they did was merely eat fresh, whole foods as their dietary staples.

It is disturbing to witness so many people today, especially children, suffering from crowded teeth, impaired dental arches, breathing through the mouth, and, of course, a mouth full of tooth decay.[15] Price's work suggests that there will be less and less healthy people in our midst if we continue to build the diet around foods that are designed with the twin objectives of pleasing the appetite and convenience.

Pottenger's Cats and Raw Foods

Dr. Francis M. Pottenger, Jr., carried Price's work forward one important step. Price observed that people who ate well had healthy dental structures and people who ate poorly had poor-quality bone structure and teeth. Pottenger conducted experiments in which he fed animals inadequate diets and carefully observed and documented the degenerative changes that took place.

Pottenger spent ten years studying four generations of cats. A total of 900 cats were divided into two groups. One group received totally raw foods, while the other group received the bulk of the diet in the form of some type of cooked food.

Animals on raw diets demonstrated good health throughout the experiment, but numerous health problems developed in the group that consumed heated foods. Problems ranged from simple infections to major respiratory and bone troubles. There were also profound changes in behavior, from hyperactivity among animals fed sugar to extreme aggressiveness among animals given cooked foods without sugar. None of the cats on processed foods survived into the fifth generation. Although many of the degenerative signs could be reversed over a period of several generations, improvements came slowly. Allergic tendencies were the most difficult degenerative trait to reverse.

There will be less and less healthy people in our midst if we continue to build the diet around foods that are designed with the twin objectives of pleasing the appetite and convenience.

Allergic tendencies were the most difficult degenerative trait to reverse.

An especially noteworthy feature of Pottenger's work was his careful documentation that poor diet produced readily observable changes in the appearance of his cats: among animals fed cooked foods the fur lost its sheen, nasal and sinus cavities narrowed, cats weighed less, bones declined in mineral content and became weaker, and degenerative diseases such as allergies, asthma, and arthritis were evident. Poor diet typically resulted in pronounced fatigue and lack of energy unless the diet contained sugar, which resulted in hyperactive animals.[16]

Pottenger's work, like that of Weston Price, provides a clue to the source of current health issues—a lack of quality foods and nutrients, not a lack of physicians! His work taught us that even moderately heated foods could incur sufficient damage to induce degenerative diseases and physical changes very similar to what is observed in people on modern diets. The full extent of this damage does not show up in the individuals who consume the altered foods, but rather in their offspring. Physical deterioration resulting from poor diet is a change which takes place over a prolonged period of time. The seventy-year-old who boasts that he or she ate sugar, smoked, and drank for a lifetime and never suffered any consequences might wish to look at his grandchildren, who may be suffering from allergies or other nutrition-related problems due to their grand-parent's indiscretions.

Damage does not always show up in the individuals who consume the altered foods, but rather in their offspring.

Pottenger was eloquent in his argument regarding the extent to which foods are destroyed by simple cooking: "What vital elements were destroyed in the heat processing of the foods fed to the cats? The precise factors are not known. Ordinary cooking precipitates proteins, rendering them less easily digested…All tissue enzymes are heat labile and would be materially reduced or destroyed. Vitamin C and some members of the B complex are injured by the process of cooking…Minerals are rendered less soluble by altering their physio-chemical state. It is possible that the alteration of the physiochemical state of the foods may be all that is necessary to render them imperfect foods for the maintenance of health. It is our impression that the denaturing of proteins by heat is one factor responsible."[17]

It is alarming to learn that even the simplest cooking can make it difficult for our body to utilize the vitamins, minerals, and protein from our diet. As a result of cooking, nutrients are either outright destroyed or subtly altered in their structures. This deterioration impairs the body's ability to digest and assimilate them properly and efficiently. What type of damage is done by more extensive food processing?

Doesn't it seem strange to you that the richest and wealthiest country in the world should have such a vast array of health conditions, expensive medical care, and one of the highest incidences of degenerative disease on earth? Could it be that we have allowed excessive tampering with our food supply? Foods in the United States today are altered in every conceivable way, from refining, heating, and irradiation, to genetic engineering. As consumers of these altered foods, our bodies are crying out for attention by often showing multiple signs that problems exist. Perhaps it is time for us to make an attempt to decipher what those signs are trying to say to us. Through the work of Williams, Sheldon, Price, Pottenger, and other researchers, we have a compass that can point us in the right direction, and show us what to look for.

Food for Thought

In what ways do sick people look sick? How do you look and feel when you are ill or stressed?

Name three signs of physical deterioration that you have observed in yourself.

How are foods altered today from their natural form? How are these changes harmful or helpful?

Body Shape: *The Big Picture*

Iremember it as if it were yesterday though the event took place a decade ago. I was riding a taxi from DFW airport into the city of Dallas. The Iranian driver and I carried on an interesting conversation. I was unprepared for his reply, though, when I asked him, "What do you find most striking about Americans?" Without blinking his eyes, he said, "Everyone is fat!"

This is how the rest of the world sees the population of the United States, where one finds more cases of obesity than any other nation on earth. It is common knowledge that weight provides clues to one's nutritional status, dietary habits, and risk factors for a multitude of diseases. An increase in weight, whether fast or slow, is evidenced by a change of body shape, and can lead to health concerns.

This chapter focuses on body signs associated with excessive or deficient calorie consumption, which often exists side by side with serious nutritional deficiencies. Three of the signs point to an increased risk of adult onset diabetes. This unwanted reward stems from an undisciplined life characterized by a diet that is low in fiber, and high in fats and concentrated sugars. A fourth sign, SMALL WAIST AND ALZHEIMER'S, would, at first glance, appear to be unrelated to the others; but in reality, millions of Americans are overfed, but undernourished. This sign provides a warning that poor nutrition, extended over time, whether from poverty, disease, or dieting, can damage the brain.

Beer Belly Syndrome

SIGN

Beer Belly Syndrome, also referred to as "central adiposity," is identified by a belly that is larger than the hips. Other endearing terms might be "spare tire syndrome," "dunlop's disease" (belly dun lop over the belt), or "furniture disease" (chest drops in the drawers).

SIGNIFICANCE

Weight gain about the middle is an indicator of Syndrome X, a pre-diabetic condition associated with excess insulin. The body's insulin production increases as soon as the fat cells refuse to answer the call of insulin's knock at the door. The more insulin the body creates, the more resistant the fat cells become. Eventually, the cascading effect of high insulin can damage the body overall by inducing high blood pressure, building dangerous levels of blood fats, damaging liver function, and boosting weight gain. Unhealthy weight gain puts pressure upon joints resulting in excessive wear and tear, deterioration, and back pain.

DISCUSSION

A spare tire around the middle is a clear indicator of insulin resistance.

To find out if you have central adiposity you can:

1. Measure the narrowest point of the waist.

2. Measure the widest point of the hips and buttocks.

3. Divide the waist measurement by the hip measurement. (A healthy measurement for women is less than 0.8, and less than 1.0 for men.)[1]

The body's insulin production increases as soon as the fat cells refuse to answer the call of insulin's knock at the door.

The "potbelly" is closely coupled to increased risk of heart disease and accumulation of fat in the liver. The amount of weight gain around the middle is more closely associated with abnormal measurements of liver enzymes (ALT and GGT) than the usual measure used to determine obesity (Body Mass Index or BMI). Dr. Saverio Stranges and his associates at the State University of New York at Buffalo found that the potbelly was a better predictor of abnormal liver function in both men and women than was body weight.[2]

A "potbelly" is the most common indicator of what scientists have come to call Syndrome X. Syndrome X, also known as "insulin resistance syndrome," is a metabolic disorder identified by Dr. Gerald Reaven of Stanford University. He wrote, "One way to guard against Syndrome X is to ignore the 'best' medical advice, to shun the low-fat, high-carbohydrate diet everyone 'knows' is good for the heart. If you have Syndrome X—and 60 to 75 million Americans do—that 'good' diet can be deadly."[3] The solution to this problem of insulin resistance is not reducing cholesterol, but rather keeping blood sugar stable.

The sudden popularity of low-carb diets in the United States is a tacit recognition that the "low-fat, high-carbohydrate" recommendations of the medical community in the last several decades have been a disastrous failure. That advice has generated uncontrolled weight gain among men and women and has done practically nothing to reduce the risk of heart disease. The core of this failure was the refusal to distinguish between refined and rapidly absorbed carbohydrates, which increase insulin production dramatically, and complex carbohydrates, which do not.

Diets high in sugar and refined carbohydrates will easily cause Syndrome X. First, you get elevated fats in your blood, then you get fat deposited around the middle of the body, and eventually these fats increase your chances of a stroke or heart attack. Fat around the middle can be a killer.

SUGGESTIONS

- Eat multiple, small meals.
- Exercise regularly.
- Restrict refined carbohydrates and sugars.

Obesity

SIGN

An excessive amount of body weight, generally greater than 20% above the ideal weight for height, is defined as obesity. In terms of percentage of body fat, obesity for women is over 30% and for men over 25%. It is estimated that more than one in three adults in the United States meet the criteria for being obese.[4]

SIGNIFICANCE

Obesity increases the risk of cancer and heart disease and causes tremendous wear and tear on the joints. This condition has become epidemic among young people and is considered a major contributor to today's high cost of medical care in the United States.

RELATED TOPICS

BINGING

DISCOLORATION OF THE SKIN OF THE LOWER LEG

DUPUYTREN'S CONTRACTURE

OBESITY

SKIN TAGS

UPPER BODY WEIGHT GAIN

Consuming too many calories, particularly those from rapidly absorbed carbohydrates, and engaging in too little exercise can bring most individuals to a state of obesity. In addition, low thyroid and other glandular imbalances can play a role in weight gain. Those who are obese usually prefer to skip breakfast, or eat a light breakfast, favoring large evening meals.[5] Weight gain resulting from this faulty dietary habit tends to decrease the desire and the ability to exercise.

Modern food processing also contributes to overeating. In *Fighting the Food Giants*, Biochemist Paul Stitt called the intentionally designed over-consumption of foods "The 'Can't Eat Just One' Syndrome." He describes how salt and sugar are added in food processing, while fiber and nutrients are removed. These changes escalate the amount of processed foods we eat because low fiber and nutrient-depleted foods simply do not fill the stomach or meet nutritional needs. Stitt perceived this food industry practice as the "conspiracy of the sales curve." The more nutritious a food, the less of it must be consumed because the nutritional needs of the cells are satisfied. Nutrient-depleted foods leave us with "hidden hungers" even after large meals. Stitt wrote, "...the food giants aren't the only ones getting huge on processed foods—you are, too."[6]

Nutrient-depleted foods leave us with "hidden hungers" even after large meals. The more nutritious a food, the less of it needs be consumed because the nutritional needs of the cells are satisfied.

Stitt, an idealist, bought a bakery and began producing highly nutritious bread. He soon found himself caught in the web of the conspiracy of the sales curve. The more nutritious his bread became the less of it he was able to sell. It satisfied appetite too well. He was forced to the edge of bankruptcy before he realized he needed to increase his marketing area to avoid insolvency.

In the same vein, Paula Geisselman at UCLA experimented on rabbits to demonstrate that large intakes of sugar or salt can double normal food consumption, disproving a commonly held assumption that sugar decreased appetite. Rabbits fed sugar or salt eat faster, longer, as well as more.[7] Other food additives also increase appetite. Dr. Johanna Budwig of Germany found that partially hydrogenated oils increased food consumption, sometimes as much as six-fold, in both animals and human beings.[8] This kind of uncontrolled eating cannot help but promote weight gain.

"...the food giants aren't the only ones getting huge on processed foods— you are, too."
Paul Stitt, Biochemist

The obesity problem in the United States is the aftermath of loading our stomachs with excessive artificial fats, salt, sugar, and other additives like MSG. (Animals fed with MSG when they are young become obese adults.[9]) Trying to

Chapter 2 – Body Shape

reduce only calorie consumption, like the heavily advertised low-fat, low-carb diets, without taking away appetite-triggering food additives is a losing proposition.

Consumer Reports summed up years of research on weight loss in a 2002 issue, concluding that taming erratic blood sugar is central to effective weight loss. One study they referenced showed an average of 4.5 pounds lost in four months in the group with a diet for blood sugar control, while those on a low-fat diet gained 2.9 pounds. Another study came to essentially the same conclusion, observing that men on a diet that stabilized blood sugar spontaneously reduced calorie intake by 25%.

A second weight loss principle, as stated in their report, is not to skimp on protein or fat. Protein and fat slow the absorption of carbohydrates, keeping blood sugar levels down. In one study 81% more calories were consumed when protein and fat intake were cut. Another study, which lasted a year and a half, found that those on a low-fat diet gained 6.4 pounds, while those on a moderate fat intake lost 9 pounds. This established that healthy fats can reduce appetite.

Avoiding dense foods, such as refined grains that have less water and fiber, also helps scale down caloric intake. When given less dense foods like vegetables and salads, participants sought out 20% fewer calories.[10]

It is almost impossible to overstate the importance of addictive allergy as a contributor to extreme weight gain. One of the consequences of having a strong allergic response to a food is oftentimes an unpleasant withdrawal. When the food is removed from the diet, one can experience depression, headaches, stomach cramps, asthma, arthritis, or painful muscle aches, and powerful emotional changes such as panic or anger.

Dr. Marshall Mandell, a pioneer in the field of allergy, described how food allergy causes weight gain, "Progressive overweight develops as the advancing state of allergic food addiction requires increasing the doses of the specific food(s) to satisfy the craving. Food at bedtime, in particular, postpones the onset of late night or early morning withdrawal symptoms, and eating between meals may become essential for comfort during the day. Intense, irresistible cravings make it impossible for the compulsive eater to follow a weight reduction program. He eats despite a complete loss of appetite from diet pills because food is his only treatment for the severe withdrawal symptoms that override his common sense and sincere desire to lose weight."[11] The individual who wishes to lose weight must consider the possibility that improperly chosen late night or between-meal snacks may contribute to weight gain. These people

Taming erratic blood sugar is central to effective weight loss.

It is almost impossible to overstate the importance of addictive allergy as a contributor to extreme weight gain.

eat certain foods as a "treatment" to avoid withdrawal, but at the tragic expense of weight gain.

While poorly chosen foods can promote weight gain, foods contaminated with pesticides may slow weight loss. Recent research suggests that accumulation of pesticides can make weight loss more difficult. A 15-week study of 15 obese people found that rising levels of 25 pesticides released from existing fat into the blood during weight loss were closely associated with a slowing of weight loss or what is commonly called a "plateau." Pesticide levels rose 23% as the body turned to stored fat for energy.[12]

Accumulation of pesticides can make weight loss more difficult.

A recent article in *Science News* revealed that fat cells may increase inflammation in the body and be responsible for chronic elevation of a chemical messenger of the immune system called tumor necrosis factor-alpha (TNF-α). This substance can cause "insulin resistance," a characteristic of obesity and adult onset diabetes.[13] In other words, the more fat cells we accumulate, the more inflammation is created in the body, which in turn increases the likelihood of weight gain. By reducing inflammation, we can improve insulin function and facilitate weight loss. The popular Hamptons diet, for example, combines a low-carbohydrate regimen, omega-3 oils for their anti-inflammatory effect, and a quality macadamia nut oil to improve assimilation of the omega-3 oils.

By reducing inflammation in the body, we can improve insulin function and facilitate weight loss.

SUGGESTIONS

- Avoid appetite-stimulating additives.
- Avoid exposure to pesticides.
- Avoid low-fat diets that are high in sugar.
- Build your diet around low-density foods (fruits and vegetables).
- Keep blood sugar stable.
- Make sure your protein intake is sufficient.
- Supplement with omega-3 oils and antioxidants to reduce inflammation.

Small Waist and Alzheimer's

SIGN

A thin waist and large hips

SIGNIFICANCE

Alzheimer's appears to be more common among those with a thin waist and large hips, rather than those with a wide waist and narrow hips. This may be due to greater malnutrition or a more unstable blood sugar among those with a thin waist or a result of the fact that those with a thin waist live a longer life.

Dementia among the elderly is an increasing problem. Treatment for Alzheimer's patients is draining on their families and costs are staggering for the health care system.

DISCUSSION

Dr. Eric B. Larson and his associates at the University of Washington in Seattle spearheaded a study on 2,500 seniors. They found that the smaller the circumference of the waist compared to that of the hips, the greater the risk of developing Alzheimer's disease. Those with the greatest difference between the two measurements were *three times* more likely to develop the disease than those that did not have a "pencil thin" abdomen. None of these people was diagnosed with Alzheimer's at the beginning of the study. The only factor that distinguished those who developed the disease was this "waist-to-hip" ratio.

Research is continuing to determine whether developmental or genetic factors are involved in this risk, or whether those with a narrow waist live longer due to decreased risk of heart disease and diabetes.[14]

A related study found that Alzheimer's is highest in individuals without diabetes. "Alzheimer's doubled in those with hypoglycemic tendencies (high insulin and low blood sugar levels)." Elevated insulin is also associated with decline in memory.[15]

Production of free radicals can contribute to Alzheimer's. According to the Cache County Study, a major research on Alzheimer's, supplementation with antioxidants, such as vitamins C and E, is beneficial. Taking vitamins C and E separately made little difference, the study revealed, but a modest intake of both supplements together resulted in a significant reduction in the onset of Alzheimer's.[16]

Other supplementation is also crucial. Foods that are high in DHA and lecithin can help repair damage and build healthy cells in the brain. Complex carbohydrates and B complex vitamins supply energy to prevent starvation of brain cells and enable them to protect themselves.

Alzheimer's doubled in those with hypoglycemic tendencies.

Those with the greatest difference between waist and hip measurements were three times more likely to develop Alzheimer's.

RELATED TOPICS

ALZHEIMER'S
SLEEP APNEA

SUGGESTIONS

- Avoid exposure to mercury or other heavy metals.
- Eat regular and sensible meals so as to *never* starve the brain.
- Maintain adequate supplementation of all antioxidants, especially vitamins C and E.

Upper Body Weight Gain

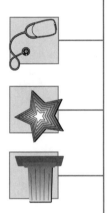

SIGN

Weight gain above the waist, especially on a woman

SIGNIFICANCE

This sign is a predictor of an increased risk of diabetes.

DISCUSSION

Ahmed H. Kissebah, M.D., of the Medical College of Wisconsin, has noted a very strong correlation between diabetes and an upper body weight gain pattern among women. His study showed that one-fourth of the 40% of American women who are overweight will have upper body weight gain. Six out of ten of these women manifested preclinical diabetes and 16% had the full-blown disease. Weight gain above the waist is generally characterized by fat cells that are curiously large, while weight gain below the waist is associated with an exceptionally large number of much smaller fat cells.[17] Large fat cells are less responsive to insulin, increasing the risk of developing diabetes.

The worst habit a high-risk woman can have is to drink sugar-sweetened beverages. A study of over 90,000 women found that soft drinks and fruit punches cause dramatic weight gain when consumption changes from one or less per week to one or more per day. Risk of diabetes nearly doubled when an individual gulped down large volumes of fruit punch or soft drinks daily.[18]

Sugar-sweetened soft drinks, comprising 7.1% of total calorie intake in the United States, have become our most popular beverage. Unfortunately, consumption of liquids high in sugar does not decrease food consumption. These beverages just provide extra calories. An excess of soft drinks is often-times accompanied by less physical activity, more smoking, and greater alcohol consumption.[19] Fruit juices do not increase risk of diabetes like sodas and fruit

Risk of diabetes nearly doubled when an individual gulped down large volumes of fruit punch or soft drinks daily.

punches, but they do cause weight gain. Tomato juice is an excellent beverage for the diabetic, as it reduces risk of heart disease.[20, 21]

A wide variety of nutrients benefit the diabetic, but recent research suggests one often-overlooked nutrient offers tremendous benefits. Scientists discovered that approximately doubling blood measurements of vitamin D improved insulin sensitivity by 60% "which is a greater increase than many anti-diabetes drugs provide."[22]

Women with this weight gain pattern should be cautious about certain types of hormone replacement therapy which can promote weight gain. It is no longer news that estrogen can promote weight gain, and women with upper body weight gain must control their weight to prevent diabetes. Fortunately, weight reduction is easier for the woman who gains weight above the waist than it is for the woman who gains weight below the waist.

SUGGESTIONS

- Avoid excessive exposure to estrogens and estrogenic pollutants.

- Drink tomato juice or water rather than sodas.

- Supplement with cod liver oil as a natural source of vitamin D if exposure to sunlight is minimal.

- Watch weight closely if you gain above the waist.

Food for Thought

The meat industry fattens animals by not allowing them to exercise, by giving them estrogens and antibiotics, and by feeding them a carbohydrate rich diet (usually corn). How do people do the same to themselves?

What are your most effective weight loss strategies?

What steps have you taken, or will you be taking, to assure that your brain is well-nourished and protected?

Consumption of liquids high in sugar does not decrease food consumption.

Scalp and Hair: *The Crown on Our Heads*

The afternoon had been spent exploring the value of hair analysis with the energetic owner of a laboratory. I learned that hair traps within its physical and chemical structure a precise record of whatever we have been eating or applying to it. Hair can reveal if we smoke, drink, or take drugs and it provides a record of behavior for several months because of its slow growth. This is why some people who take drugs shave their heads.

The stocky frame of my guest at the dinner table tilted toward me as I asked, "Have you ever seen a 'perfect' hair analysis?" He answered with a chuckle, "Some of the most 'perfect' hair analyses I have seen came from engaged couples or newlyweds. Perhaps the euphoria of love improves their nutritional status as well as their emotional well-being."

While good attitudes and feelings can favorably impact utilization of nutrients, it is even more axiomatic that poor nutritional intake and toxic exposures result in unpleasant behaviors and attitudes. Virtually anyone who works with hair analysis has observed that hair has often accumulated patterns of heavy metals when individuals are emotionally disturbed or skewed toward violence.[1] In addition, professional diagnoses of attention deficit disorder often match very closely with the quantity of lead in the hair.[2]

Nutritionally compromised children and adults are those most susceptible to the wide range of toxic substances in our environment.[3] Nutrients, such as calcium, zinc and vitamins C and E, have been found to be effective in counteracting lead buildup. Other nutrients are similarly protective against other toxic metals. Examination of hair reveals not only the accumulation of toxic substances, but also deficiencies of many of the protective minerals.

The scalp and hair resemble mirrors reflecting the body's nutritional status. The scalp is the active tissue that produces the hair, and impaired blood flow to this area will result in inferior hair. Because of this bond to our circulation, the hair provides clues to the condition of the heart and circulatory system.

I am reminded of an individual who looked like a heart attack waiting to happen. He developed such bad dandruff and lesions on his scalp that he could not grow hair. After supplementing with what I refer to as "chain of life" nutrition (the complete spectrum of essential nutrients) this man not only lost considerable weight, but he grew a glorious head of hair!

A wide spectrum of nutrients is necessary for a healthy scalp and hair. Quality fats improve circulation and keep the scalp healthy. Hair consists of protein and minerals and reflects a lack of these nutrients. Faulty digestion, particularly of protein, can cause loss of hair or its deterioration.

This chapter unearths the volume of nutritional information buried in our scalp and hair. We shall see how important adequate intake of protein, vitamins, and minerals are for a luxuriant head of hair—and how the use of these nutrients stands or falls with the proper functioning of the glandular and circulatory systems.

Baldness

SIGN

No hair, or premature and/or temporary hair loss (Scientific term: alopecia)

SIGNIFICANCE

Some types of baldness have been linked to heart disease. Early intervention reduces the risk tied to this cold-blooded killer. Premature hair loss in women has been associated with poor nutrition, especially iron deficiency. Immune irregularities caused by immunization can contribute to loss of hair as well.

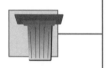

DISCUSSION

Samuel Lesko, M.D., conducted a study of baldness among men. He compared 665 men admitted to a hospital with a heart attack with 772 men admitted without a heart attack. Frontal baldness showed no association with heart attack, but the greater the degree of baldness on the top of the head, the greater the risk that a man would have a heart attack.[4]

The conclusion we can draw from this study is that a lifestyle that causes baldness on the top of the head may also be damaging the circulatory system. These lifestyle factors age the skin and scalp, damage hair, and age the circulatory system. Wrinkling of the skin and gray hair have also been associated with increased risk of having a heart attack and dying at a younger age.[5]

Another study by Dr. Janet L. Roberts, a physician who specializes in treatment for hair loss, indicates just how important nutrition is for a head of healthy hair. She studied 153 women and found iron deficiency to be the main determinant of hair loss in almost three-quarters (72%) of pre-menopausal women and over one quarter (29%) of post-menopausal women. Almost half (49%) of post-menopausal women lose their hair as a result of side effects of prescription drug use.[6]

Because excess iron can act as a powerful free-radical and increase the risk of heart disease, men in particular should not supplement with iron overzealously. Any serious deficiency of zinc and protein may also evoke various degrees of hair loss.[7]

Immunization may cause temporary hair loss, according to Dr. Robert Wise. In an evaluation of 60 cases of hair loss, 46 of them had received the hepatitis B vaccine. This hair loss was only temporary in most of the cases.[8] This kind of alteration in immune function, here accompanied by hair loss, is one reason why some scientists are still debating today whether immunization does more harm than good.[9]

SUGGESTIONS

- Maintain healthy circulation with regular exercise and good diet.
- Supplement with nutrients known to improve circulation and prevent heart disease.
- Maintain a healthy antioxidant intake to slow aging.
- Women with hair loss should be tested for or suspected of having iron deficiency.

Iron deficiency appears to be the main cause of hair loss in pre-menopausal women.

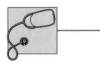

Dandruff

SIGN

Dry flaky scalp with an excessive number of dead cells

SIGNIFICANCE

Dandruff is commonly associated with poor nutrition in both laboratory animals and human populations. This sign has little to do with the cleanliness of the scalp, but a great deal to do with the dysfunction of the oil-secreting glands and the dehydration of skin cells.

DISCUSSION

Dr. Donald Rudin, in his book *Omega-3 Oils*, shared an experiment in which capuchin monkeys in Britain were deprived of omega-3 oils for two years. The researchers found that "All the monkeys developed dandruff and patchy hair loss."[10] Lack of omega-3 oils or other essential fatty acids is the first deficiency that comes to mind when I see a bad case of dandruff.

Dr. Michael Schmidt, author of *Smart Fats*, also listed dry skin, dandruff, and dry unmanageable hair as indicators of fatty acid imbalance in the diet. Nutrients, such as zinc, magnesium, vitamins B3, B6 and B12, folic acid, biotin, and vitamin C, are all essential for the proper working of fats in our body. Lack of any of these nutrients may contribute to dandruff. Dr. Schmidt noted that high intake of sugar, alcohol, or faulty digestion are all roadblocks to efficient use of fats.[11]

Selenium, while quite toxic in excess, may reduce dandruff, which is why it is often added to shampoos by their manufacturers. Selenium boosts immune function and dandruff may be accompanied by overgrowth of bacteria or fungi.[12]

SUGGESTIONS

- Avoid over-using harsh shampoos which can dry the scalp.
- Consume good fats, especially omega-3 oils and phospholipids, while avoiding junk fats.
- Supplement with a well-balanced vitamin-mineral.

RELATED TOPICS

BUMPS ON THE
BACK OF THE ARM

CALLUSES

ROUGH ELBOWS

High intake of sugar, alcohol, or faulty digestion are all roadblocks to efficient use of fats.

Chapter 3 – Scalp and Hair

Excess Facial Hair

SIGN

Excess facial hair on a woman's face (Scientific term: hirsuitism)

SIGNIFICANCE

Excessive sugar and caffeine, or undue emotional stress, can over-stimulate the adrenal glands and cause excess facial hair in women. Overstimulation of the adrenal glands may result in failure to ovulate leading to estrogen dominance.

DISCUSSION

Under normal circumstances, the hair follicles on a woman's face produce no hair or very fine, almost invisible hairs. A superabundance of male hormones (androgens) in women is a central contributor to the proliferation of hair on the face. Deborah Chase, author of *The Medically Based No-Nonsense Beauty Book*, wrote, "Androgens are, in fact, the most important hormone of the adrenal glands when considering problems of excess hair. It is the level of androgens in the body that directly controls the activity of the hair follicles. The greater the amount of androgen, the more hair will grow."[13]

Anything, tumor included, that increases adrenal activity, particularly its secretion of androgen, can increase facial and body hair. Less recognized is the ability of sugar, caffeine, and strong emotions to generate excess adrenal activity. Dr. John Yudkin reported in the 1970s that high sugar intake could increase increase corticosteroids by 300 to 400%.[14]

Sugar intake in the average diet is like an iceberg. Eighty percent of the sugar we consume is hidden in foods. For example, catsup is almost one-third sugar. Most of us consume far more sugar than we know because of this hidden aspect of sugar intake. The total amount of the sugar in the blood at one time is only 1 to 3 teaspoons. Consuming vastly greater amounts of sugar than this at one sitting sets up a profound disturbance in the delicately balanced glandular system that governs our overall health and well-being.

Excess adrenal activity not only increases the likelihood of excessive facial hair, but can also contribute to irregular menstruation and underdeveloped breasts.[15] Overstimulation of the adrenal gland to the extent that excess male hormones are produced may trigger anovulatory cycles—menstrual cycles

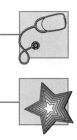

RELATED TOPICS

BREAST CANCER

CRAVING FOR SALT

DIZZINESS UPON RISING

SENSITIVITY TO BRIGHT LIGHT

Sugar intake in the average diet is like an iceberg. Eighty percent of the sugar we consume is hidden in foods.

without the release of an egg. Failure of ovulation results in progesterone deficiency and estrogen dominance—a scenario that increases the risk of hormone-linked cancers and a wide range of other health problems.[16]

SUGGESTIONS

- Avoid refined carbohydrates, sugar, and caffeine.
- Avoid entertainments, habits and hobbies that overstress and over-stimulate the adrenal glands.
- Support adrenal function with adequate protein and complex carbohydrate.
- Supplement with vitamins B complex and C, and plant fats (phospholipids and phytosterols).

Flag Sign

SIGN

The hair, particularly of a child, loses its pigment.

SIGNIFICANCE

The flag sign indicates periodic deficiency of protein intake or inability to utilize the amino acids. Hair color fluctuates with the deficiency, creating a flag effect. Brown hair may become rusty red and light-colored hair blonde during protein deficiency. This sign is often accompanied by a poor utilization or deficiency of other nutrients. Protein is necessary for building muscle, critical immune factors, and endocrine hormones.

DISCUSSION

The word *protein* is from the Greek, meaning "first." Protein is built from 22 building blocks called amino acids. Insufficient amino acid intake results in numerous health problems. Lack of a single amino acid can alter important body functions. For example, lack of the amino acid cysteine can cause a drop in the body's production of glutathione—our most important internally synthesized antioxidant. This compromises immune function. Lack of tryptophan may lead to serotonin deficiency and depression. Tyrosine is essential for the functioning of the adrenal glands, our means of coping with stress.

Severe protein malnutrition causes hair to lose its color. Gray hair can sometimes be darkened by an increase of protein in diet.[17] Protein deficiency severe enough to alter the pigmentation of the hair is most common among malnourished children, long-term drug addicts, or extreme dieters.

Protein deficiency causes the most problems when requirements are high, as in the body of a growing child. Inadequate intake at this time may result in permanent impairment in both physical and mental development. Abram Hoffer used the illustration of a bricklayer to describe the importance of a sufficient supply of all the amino acids. The bricklayer may need three bricks to complete a wall. Excess bricks will not hinder his work, but lack of one kind of brick may stop his work. He concluded, "Lack of quality protein is serious, a state that the functioning body will not long endure without showing deficiency symptoms."[18] The high-carbohydrate, low-protein diet of many young people in the United States puts them at risk for protein deficiency, which is often evidenced by weak, flabby muscles.

Dr. Alfred Libby and vitamin C researcher Irwin Stone suggested that drug addicts suffer from kwashiorkor, a scientific term for protein deficiency. In their studies, they noted astonishing improvement in the ability to break drug habits when protein, accompanied by generous quantities of vitamin C, was abundantly supplied to the diets of addicts.[19]

Protein supplementation may also help those who are addicted to foods. A study was conducted many years ago in which a small dose of amino acids (8 grams) administered a half hour before meals reduced calorie consumption of obese patients by 22.5%.[20] Amino acids are valuable tools for breaking addictions to both foods and narcotics.

Research agrees with my own experience that the best protein in the marketplace, for those with compromised digestion or serious health conditions is one that is partially predigested. As we age, we lose the ability to digest our food well, and this kind of protein can lift a tremendous burden off the digestive tract, improve protein absorption, and greatly speed healing from injury or surgery.[21]

A number of years ago a family member was diagnosed with bowel cancer and a large segment of the digestive tract was removed. Despite the fact he was being fed by tube, his health deteriorated until he weighed only a little over 80 pounds. Every food he was given resulted in diarrhea. My brother's wife went into the hospital and asked permission from the physician to provide her brother with a partially predigested protein. The physician assured her that the

Severe protein deficiency may be indicated by fluid retention and increased susceptibility to infection.

"Lack of quality protein is serious, a state that the functioning body will not long endure without showing deficiency symptoms." Abram Hoffer

RELATED TOPICS
BLOATING, BURPING AND BAD BREATH

protein would do no good as he was being given all the protein he needed. Nevertheless, he permitted her to administer the predigested amino acid formula. The young man's stool solidified within two hours and he staged a miraculous complete recovery. Those who are ill should be provided with forms of supplementation that are easily used by the body.

SUGGESTIONS

- Increase protein intake, preferably a food or product easy to digest.
- Supplement those with strong cravings or addictions with generous quantities of amino acids and vitamin C.

Prematurely Gray Hair

SIGN

Hair turns white or gray at a young age

SIGNIFICANCE

Prematurely gray hair may reflect vitamin D inadequacy, increased risk of bone loss and osteoporosis.

DISCUSSION

I would have regarded some of the nutritional literature on darkening of gray hair with suspicion if I had not witnessed the change in my parent's hair. My mother was told by her physician at the age of 43, after having suffered a broken elbow, that she had broken her bones like "a little old lady." She had seen her grandmother die as a result of complications from a broken hip. Due to this experience, when she received her own diagnosis, she began what she considered a dramatic life change—supplementing with whole food supplements. Not only did her hair darken, but her bones healed in half the time the doctor expected.

According to Dr. Clifford Rosen at the Maine Center for Osteoporosis Research and Education, those who experience graying of hair in their teens and twenties usually have a family history of premature graying. This is not true of those who become gray in their thirties. He finds that individuals who have prematurely gray hair (half of the hair gray by age of 40) are 4 1/2 times more likely to develop osteoporosis than those who are not prematurely gray. Dr. Rosen further uncovered a startling number of endocrine problems,

Individuals who have prematurely gray hair are 4 1/2 times more likely to develop osteoporosis.

especially those of the thyroid, in individuals with prematurely gray hair. Individuals with early gray hair are also more prone to vitiligo—a loss of pigment in the skin.

It appears that those with more skin and hair pigment have denser bones across the board. There is no doubt that exposure to sunlight, which provides vitamin D, darkens the skin. Rosen goes one step further, suggesting that loss of pigment in the hair and osteoporosis may both be associated with vitamin D deficiency.[22]

SUGGESTIONS

- Expose the skin to sufficient sunlight or supplement with vitamin D.
- Obtain all essential nutrients to slow the aging process.

RELATED TOPICS

OSTEOPOROSIS

PAIN IN THE JOINTS AND MUSCLES

RICKETS

VITILIGO

Food for Thought

Dandruff is common in malnourished laboratory animals. How common do you think it is in humans? What does this say about our nutritional intake?

How many of the foods you eat probably contain hidden sugars? What foods in your diet might contain more than 3 teaspoons of sugar?

When was the last time your skin was allowed relaxed exposure to sunlight without hindrance from sunscreen or glass? What could be some alternatives to receiving adequate exposure of the skin to sunlight in order to meet your vitamin D requirements?

Eyes and Forehead: *Windows of the Soul*

For thousands of years men have looked into the eyes of their neighbors for clues to physical and spiritual condition. In the Far East they looked for "sanpaku" (Japanese for three "san" and whites "paku"). The Japanese believed "a man's entire system—physical, physiological, and spiritual—was out of balance" when they saw white beneath the iris as he looked straight ahead.[1]

George Ohsawa, a student of sanpaku, identified the trait in John Kennedy shortly before his assassination. The trait was also seen in Abraham Lincoln. Both of these men suffered major health problems, indicating that this sign may be linked to poor health. President Kennedy suffered with adrenal failure, osteoporosis, and terrible back pain, while Lincoln suffered with Marfan's syndrome, which affects the heart and eyes.[2] Lincoln is believed to have taken a medication called "blue mass" for frequent bouts of depression. This patent medicine of his time contained 9,000 times the level of mercury considered safe today. Lincoln quit taking the medication after being elected president because it made him cross.[3] He might not have been noted as the "steady hand at the helm of government" during the civil war had he continued this medication.

The Mediterranean world lived in fear of the evil eye. It was believed that some individuals could transmit a curse by their malevolent gaze. This idea may have originated from the observation that evil or cruel people manifested an altered appearance to the eyes.

The eyes of assassins and terrorists often have a strange appearance. A *Newsweek* photographic essay noted that John Hinkley, the man who attempted to end Ronald Reagan's life, ate a diet consisting primarily of milk shakes and hamburgers. The look in Hinkley's eyes is very similar to sanpaku.[4]

One sees the same kind of strange look in the eyes of many of the terrorists who flew into the twin towers on September 11, 2001.

Even the Bible speaks of how dietary habits alter the appearance of the eyes. The Biblical Book of Proverbs describes red eyes caused by excess alcohol consumption:

> *"Who has redness of eyes?*
> *Those who linger long at the wine,*
> *Those who go in search of mixed wine."*[5]

Examination of the eyes is popular in alternative medicine. Sclerology, study of the white part of the eye, and iridology, study of the iris, are not considered here because there is little information or support for them in the medical literature at this time.

A clue to our societal malnutrition is the frequent incidence of nearsightedness.

A clue to our societal malnutrition is the frequent incidence of nearsightedness. The eye simply develops differently when nutrition is skewed. An eye that does not mature properly cannot function normally. Societies with a high intake of sugar contain many people with visual problems.

The area around the eye also changes appearance in concert with diet. Poor diet and allergic responses can cause the delicate tissue around and under the eye to become red or dark, to form creases, or to swell and become puffy. Digestive problems, which often accompany allergy, may cause creases in the forehead.

The healthy eyeball is constantly lubricated. The eye provides an open doorway to view how efficiently the body is lubricating different tissues. This is revealed by whether the eye is dry or moist and shiny. The eye's visual apparatus also has remarkable complexity and specialized need for nutrients to function properly and maintain a state of health. Lack of these nutrients may increase the risk of cataracts, night blindness, or macular degeneration.

Cataract

Sign

An opaque or cloudy condition of the lens of the eye

SIGNIFICANCE

Cataract, which can lead to blindness, is usually treated with surgery at considerable expense.

DISCUSSION

Diabetics, especially of the juvenile type, are predisposed to develop cataracts, damage to the retina that leads to blindness and kidney damage. This is due largely to an enzyme called aldose reductase which converts glucose to sorbitol. Sorbitol is a sugar alcohol that is added to some diet foods as well as being produced in the body itself. High levels of sorbitol damage tissue, causing diabetic complications. Fortunately, vitamin C intake as low as 100 mg a day has been shown to prevent buildup of sorbitol in red blood cells, making vitamin C an important nutrient for diabetics.[6] There are pharmaceutically developed sorbitol inhibitors, but they neither provide the nutritional benefits of vitamin C nor are they as safe.

Vitamin C occurs in nature accompanied by flavonoids that are also powerful antioxidants. Vitamin C combined with citrus extract was 41% more effective than vitamin C alone in reducing risk of cataract in rats, especially at the lower levels of vitamin C intake. It is quite remarkable that vitamin C and flavonoids would reduce risk of cataract in rats at all since they synthesize their own vitamin C in rather large quantities! The benefit of flavonoids in this research is a powerful argument for making an attempt to obtain nutrients from natural complexes rather than as isolated synthetic nutrients.[7]

The benefit of flavonoids in this research is a powerful argument for making an attempt to obtain nutrients from natural complexes rather than as isolated synthetic nutrients.

Cataracts in those who are not diabetic most often result from oxidative damage to the eyes—usually from exposure to sunlight. Nutritional antioxidants including vitamins C, E, and carotenoids offer powerful protection. If the development of cataracts could be delayed only 10 years, and adequate antioxidant intake offers this promise, half the surgeries for this condition would be eliminated.[8]

SUGGESTIONS

- Diabetics should supplement with vitamin C and flavonoids.
- Eat a diet rich in fruits and vegetables.
- Supplement with antioxidants.
- Presence of cataract may be a clue to blood sugar problems.[9]

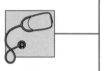

Dry Eyes

SIGN

Dryness and loss of sparkle to the eye

SIGNIFICANCE

The eye loses its glow with deficiency of omega-3 oils, vitamin A, and zinc. Dry eyes may also provide an early clue to autoimmune disease.

DISCUSSION

People with bright eyes are perceived to possess a vibrant personality, but bright eyes also reflect good health. The moisture that confers the shine to the eye is composed of mucous, water, and lipids or oils. Lack of vitamin A or zinc can hinder mucous secretion, resulting in drying of the eyes.[10] These nutrients are partners with omega-3 oils, which concentrate in eye tissue, supply the lipid portion of eye secretions, and are often found deficient in those with dry eyes.[11] Omega-3 oils are often helpful for dry eyes caused by autoimmune activity.

Autoimmune disorders often improve when the effects of excessive levels of estrogen are blocked. Estrogen tends to switch the immune system on, which is why a number of autoimmune diseases are much more common in women than men. Testosterone and progesterone tend to switch the immune system off. It is very important to have the proper balance of these different hormones. Suggestions for dry eyes caused by autoimmune activity include establishment of hormone balance and supplementing with vitamins B12 and D.[12, 13]

Dehydration due to inadequate water consumption can contribute to dry eyes. Young people may become dehydrated when they replace water with soda pop as their primary beverage choice. Older people are more prone to dehydration and often lose their sense of thirst, resulting in dehydration. This can be seen in the eyes by a loss of sparkle.

The frequency of dry eyes has increased significantly with the progress of our technologically advanced world. Eyes become significantly drier while using a video display than when reading a book. When working at a display terminal, eyes open wider, tear evaporation is greater, and blinking is less frequent. Those who wear contact lenses and work or play at computer terminals may find the eyes dry and irritated.[14]

People with bright eyes are perceived to possess a vibrant personality, but bright eyes also reflect good health.

RELATED TOPIC

MACULAR
DEGENERATION

Chapter 4 – Eyes and Forehead

Dry eyes decrease the protective film over the eye, increasing the likelihood of experiencing inflammation and oxidative damage.[15] Eyes robbed of their moisture not only risk closing our window on the world through a greater probability of eye damage, but this dryness also decreases some of the "sparkle" of our personality.

SUGGESTIONS

- Drink adequate quantities of water.
- Supplement with antioxidants.
- Supplement with cod liver oil and omega-3 oils.
- Take a break and rest the eyes while working at video display terminals.
- Use a vitamin-mineral supplement.

Floaters

SIGN

Lines or spots appear to move across the field of vision

SIGNIFICANCE

Floaters reflect poor nutrition and accumulation of debris within the eye.

DISCUSSION

I experienced floaters as a youngster. These most frequently looked like wiggling worms although floaters can appear as a fine line, spot, or zigzag line slowly floating across the field of vision.

Floaters in the young are often caused by cellular debris that sloughs off the retina. This debris floats in the jellylike substance that fills much of the eyeball. As a person ages the jellylike substance in the eye can actually begin to change. This may result in floaters as well.

Dr. Jonathan Wright suggested flavonoids, choline, inositol, and vitamin K as important nutrients for the prevention of floaters. Lecithin is a rich source of choline and inositol. The most abundant fats in the eye are lecithin and omega-3 oils, both of which would be likely to benefit this condition.[16] The eye contains large quantities of highly unsaturated fats. Generous intake of antioxidants is

RELATED TOPICS
BUMPS ON THE ARM
NIGHT BLINDNESS

essential to prevent oxidative damage to these fats. Floaters may be an early warning that nutrient intake is inadequate to build or maintain healthy eye tissue.

If flashing lights, a sudden onset of floaters, or a rapid increase in the number of floaters takes place, serious eye problems requiring a visit to an ophthalmologist may be indicated. The problem is more likely to be serious if it is confined to one eye or if floaters appear in large clumps. Sudden changes in vision can indicate the retina has come loose or is detaching. This may result in blindness if left untreated.[17]

RELATED TOPICS
DRY EYES
NIGHT BLINDNESS

SUGGESTIONS

- Eat a diet rich in protein and low in sugars.
- Eat fruits and vegetables, including leafy greens, which supply vitamin K.
- Consume fish or other sources of omega-3 oils.
- Supplement with lecithin and cod liver oil.
- Use a good-quality multiple with antioxidants.

Forehead Furrows or Wrinkles

SIGN

Deep vertical creases, wrinkles, or furrows in the forehead, more obvious when an individual frowns

SIGNIFICANCE

Vertical furrows in the forehead may be an indicator of ulcer risk. Ulcers in the stomach are called gastric ulcers, while those below the stomach in the duodenum are called duodenal ulcers. The term peptic ulcer designates both types.

DISCUSSION

Nelson Trujillo and Thomas Warthin wrote in the *Journal of the American Medical Association* in 1983 that when there are four vertical creases within about half an inch of the midline of the forehead there is a risk of duodenal ulcer. This body sign is much more reliable if there is also the presence of upper abdominal pain.[18]

Dr. Barry J. Marshall is an Australian Professor of Clinical Microbiology. Traditional medicine had long assumed that ulcers were caused by stress, spicy foods, or excess stomach acid. A common treatment was antacids. Dr. Marshall's research has led many scientists to the conclusion that both gastric and duodenal ulcers are frequently caused by bacterial infection.

Dr. Marshall discovered that bacteria called *Helicobacter pylori* were responsible for many cases of stomach ulcers. He suggested that the proper treatment was antibiotics rather than antacids. He was ridiculed by establishment scientists and doctors for years.

In July of 1984 Dr. Marshall, then 32 years of age, drank a cocktail of *H. pylori* bacteria and gave himself ulcers. His immune system fought off the bacteria and he eventually recovered. Traditional medicine was forced to pay attention to his theory. In 1994 the National Institutes of Health endorsed antibiotics as the standard treatment for ulcers.

There is a worthwhile lesson in Dr. Marshall's ability to recover from ulcers without treatment. The bacterial causation of ulcers was initially rejected by the medical profession because it was assumed bacteria could not live in the acid environment of the stomach. A drop in the strength of stomach acid removes this normal protective mechanism, allowing invasion by potentially disease-causing microbes. This assumption is generally correct; although *H. pylori* are adapted to survive in an acid environment.[19] Decreased strength of the stomach acid may set the stage for the initial infection with *H. pylori*.

Robert Koch, the father of bacteriology, discovered the important role stomach acid plays in protecting the digestive tract from invasion by microbes in 1885. He learned he could predictably infect guinea pigs with cholera if the germs were administered with bicarbonate. The antacid reduced the number of cholera organisms necessary to create an infection 10,000 fold.[20] Weak stomach acid increases both the severity and likelihood of infection from *E coli*, salmonella, and giardia.

Repeated studies have shown the immense power of stomach acid to suppress bacterial growth in the upper portion of the digestive tract. One study found that nitrates in foods could be converted to nitrosamines, which are potent carcinogens when stomach acid is low. Low stomach acid allowed bacteria to proliferate in the stomach and generate the nitrosamines.[21] Supplementation with hydrochloric acid killed the bacteria and ended bacterial carcinogen formation.

The antacid reduced the number of cholera organisms necessary to create an infection 10,000 fold.

The bacterial causation of ulcers was initially rejected by the medical profession because it was assumed bacteria could not live in the acid environment of the stomach.

Supplementing an individual with active ulcers with hydrochloric acid is probably not a good idea, nor is the use of antibiotics ideal. Antibiotics kill beneficial bacteria in the digestive tract and open the door to proliferation of antibiotic-resistant organisms and fungi that are usually resistant to antibiotics. Fortunately, a number of natural substances inhibit *H. pylori*.

Broccoli contains a substance called sulforaphane that inhibits growth of over 90% of the strains of *H. pylori*, even those that are resistant to antibiotics. Sulforaphane not only decreases the risk of gastric and duodenal ulcers, but also functions to prevent stomach cancer.[22]

Garlic is also a powerful ulcer preventative. Compounds called thiosulfinates in garlic have been shown to inhibit *H. pylori* at a dosage as low as the equivalent of two small cloves of garlic (5 grams). Stomach cancer is lower in parts of the world where there is a higher consumption of allium vegetables (garlic, onions, leeks, and chives).[23]

Mastic gum is a natural resin derived from a Mediterranean tree, *Pistacia lentiscus*, and has been used for centuries to improve digestive function. A few studies indicate this resin can effectively kill *H. pylori* in a short period of time.[24]

Dietary changes other than consuming broccoli, garlic, and mastic gum can greatly reduce the risk of ulcers. Soluble fiber from fruits and vegetables protects against ulcers while a diet high in sugar and refined carbohydrates greatly increases the risk.[25] A research study published in 1976 showed that high sugar intake could suppress immune function for several hours, which may be one of the means by which it increases the risk of infection by *H. pylori*.[26]

The stomach acid and white blood cells of those with duodenal ulcers have been shown to be lower in vitamin C than the stomach acid and white blood cells of those without ulcers. In view of vitamin C's role in prevention of wrinkling, this could provide a partial explanation for the formation of this furrowed forehead sign.[27] Forehead wrinkles may also be a response to intense pain.

Consumption of essential fatty acids appears to be highly protective against ulcers.[29] Fish oils have been shown to hasten healing when someone has ulcers.[30] These quality oils not only suppress inflammation, but they also make cells healthier by improving cell membrane function.

Nonsteroidal anti-inflammatory drugs (NSAIDS) increase the risk of developing ulcers because they interfere with the production of mucous and bicarbonate. Even aspirin is known to cause damage to the stomach lining, which can lead to ulcers.

Broccoli contains a substance called sulforaphane that inhibits growth of over 90% of the strains of H. pylori, *even those that are resistant to antibiotics.*

Compounds called thiosulfinates in garlic have been shown to inhibit H. pylori *at a dosage as low as the equivalent of two small cloves of garlic (5 grams).*

Dehydration greatly complicates an ulcer situation by disabling the normal mucous layer that protects the surface of the stomach from the hydrochloric acid released in the process of digestion. Dr. F. Batmanghelidj, who learned he could eliminate ulcer pain within about 20 minutes with two or three glasses of water, provides the following description of the protective role sufficient water intake plays in an ulcer situation:

"The mucous covers the glands layer of the mucosa, which is the innermost layer of the structure of the stomach…Mucous consists of 98 percent water and 2 percent the physical 'scaffolding' that traps water. In this 'water layer' called mucous, a natural buffer state is established. The cells below secrete sodium bicarbonate that is trapped in the water layer. As the acid from the stomach tries to go through this protective layer, the bicarbonate neutralizes it. The outcome of this action is a greater production of salt (sodium from the bicarbonate and chlorine from the acid)."

Dr. Batmanghelidj goes on to explain that as salt builds up it causes a deterioration of the mucous layer. Intake of adequate water flushes the salt out of the mucous layer and also promotes the secretion of additional mucous. Adequate intake of pure water is the key that unlocks the action of the body's own natural antacid protection program—providing protection for the lining of the stomach in a much more natural and effective way than any antacid.[31] Dr. Batmanghelidj successfully treated 3,000 cases of stress-induced ulcer with water alone while imprisoned in Iran.

SUGGESTIONS

- Avoid sodas and caffeine containing beverages that dehydrate the body.
- Drink adequate water.
- Eat garlic and cruciferous vegetables.
- Test for bacterial infection.
- Support normal stomach function with essential nutrients including vitamins A and B complex, trace minerals, and easily digestible protein.
- Supplement with antioxidants and omega-3 fish oils.

RELATED TOPICS

BLOATING, BURPING AND BAD BREATH

BRITTLE NAILS

OSTEOPOROSIS

STOMACH ACID SELF-TEST

Macular Degeneration

SIGN

Macular degeneration is a corrosion or deterioration of an area in the back of the eye called the macula lutea, resulting in loss of central vision. There are two types of macular degeneration: a "dry" form and a "wet" form in which deterioration of the retina is accompanied by leaking of fluid from blood vessels under the center of the retina.

SIGNIFICANCE

Macular degeneration is the leading cause of blindness of persons 65 and older in the United States.

DISCUSSION

Speaking to those with macular degeneration, including support groups, has made me aware of the large numbers of people who develop vision problems as they age. This condition also creates anguish among those who receive the diagnosis. This deterioration of the eye can be largely prevented or delayed by wise dietary choices.

The macula lutea is the site in the back of the eye where light focuses with its greatest intensity. Studies show that habitual intake of the carotenoids (lutein and zeaxanthin) in leafy green vegetables such as spinach can protect this area from damage as we age. These carotenoids have an affinity for the surface of the macula lutea where light focuses in the back of the eye. They protect underlying structures from damage.

Professor Richard W. Young, Ph.D., professor emeritus at UCLA and a member of the Jules Stein Eye Institute, wrote me the following in a personal communication in 1996, "…lutein and zeaxanthin are found in relatively large amounts (in the human retina), concentrated in the yellow spot (macula lutea) directly in the center of the retina, where visual acuity is greatest. This is precisely the region of degeneration and visual loss in AMD (age-related macular degeneration). The xanthophylls appear to have the triple function of (1) absorbing violet/blue light before it can damage the visual cells and retinal pigment epithelium (the cells which deteriorate in AMD), (2) acting as retinal antioxidants, and (3) being situated in just the right place for protection against

"…lutein and zeaxanthin are found in relatively large amounts (in the human retina), concentrated in the yellow spot (macula lutea) directly in the center of the retina, where visual acuity is greatest." Richard Young, Ph.D.

Chapter 4 – Eyes and Forehead

AMD—front and center in the retina."[32] I am often amazed at the remarkable specificity with which nutrients sometimes operate in the human body.

The highest levels of lutein and zeaxanthin intake in the diet have been associated with a 75% reduction in the risk of developing macular degeneration. The number of those with macular degeneration is approaching 2 million, and modern medicine has little to offer in the way of prevention. The ability of nutrients to dramatically reduce risk is encouraging and welcome news. Increased intake of greens in the diet and supplementation with the appropriate carotenoids is an entirely prudent course of action.[33]

Carotenoids are not the only phytonutrients (plant-derived nutrients) that can protect the eyes from macular degeneration. A recent study found that a compound called sulforaphane in cruciferous vegetables such as broccoli protects the retina from degeneration in a dose-related manner.[34] Broccoli is one of the healthiest vegetables we can eat.

The eye contains very large quantities of omega-3 oils and these oils have a demonstrated ability to improve visual acuity as well as reducing risk of macular degeneration.[35] DHA, an omega-3 oil found primarily in coldwater fish, is a major building block of healthy eye tissue.

Other nutrients, including zinc, vitamins C and E, and beta-carotene, reduce the risk of macular degeneration.[36] All of these nutrients are antioxidants and others would doubtless be beneficial as well. Flavonoids in particular strengthen blood vessels and may be protective where the "wet" form of macular degeneration exists.

Underlying the importance of nutrients in the prevention of macular degeneration is the central issue of the ability to utilize these nutrients. Scientific studies have shown that antacid use is an *unexpected* risk factor for macular degeneration. This suggests that those with this condition should be examined for digestive insufficiency. Inadequate stomach acid will interfere with the utilization of a wide spectrum of nutrients and may well be an underlying issue in many cases of macular degeneration.[37]

SUGGESTIONS

- Avoid sweets.
- Consume a serving of cruciferous vegetables daily.
- Consume eye-protecting omega-3 fish oils.

The highest levels of lutein and zeaxanthin intake in the diet have been associated with a 75% reduction in the risk of developing macular degeneration.

Sulforaphane in cruciferous vegetables such as broccoli protects the retina from degeneration in a dose-related manner.

Antacid use is an unexpected risk factor for macular degeneration.

RELATED TOPIC
CATARACT

- Eat two servings of leafy green vegetables each day or supplement with the carotenoids found in leafy greens.
- Supplement with all antioxidants.
- Test for deficiency of hydrochloric acid.

Nearsightedness

SIGN

Inability to see things well at a distance

SIGNIFICANCE

Nearsightedness has been associated with a diet low in protein and high in sugar and refined carbohydrates.

DISCUSSION

Myopia or nearsightedness provides an excellent illustration of the way in which health problems do not occur in isolation, but tend to form clusters. Myopia is linked to increased risk for diabetes, tooth decay, and precocious puberty.

Researchers discarded the notion that a low-protein diet caused deterioration of eyesight until Dr. John Yudkin conducted an enlightening experiment. He fed rats a diet low in protein and high in sugar. The rats became nearsighted. Dr. Yudkin demonstrated that sugar can quickly damage the eyes in both animals and human volunteers when protein intake is low. Consumption of protein with sweets was protective, presumably because it reduced insulin production and blood sugar swings.[38]

Long-term consumption of sugar, particularly in young people, predisposes toward nearsightedness. Collaborative work by a number of researchers suggests that high intake of sugar and refined carbohydrates damages the eyes of the developing child by increasing insulin-like growth factor (IGF-1). Excessive levels of this hormone allow the eyeball to grow too long by reducing the effectiveness of a vitamin A–derived substance that limits cell growth. This results in an elongated eyeball and nearsightedness. Sugar does most of its damage to the eyes during periods of rapid growth.

Nearsightedness has a strong association with a number of other health problems. The more myopic an individual becomes, the greater the likelihood

Myopia is linked to increased risk for diabetes, tooth decay, and precocious puberty.

Sugar does most of its damage to the eyes during periods of rapid growth.

of becoming obese or developing adult-onset diabetes. Those who are myopic have more dental decay. The greater the degree of nearsightedness, the greater the severity of tooth decay tends to be. Those with growing severity of myopia have more rapid tooth decay than those whose eyesight is stable.

Children who are nearsighted grow taller and reach puberty at a younger age. Myopic girls will tend to have earlier menstrual cycles. Numerous studies show that both protein and fiber intake favor reduced insulin levels and a decreased tendency to develop these degenerative changes.[39]

Dr. Yudkin observed that a high-sugar diet can damage the retina as well as cause alterations in near and far vision. This explains the severe retinal disease associated with diabetes, which can lead to blindness. High-starch diets had none of these detrimental effects on the eyes in Dr. Yudkin's work.[38]

Nearsightedness is more common among those who are highly educated. One cannot rule out environmental factors as contributors to nearsightedness. Close work by itself may not be enough to greatly increase the risk of nearsightedness, while a high-sugar, low-protein diet increases likelihood of nearsightedness even if no closeup work is being performed.[39]

Faulty vision is commonly treated with laser surgery. Many of those who undergo this surgery are quite delighted with the results, but not everyone. Many who undergo laser surgery require corrective lenses at least part of the time. Some also suffer chronic pain after the surgery or experience corneal infections. The long-term effects of this surgery have not been well examined.

SUGGESTIONS

- Consume protein and fiber in conjunction with sweets.
- Minimize or eliminate sugar and refined carbohydrate intake.
- Supplement with omega-3 oils.

Night Blindness

SIGN

Night blindness consists of difficulty seeing at night or seeing well when moving from a well-lit situation to a dimly lit one. An indication is how well one can see after walking into a dark theater on a bright day.

The more myopic an individual becomes, the greater the likelihood of becoming obese or developing adult-onset diabetes.

RELATED TOPICS

BEER BELLY SYNDROME

MACULAR DEGENERATION

NIGHT BLINDNESS

OBESITY

TOOTH DECAY

UPPER BODY WEIGHT GAIN

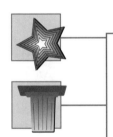

SIGNIFICANCE

This sign is associated with vitamin A deficiency.

DISCUSSION

Night blindness can increase risk of night driving, reducing vision in the dark, and making oncoming headlights temporarily blinding. The retina in the back of the eye consists of rod and cone structures. The periphery of the retina consists primarily of rods that enable us to see in poor light when a vitamin A–derived compound called visual purple comes in contact with the rods. Vitamin A deficiency blocks this visual process. Other signs of vitamin A deficiency include dryness of the eyes, the tendency for the lids to become crusty, and white foamy plaques on the cornea called Bitots spots.[40]

Some carotenoids can be converted into vitamin A, but carotenoids should not be equated with vitamin A.

Some carotenoids can be converted into vitamin A, but carotenoids should not be equated with vitamin A. Carotenoids have very little risk of toxicity, while excesses of vitamin A are toxic. A second important distinction is that some people have a very difficult time converting carotenoids to vitamin A. Even with a substantial intake of carotenoids, these people may still evidence signs of deficiency of vitamin A, including night blindness. Vitamin A is easily supplemented, fat soluble, and can be stored in the body for a considerable period of time. Zinc is essential for removing vitamin A from liver storage, and deficiency of this mineral can impair vitamin A utilization, resulting in deficiency symptoms.

Cod liver oil is generally the safest and most effective means of vitamin A supplementation. Vitamin A is available in a water-miscibilized (broken into tiny dots) form which may be better used by those who suffer from fat utilization problems as can happen with gallbladder removal or diabetes. It is not recommended that a pregnant woman take more than 10,000 IU of vitamin A daily, as it may increase the risk of birth defects.

Experimental animals deprived of vitamin D and calcium develop a condition comparable to retinitis pigmentosa.

Retinitis pigmentosa is a genetic disorder characterized by loss of peripheral vision and poor night vision. Experimental animals deprived of vitamin D and calcium develop a comparable condition. Dr. Arthur Knapp, after observing these animal experiments, treated this condition with vitamin D and calcium and found that every patient improved.[41] A nutritional approach such as this is worth a trial in this difficult disorder where little in the way of medical treatment is available. Cod liver oil is an excellent source of both vitamins A and D.

RELATED TOPICS

CALLUSES

DRY EYES

SUGGESTIONS

- Beware of supplementing with excess vitamin A.
- Don't rely on carotenoids to meet a vitamin A requirement.
- Supplement with cod liver oil or vitamin A.
- Use a multiple vitamin-mineral with zinc.

Puffy, Dark, Inflamed, or Wrinkled Under the Eyes

SIGNS

Puffy or swollen tissue beneath the eye (Scientific term: periorbital edema)

Wrinkles or folds on the lid below the eye (Scientific term: Dennie's sign)

Dark circles under the eye (Scientific term: allergic shiners)

Inflammation of the eyelids (Scientific term: blepharitis)

SIGNIFICANCE

These signs are all common allergy indicators. Puffiness under the eye can also indicate kidney problems.

DISCUSSION

Dr. Doris Rapp observed that the skin under the eye tended to be rather loose, becoming puffy or forming wrinkles if the body is holding water. Many of these signs around the eyes come and go when exposure to allergens is involved and exposure is not constant.[42] Disappearance of the signs, however, may not immediately follow avoidance of an allergen.

Puffy eyes may be the only indication of milk intolerance, especially in children.[43] Fluid retention under the eye commonly accompanies allergy and less frequently indicates damage to the kidney. The tendency to accumulate water as a result of allergic response can result in a weight gain of as much as 2 to 6 pounds in a single day. This weight may persist for two or more days until the body has rid itself of the remnants of the food that triggered the allergic response.[44]

Puffy eyes may be the only indication of milk intolerance, especially in children.

Allergic eye folds result from swelling of the tissue and folding of the eyelid. Dark circles often accompany eye folds and result from congestion of blood flow around the eyes. This sign is often coupled with recurrent middle ear infections, congestion of the sinuses, swelling, and mouth breathing, which can lead to sore throat.[45] Dark circles may also be caused by fatigue and lack of sleep. African Americans may develop dark circles under the eyes in conjunction with anemia with no other symptoms.[46]

Inflammation of the eyelids may result from allergy, drying of the tears, or bacterial infection.[47] Omega-3 oils, amino acids, and vitamin B12 are useful nutrients for this condition.[48] Hot compresses applied to the eyes to melt and loosen dried oils clogging the base of the eyelashes prevents intensification of the condition.

SUGGESTIONS

■ Avoid suspect foods or inhalants and note if the eye signs disappear.

■ Puffy eyes may indicate the need for evaluation of kidney function.

■ Use essential fatty acids from fish oils, antioxidants, and trace minerals.

■ Young children should be tested for tolerance to milk.

Vitamin B2 deficiency can lead to sensitivity to bright light.

Red Eyes

SIGN

Capillary growth in the white of the eye, commonly seen in alcoholics, sometimes accompanied by a red nose

SIGNIFICANCE

This sign may be the result of a vitamin B2 or riboflavin deficiency.

DISCUSSION

While eyes can and often do become red as a result of irritation, chronic redness with visible blood vessels in the white of the eye, on the cheeks, and/or on the nose can signify shortage of vitamin B2. The stereotypical red nose and cheeks of the alcoholic are a result of this deficiency. Vitamin B2 deficiency results in sensitivity to bright light.

Vitamin B2 carries oxygen to the surface of the skin. When the vitamin is inadequately supplied in the diet, blood vessels grow to supply oxygen to surface tissues, including the white of the eyes. Alcoholics run the risk of

Chapter 4 – Eyes and Forehead

becoming deficient not only in vitamin B2, but also in vitamin B6 and magnesium, which are believed to be associated with delirium tremens.[49]

If blood vessels pop in the eye, this may indicate high blood pressure or weakened blood vessel walls due to inadequate intake of vitamin C, flavonoids, and other nutrients involved in construction of healthy connective tissue. Blood pressure should be checked since untreated high blood pressure can have serious consequences, including blindness.

SUGGESTIONS

- Reducing refined carbohydrates and increasing protein intake may decrease desire for alcohol.
- Supplement with B complex vitamins.

Sensitivity to Bright Light

SIGN

Bright light makes the eyes uncomfortable, sometimes to the point of needing to wear sunglasses

SIGNIFICANCE

This sign suggests weak adrenals.

DISCUSSION

Those with weak adrenal glands can often be picked out of a crowd because they tend to wear sunglasses in order to cope with an increased sensitivity to bright light. The adrenal glands control contraction of the iris when the eye is exposed to light. Dr. George Goodhart reported that shining an examining light into the eye of someone with low adrenal function for 30 to 40 seconds will often result in a dilation (rather than a contraction) of the pupil or an alternating contraction and dilation. He commented that this explains "why some patients can't stand bright lights."[50]

Another sign of weak adrenal is a white line produced by drawing a fingernail across the abdomen. This is called Sergent's white adrenal line. The mark on the abdomen is usually drawn about six inches. The line will normally turn red in a few seconds. If the person has a weak adrenal, the line will oftentimes stay white for up to two minutes and also become wider.[51]

RELATED TOPICS

CRAVING FOR SALT

DIZZINESS UPON RISING

RED EYES

SUGGESTIONS

- A quality supplement of adrenal glandular may be helpful.
- Avoid refined carbohydrates.
- Consume adequate protein, complex carbohydrates, fruits and vegetables.
- Supplement with quality oils, vitamin B complex, and vitamin C.

Up and Down, Side to Side Eye Movement

SIGN

This syndrome is indicated by a movement of the eyes from side to side, up and down, or in a rotary motion. (Scientific term: Wernicke-Korsakoff Syndrome)

SIGNIFICANCE

This is a vitamin B1 or thiamine deficiency, common in alcoholics.

DISCUSSION

I have had a friendship for years with a woman who once told me she served a B complex vitamin with every cocktail at her parties. The woman's guests reported they did not suffer from a hangover the next day.

Another woman at one of my seminars worked as a nurse for one of the great nutrition pioneers. She shared that this man greatly enjoyed drinking alcohol. He would blend raw liver with synthetic B vitamins, drink the mixture, and then go out and party to his heart's content. He believed that B complex vitamins greatly aided the body's detoxification of harmful substances such as alcohol. This man's concoction obviously contained a good deal of vitamin B1, although I draw the line at gulping down raw liver!

Dessicated or dried liver, on the other hand, is easy to use and an excellent source of very fine protein and B complex vitamins. A number of years ago, Dr. Benjamin Ershoff conducted an amazing experiment which he shared with me in a phone conversation. He dropped rats in a barrel of cold water and tested endurance on several types of diets. Rats fed a basic diet, or the diet with added synthetic B complex vitamins, swam for a little over 13 minutes. Only 3 of 12 rats fed dried liver swam for less than two hours! These three swam 63, 83, and 87 minutes. Dr. Ershoff told me that he did not know what nutrients in the liver were responsible for the amazing performance of these animals because liver is a treasure trove of amino acids, vitamins, minerals, and enzymes.[52] Desiccated or dried liver is a wonderful supplement not only for those seeking a little extra stamina, but also for those seeking to build the health of the liver in its ability to detoxify harmful substances such as alcohol.

Sufferers from Wernicke-Korsakoff syndrome develop eye signs, including nystagmus, a condition in which the eyeballs move "from side to side, or less commonly up and down, or a rotary motion which is a combination of the two."[52] Double vision and paralysis of eye muscles or even the eyes can develop.

Korsakoff's psychosis is a condition in which short-term memory is lost and is often concealed by elaborate stories. It is closely coupled to Wernicke's disease and both respond to vitamin B1. Failure to treat this condition leads to irreversible brain damage. The B complex vitamins are absolutely essential for healthy brain and nerve function. Excessive alcohol consumption leads to clogging of blood vessels all over the body, including the brain. This can result in death of brain cells and an irreversible spiral of mental decline.

Alcoholism by its very nature is the antithesis of sound nutrition. It involves consuming large quantities of naked calories without the nutrients required to properly metabolize them. Dr. Roger Williams, author of a number of books on biochemistry, wrote "I will…positively assert that *no one who follows good nutritional practices will ever become an alcoholic.*" Dr. Williams found that alcoholics suffered from multiple nutrient deficiencies. Among the nutrients shown to benefit alcoholics are not only the B complex vitamins, but also magnesium and the amino acid glutamine, which decreases alcohol consumption by laboratory animals.[54]

SUGGESTIONS

- Eat sufficient protein and reduce consumption of refined carbohydrates.
- Supplement with a quality dried liver, vitamin B complex, and magnesium.
- Supplement with a good-quality multiple.

The B complex vitamins are absolutely essential for healthy brain and nerve function.

"I will…positively assert that no one who follows good nutritional practices will ever become an alcoholic." Roger Williams, Ph.D.

Food for Thought

Adrenal exhaustion appears to be epidemic in the modern world. The word stress is on the tip of everyone's tongue. In what ways could the following be considered stressors or contributors to adrenal exhaustion: sugar, coffee, a horror movie, a roller coaster ride, and an argument with a family member?

Dr. Archibald Hart in his book *Adrenalin and Stress* writes, "For some of you, adrenalin management will mean unlearning an 'addiction' to your own adrenalin; you may have become so dependent on the 'high' your adrenalin gives you that you have difficulty giving it up."[55] Have you ever felt the addictive nature of your own adrenalin?

Prevention of macular degeneration and blindness by a regular intake of carotenoid-rich leafy green foods and sulforaphane-rich cruciferous vegetables is a good example of a lifetime nutrition habit that can improve the quality of life as we age. Do you think the benefits of good nutrition are worth the cost in this instance? What steps would you be willing to take to achieve protection of your eyesight?

Nose and Ears: *Our Ventilation and Sound Systems*

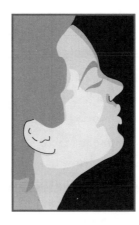

Several years ago I conducted a seminar in the lovely home of a Los Angeles lawyer. The skyline was hazy and the colors of the land were muted by the dense smog that blanketed the valley. Conversation turned to the polluted air and I learned of an environmental case built around the fact that young people in this city were found to have holes in their lungs resulting from damage due to air pollution. The health of these young people is being impacted by the collision of two powerful forces—increasing environmental pollution and a deteriorating quality of nutritional intake. The damage to the lungs of these adolescents was a direct result of the air pollution in that great city, but dietary intake was also a collaborator in the epidemic of respiratory troubles they experienced.

Young people rarely eat adequate quantities of fruits and vegetables, our major source of lung-protecting antioxidants. A front page story in *USA Today* (1/15/1996) announced that 25% of the vegetables children consume are French fries and only 1 in 5 children consumes the minimal recommendation of five servings of fruits and vegetables each day. The most frequent fruit consumption was fruit juice, which is high in sugar. Faulty nutrition is a contributor to some of the respiratory issues discussed in this chapter.

In this chapter you will see that compromised breathing is not only an unpleasant experience, but can put health in jeopardy. Oxygen is a nutrient more important than any other. Our life would cease in several minutes without it. Oxygen must be delivered to the cells and the sign of the EARLOBE CREASE may indicate that the circulatory system is undergoing damage, blocking delivery of nutrients and oxygen to the tissues of the body. It is not the abundance of nutrients available that determines health, but how efficiently these nutrients are delivered to the tissues that need them. Damage to the

Compromised breathing is not only an unpleasant experience, but can put health in jeopardy. Oxygen is a nutrient more important than any other. Our life would cease in several minutes without it.

circulatory system cannot only lead to death, but it may also result in a more subtle problem—faulty delivery of nutrients to the tissues of the body.

A regular intake of quality nutrition is mandatory for normal maturation of the sinuses and inner ear. Poor nutrition during development may lead to incomplete or delayed development of the sinus cavities and ear canal. This may result in a lifetime of breathing difficulties or ear infections, which can easily cause hearing damage.

Environmental factors may also threaten hearing. Loud noises are responsible for an epidemic of hearing loss. I recently spoke with a woman who spent a day at a rifle range. Even though she wore earplugs, her hearing was seriously impaired for a month and in the opinion of her physician her hearing might not fully recover for three months or longer.. This woman worked in sales and shared how frustrating it was to endeavor to understand her customers without the ability to hear. She also found herself isolated and alone and could not enjoy television because the voices were being seriously distorted.

Hearing experts suggest *no more* than about 15 minutes of exposure to a loud rock concert (115 decibels) without protection. A gun muzzle blast (140 decibels) is the maximum safe sound *with* hearing protection. Many people unknowingly expose themselves to sounds that gradually erode the ability to hear. Once hearing is destroyed, not even a hearing aid can restore the full quality of normal hearing.

Hearing loss is often gradual and difficult to detect and sufferers learn to read lips, often believing those around them are speaking in a low voice. Jacqueline Krohn, M.D., suggested the following simple test for loss of hearing in the high-frequency area: "Hold your hand next to your shoulder as though you are taking an oath. Rub your thumb and forefinger together. If you cannot hear a distinct rubbing sound, you may have some high frequency range hearing loss. Be sure to check both ears."[1] Suspicion of hearing loss should be confirmed by a qualified professional.

Allergic Salute

SIGN

The "allergic salute" results in a wrinkle normally formed about 1/2 inch above the tip of the nose. It is often marked by blackheads in adolescents.

SIGNIFICANCE

The allergic salute is a common allergy indicator resulting from a runny nose.

DISCUSSION

A creased nose is developed in response to wiping or rubbing the nose due to clogged sinuses as a consequence of allergy.[2] Dr. Doris Rapp, a leader in allergy research, described this process, "Pushing the nose up with the fingers or wrist repeatedly, or doing 'the allergic salute,' in response to chronic or sudden nasal secretions, is how the allergic nose wrinkle is created."[3] Intolerance to milk is a common source of clogged sinuses, especially in young people.

Make every effort to find the cause of clogged sinuses and runny nose and correct the problem. The brain desperately needs all the oxygen it can obtain. Any impairment of breathing impairs thinking.

SUGGESTIONS

- Avoid sugar and foods that make the sinuses run.
- Consume a nutrient-rich diet.
- Supplement with cod liver oil, omega-3 oils, and antioxidants.

Ear Infections

SIGN

Swelling and inflammation of the inner ear, often accompanied by bacterial infection (Scientific term: otitis media)

SIGNIFICANCE

Ear infections are the most common occasion for visits to a pediatrician and involve considerable expenditure.

DISCUSSION

One of my painful childhood recollections is recurrent ear infections which resulted in repetitious visits to the doctor's office for antibiotic treatments. Many years later a woman who ran a daycare center shared that the children she cared for rarely developed ear infections when they were given cod liver oil.

RELATED TOPICS
LONG FACE SYNDROME
MOUTH BREATHING
RUNNY NOSE
SLEEP APNEA

A study by allergy investigator Dr. Talal Nsouli, found that 78% of patients with recurrent ear infections had food allergy as a contributing factor.

Research supports the use of cod liver oil, vitamin A, and selenium in reducing ear infections.[4] Vitamin A deficiency leads to ear infections in animal studies.[5]

Allergy is a prime contributor to inflammation of the lining of the inner ear. A study by allergy investigator Dr. Talal Nsouli, found that 78% of patients with recurrent ear infections had food allergy as a contributing factor. Elimination diets resulted in improvement in 86% of these people. Reintroduction of the foods identified as causing the problem provoked a return of inner ear problems in 94% of the patients. The most common offending foods in order were milk (38%), wheat (33%), egg white (25%), peanut (20%) soy (17%), corn (15%), orange (10%), tomato (5%), chicken (5%), and apple (4%).[6]

Other studies have found an even higher incidence of allergy in children with ear infections. Allergies and sensitivities to foods are difficult to identify because there are so many possible substances to which one can react. These triggers can include not only foods, but also mold, animal hairs and saliva, and environmental chemicals.

Early identification and treatment of allergies in children prevents health problems later in life. Clues to allergy in young people include a "Jekyll and Hyde" personality, sleep disturbances, skin problems, digestive complaints, leg aches, elevated pulse, fatigue, clucking sounds in the throat, wrinkling of the nose, red earlobes, circles or puffiness under the eyes, and "wiggling" legs.[7]

Breastfeeding provides children substantial protection against ear infections. Risk of ear infections increases shortly after breastfeeding is discontinued, and after 12 months risk for bottlefed and breastfed infants is identical.[8] Prolonging the period of time during which children are breastfed reduces the risk of ear infections. The older a child becomes, the less likely he or she is to develop an ear infection.

SUGGESTIONS

- Reduce sugar consumption.
- Identify and avoid allergens.
- Supplement with cod liver oil.
- Supply all essential nutrients.

Earlobe Crease

SIGN

A diagonal crease in the earlobe

SIGNIFICANCE

The earlobe is rich in blood supply. Creases in the earlobe may reflect an increased risk of heart disease as a result of oxidative damage to the circulatory system. Wrinkling in general is associated with oxidative damage and increased risk of heart disease.

DISCUSSION

Dr. S. T. Frank first reported a link between creases in the earlobes and heart disease in 1973. A year later, Dr. Edgar Lichstein wrote, "The diagonal earlobe crease appears more commonly in patients with coronary heart disease and should be regarded as a coronary risk factor…this crease is easily noted and serves to identify this high risk group."[9]

Dr. Jack Sternlieb noted the importance of linking this sign with pains in the chest. He wrote, "…a person with the crease who has coronary signs, such as pains in the chest, has about a 90 percent chance of having coronary artery disease…the person who has symptoms of heart disease and does not have the earlobe crease has about a 90 percent chance of being free of coronary artery disease…the greatest significance of our research is for men between 45 and 60…"[9,10] In other words, this sign provides a risk indicator for a segment of the population with the greatest chance for having a heart attack.

Creases in the earlobe rich in blood vessels may reflect underlying damage to the circulatory system. Oxidation of blood vessels reduces their flexibility and leads to increases in blood pressure. Among the causative agents promoting this process are rancid fats and alcohol in the diet.[10, 11]

Dr. David Bresler found a different significance in the earlobe crease. The vagus nerve that controls the heart has a branch in the earlobe. Dr. Bresler suggested a crease in the earlobe may indicate damage to this nerve. Heart attacks can be triggered by abnormal rhythms in the heart triggered by the vagus nerve.[10]

Dr. Toshiharu Ishii and his associates noted that the deeper the crease in the earlobe, the more serious hardening of the arteries near the heart tended to be. The depth of earlobe creases also correlated with elevation of cholesterol levels.[12]

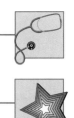

RELATED TOPIC

HAIR IN THE EAR

"…a person with the crease who has coronary signs, such as pains in the chest, has about a 90 percent chance of having coronary artery disease."
Jack Sternlieb, M.D.

Dr. Toshiharu Ishii and his associates noted that the deeper the crease in the earlobe, the more serious hardening of the arteries near the heart tended to be. The depth of earlobe creases also correlated with cholesterol levels.

Dr. Kilmer McCully pinpointed homocysteine, a byproduct of protein metabolism, as a key factor damaging blood vessel walls. He noted that even children with elevated blood levels of this end product of protein metabolism suffered extensive damage to the arteries and heart.[13] He further observed that accumulation of this protein in the blood resulted from nutritional deficiencies of vitamins B6, B12, folic acid, and betaine. Suggesting that heart disease could be prevented by vitamins did not go over well with pharmaceutical companies making a fortune selling cholesterol-lowering drugs. Nevertheless, Dr. McCully was unrelenting in his research and we now know that the genetic predisposition to accumulate homocysteine occurs in about 1 or 2 per 100 individuals.[14]

We have all been taught that cholesterol causes heart disease. In actuality, all the early studies linking heart disease to cholesterol were done with an oxidized product that is about 500 times more damaging to the arteries than is pure or non-rancid cholesterol.[15] Modest intake of unoxidized cholesterol is not a major risk factor for heart disease. Unfortunately, much of the cholesterol we do consume is oxidized. This includes aged meats and cheeses, butter allowed to sit too long, and highly heated fats. Robert Ford, president of Magnolia Laboratory, conducted extensive research decades ago that clearly demonstrated that a major cause of heart disease was stale or oxidized food. He wrote, "By feeding experiments with animals and human beings consuming nearly a quarter million dollars in labor and materials over a period of seven years I finally determined that the true cause of arteriosclerosis is simple: STALE FOOD."[16] Consuming fresh foods would dramatically reduce the incidence of heart disease in the United States, although it is difficult to persuade people to give up what many consider their favorite foods.

Antioxidants prevent cholesterol from turning rancid both in foods and also inside the human body. Vitamins C and E, carotenoids, and flavonoids have all been shown to protect from heart disease. Matthias Rath, a physician who worked with Linus Pauling, found vitamin C critical for the structure of the blood vessel wall. His book *Eradicating Heart Disease* offers stunning pictures of the difference between the blood vessel walls of guinea pigs on low versus high vitamin C intake. Blood vessel walls formed in the absence of vitamin C lack integrity and elasticity. They are more prone to damage, to buildup of fatty deposits, and to life-threatening clots.[17]

Vitamin C intake is significant beyond the nutrient's role in the formation of healthy connective tissue. Vitamin C also has the ability to support, protect, and regenerate other antioxidants such as vitamin E, glutathione, and carotenoids.[18] Vitamin C in nature is always accompanied by flavonoids, which have been shown to do the following:

- ► Improve the ability of the body to use vitamin C.
- ► Prevent death from heart disease.[19]
- ► Reduce the tendency of red blood cells to clump together by 40%.[20]
- ► Prevent cholesterol from oxidizing.[21]
- ► Strengthen connective tissue and block enzymes that can destroy it.[22]

Fat-soluble antioxidants are also important in the prevention of heart disease. Under normal circumstances, vitamin E is the most abundant antioxidant in what is generally regarded as "bad" or LDL cholesterol.[23] In one study, doctors were stunned to find that "vitamin E seems to reduce heart attacks by 75 percent when taken by people with bad hearts."[24] A natural vitamin E complex provides the best all-around benefit, as evidenced by the fact that tocotrienols, part of the vitamin E complex often missing in supplements, inhibit the critical enzyme involved in cholesterol synthesis.[25]

Carotenoid levels in blood and in LDL cholesterol can be easily elevated with appropriate supplementation.[26] In one study men taking a minimal dose of only one carotenoid, beta carotene, "suffered half as many major cardiovascular events, such as heart attack and stroke, as men taking placebo pills."[27] Supplementation with a natural carotenoid complex has been shown to reduce cellular oxidation significantly.[28]

Supplementation with a natural carotenoid complex has been shown to reduce cellular oxidation significantly.

SUGGESTIONS

- ■ Eat fresh foods.
- ■ Obtain all necessary nutrients emphasizing B complex vitamins and antioxidants.
- ■ Supplement generously with vitamin C.

Hair in the Ear

SIGN

Hair growing in the ear

SIGNIFICANCE

Ear hair suggests an increased risk of heart disease.

DISCUSSION

This sign is most reliable when accompanied by some of the other body signs indicating increased risk of heart disease such as the earlobe crease. Richard Wagner and his associates noted that combining the earlobe crease and ear-canal hair yielded the greatest sensitivity (90%) and the lowest false negative rate (10%).[29]

Wagner suggested that testosterone, indicated by ear hair, contributed to heart disease. This does not square with research done by Dr. Jonathan Wright, who argued that the evidence regarding testosterone is quite to the contrary. Natural testosterone is actually a primary factor necessary for the health of the heart and blood vessels. The risk of atherosclerosis goes down as free testosterone levels go up.[30]

The following may accompany low testosterone levels:

- ▸ Chest pains (angina)
- ▸ Hardening of the arteries
- ▸ Elevated blood sugar
- ▸ Elevated blood fats (cholesterol and triglycerides)
- ▸ High blood pressure
- ▸ Obesity
- ▸ Increased tendency of blood to clot[30]

RELATED TOPIC

EARLOBE CREASE

SUGGESTIONS

- ■ Do not rely on just one sign as an indicator of a problem.
- ■ Men with heart disease may have low levels of testosterone.

Hearing Loss

SIGN

Loss of the ability to hear

SIGNIFICANCE

One of the great untold stories of modern technology is the amount of hearing loss resulting from music amplifiers, firearms, and heavy equipment. The sensory cells of the ear are damaged by both the intensity of noise and also by the length of exposure to loud sounds. Loss of hearing isolates people and has been associated with depression.

DISCUSSION

The best protection for hearing is to avoid loud noises, although proper nutrition can provide considerable protection against the chance that loud noise will destroy hearing. It is believed that hearing loss results from free-radical damage in the ear as the result of loud noises. Antioxidants such as glutathione have been shown to help prevent hearing loss when animals are exposed to deafening sounds[31] The amino acid cysteine, vitamin C, and lipoic acid have all been shown to increase levels of glutathione in the body. Magnesium, at least in guinea pigs, appears to provide significant protection against hearing loss.[32] Vitamin B12 and folic acid deficiencies may be involved with hearing loss in older women.[33]

SUGGESTIONS

- Avoid prolonged or very loud sounds.[34]

- Maintain adequate protein, vitamin B complex and magnesium intake.

- Supplement with vitamin C, lipoic acid, and other antioxidants when exposed to loud noises.

Long Face Syndrome

SIGN

The face is long and narrow.

SIGNIFICANCE

This sign reflects early malnutrition, particularly in nutrients involved in bone building. Narrow faces are linked to crowding of the teeth and other dental abnormalities that can make chewing difficult or cause other dental difficulties.

DISCUSSION

Dentist James F. Garry, a national and international lecturer on airway obstruction and sleep apnea, discovered that difficulty breathing created defor-

The best protection for hearing is to avoid loud noises.

mities of the mouth and teeth. He also observed that a compromised airway is associated with "long face syndrome."[35] A long, narrow face often indicates a pinched sinus cavity.

It makes sense that deficiencies of nutrients involved in bone building, such as calcium and vitamin D, would lead to a narrower face. The smaller jaw, in turn, can result in crowding of the teeth in the mouth. Westin A. Price links a narrow face to early malnutrition in his encyclopedic volume *Nutrition and Physical Degeneration*.[36]

Dr. Francis M. Pottenger, Jr., conducted a feeding study in which he malnourished cats by cooking their food over four generations. The second-generation animals on the cooked foods had longer and narrower faces with a retraction or depression of the middle third of the face. The frontal sinuses were incompletely formed and overbites and underbites were common. Bones lost a good deal of density after two generations of poor diet. There was also insufficient room for a complete set of teeth. Pottenger wrote, "As the jaw does not expand or widen to make room for the permanent teeth, these teeth show considerable crowding, twisting, and impaction."[37]

The narrowing of the face observed in Pottenger's cats is very similar to what is observed in many people—perhaps providing a clue to a family history or upbringing stunted by poor nutrition. It is not impossible that the face could widen, particularly in young people, if the diet is improved.

RELATED TOPIC

MOUTH BREATHING

SUGGESTIONS

■ Eat a wholesome diet with as many raw foods as possible.

■ Supplement or obtain in the diet essential nutrients for bone building, including calcium, magnesium, protein, cod liver oil, and trace minerals.

Mouth Breathing

SIGN

An individual has difficulty breathing through the nose and therefore breathes through the mouth.

SIGNIFICANCE

Mouth breathing is often a clue to allergy or malnutrition that is inhibiting proper development or functioning of the sinus cavities.

DISCUSSION

Dentist James Garry suggested that airway obstruction pushes the tongue forward, resulting in deformities of the face and teeth. Airway obstruction can result from food or inhalant allergies or by enlarged tonsils or adenoids—a condition that can be caused by allergies. Those with obstruction of the nasal passages tend to become mouth breathers. This can alter the development of the face and the alignment of the teeth. Dr. Garry estimated that in the United States "obstructions in the nasal cavity exist in 85% of all children."[35]

Breathing patterns are best detected after an individual is sleeping: Mouth breathers sleep with their lips apart or open while nasal breathers sleep with their lips together. Nasal breathers have more relaxed facial muscles. Mouth breathers will often sleep with their head and shoulders forward, contributing to headache and poor postural alignment.

Chronic mouth breathing results in deterioration of health. Habitually breathing through the mouth alters the pH of the blood and decreases oxygen saturation, resulting in 20% more carbon dioxide and 20% less oxygen in the blood. These changes contribute to sleep apnea, grinding of the teeth, hyperactivity, difficulty in swallowing, and bed wetting.[35]

Dr. Garry suggested that breastfeeding is optimal for the facial development of the infant and promoted La Leche, an organization that advocates breastfeeding. Sucking an appendage or a bottle "can act as an orthodontic appliance," altering the alignment of the teeth and creating malocclusions.[38] Milk of a well-nourished mother taken from the breast continues to be the best source of nutrition for the developing infant.

SUGGESTIONS

- Breastfeed infants.
- Eliminate mouth breathing by elimination of allergens or whatever other measures are necessary.
- Purify the air in the home or car to decrease inhalant allergic responses.

Runny Nose

SIGN

The nose drips or runs a good deal of the time

Habitually breathing through the mouth alters the pH of the blood and decreases oxygen saturation, resulting in 20% more carbon dioxide and 20% less oxygen in the blood.

RELATED TOPICS

LONG FACE
SYNDROME

SLEEP APNEA

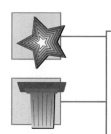

Chocolate was by far the most frequent trigger for nasal symptoms.

Nasal symptoms are quite common in those with chemical sensitivity.

SIGNIFICANCE

Runny nose is often connected to allergy.

DISCUSSION

One of my associates suffered with a continuously runny nose and suppressed the symptoms with large amounts of vitamin C. He later discovered that his difficulty was a result of intolerance to white potato.

A research study of 142 subjects found that the foods that created the strongest and quickest nasal reactions were chocolate, banana, and corn. Chocolate was by far the most frequent trigger for nasal symptoms. Other problem foods included wheat, milk, citrus fruits, eggs, plants of the cabbage family, tomatoes, apples, pork, onions, peas, beans, coffee, cola, and tea.[39] A diet free of cereal grains is often all that is necessary to clear up nasal symptoms.

Some interesting patterns were observed in these allergy studies. Foods could create reactions up to five days after they were eaten. Some subjects had worse symptoms in cold weather than in warm weather. Dietary items in concentrated form could trigger symptoms while such might not be the case when the foods were mixed with other foods. An example would be eating a banana by itself as opposed to having banana in a fruit salad.

Sometimes foods would trigger problems only when eaten first thing in the morning. In other situations, foods would create symptoms only when eaten at night. Some people had symptoms only when they were reacting to something else at the same time. Symptoms could include itching, obstruction of the nasal passages, sneezing, and discharge.[39] These observations suggest that identification of substances to which one is allergic may be very difficult.

Nasal symptoms are quite common in those with chemical sensitivity.[40] Dr. Stephen Levine, Ph.D., was almost totally incapacitated with chemical sensitivity for three years. He was forced to live in a wooden shack away from all chemicals for over three months. He discovered that Pacific kelp, rich in selenium, enabled his recovery. His discovery that the entire spectrum of antioxidants, including selenium, is important for dealing with chemical sensitivity and allergy is discussed in his book *Antioxidant Adaptation*.[41] Antioxidant levels are generally depressed in those with chronic sinus problems.[42]

Supplementation with fish oils rich in EPA significantly decreases the amount of nasal discharge in response to allergic exposure.[43] EPA is wellknown to decrease production of powerful inflammatory compounds at the cellular level.

SUGGESTIONS

- Avoid allergens.
- Nasal sprays containing saline solutions or xylitol may be helpful.[44]
- Purify the air indoors.
- Stay away from sugar.
- Supplement with antioxidants and other essential nutrients.
- Supplement with fish oils.

Sleep Apnea

SIGN

Breathing repeatedly stops while sleeping

SIGNIFICANCE

The individual with sleep apnea must partially wake up each time breathing stops and gasp for air. This results in sleep deprivation. Sleep apnea causes a depletion of oxygen at night, possibly contributing to its strong linkage to development of heart disease and Alzheimer's disease.

DISCUSSION

Dr. Emmanuel Mignot and his colleagues at the Center for Narcolepsy at Stanford's Center for Human Sleep Research have discovered a gene linked to sleep-disordered breathing. The gene is called ApoE4 and is also linked to heart disease and Alzheimer's. Alzheimer's patients often suffer from serious sleep disorders.[45, 46]

Those with sleep apnea are at greater risk for heart disease if homocysteine level is elevated, indicating deficiencies of folic acid, vitamin B6, and B12.[47] Lack of vitamin B1 has also been associated with congestive heart failure and sleep apnea.[48] Supplementation with B complex vitamins may protect from some of the risks associated with this breathing difficulty.

Physical activity and weight loss can prevent complications from sleep apnea.[49] Physical activity improves the functioning of the breathing apparatus, while weight loss reduces any obstruction in the respiratory tract. Physical activity may be difficult if thyroid function is low and low thyroid function is a

RELATED TOPICS

ALLERGIC SALUTE

LONG FACE SYNDROME

MOUTH BREATHING

The individual with sleep apnea must partially wake up each time breathing stops and gasp for air. This results in sleep deprivation.

Sleep apnea is associated with increased risk for heart disease and Alzheimer's disease.

Caffeine consumption tends to be almost three times higher in those with severe apnea symptoms.

well-recognized cause of sleep apnea. Those with this condition should have the function of the thyroid gland checked.[50]

Apnea makes obtaining a good night's sleep more difficult, but many of those with this disorder make the situation worse by excessive caffeine consumption, which tends to be almost three times higher in those with severe apnea symptoms than in those without problems.[51] Caffeine is a stimulant and should be avoided by those who have difficulty sleeping, especially those with sleep apnea.

Children may have difficulty resulting from caffeine consumption, although children are more likely to suffer with sleep apnea because they are allergic.[52] Allergic responses easily interfere with normal breathing.

Men often have a greater exposure to chemicals and contact with organic solvents increases risk of apnea. Solvents interfere with the nerve function that supports normal breathing.[53]

Combinations of signs often indicate increased risk. The earlobe crease has been associated with both sleep apnea and heart disease.[54]

SUGGESTIONS

- Avoid solvents.
- Avoid caffeine and sugar.
- Eliminate allergens from the diet.
- Supplement with B complex vitamins and omega-3 oils.
- Supplement with antioxidants.

Food for Thought

Relax and breathe deeply for a few minutes. In what ways do you feel differently? How do clogged sinuses make life more difficult?

Why do you think hearing loss is becoming so common in our society? What steps can you take to reduce your risk of losing your hearing?

Breastfeeding is one of the best preventatives of recurrent ear infections. What measures do you think our society could take to make it easier for mothers to breast-feed their children?

Heart disease is the number one killer today, although it was virtually unheard of a century ago. What factors do you think have led to the rapid increase in heart disease? What steps have you taken to protect your heart?

Mouth and Teeth: *Our Megaphone*

Neither dentists nor doctors could provide any explanation for the frequent occurrence of canker sores in my family while I was growing up—nor were any of their suggestions effective. Many years later I learned that the mouth is the first point of contact the body has with the foods we eat, making it the logical site for the body's early warning system that a food is not going to be well tolerated.

Eventually I discovered that my own outbreaks of canker sores were primarily a consequence of allergic response to gluten found in wheat, rye, oats, and barley. I learned this by fasting for several days. Subsequent to the fast I added foods back one at a time. Wheat, one of my dietary staples in those days, created such a severe negative response that I had no doubt it was not being well tolerated. Minimizing my exposure to gluten has not only eliminated canker sores, but my health is much improved in many other ways as well.

The tissues of the mouth can actually speak with a megaphone if we are willing to listen—providing remarkable insights into our nutritional history and current nutritional state. Not only do the soft tissues of the mouth provide clues to how well we are tolerating foods, but the gums tell us about the health of the circulatory system and the risk of heart attack. We can visually see an example of internal mucous producing epithelial tissues that line the entire digestive tract by glancing in the mouth.

The teeth also provide clues to adequacy of mineral intake and utilization. Decayed teeth provide a warning of profound glandular and nutritional problems. Minerals are either inadequately supplied, poorly used, or an overly acid diet is leaching the minerals out of the body. A look at the teeth may also provide a clue to the health of the bones and how adequately they are being mineralized.

The mouth is the first point of contact the body has with the foods we eat, making it the logical site for the body's early warning system that a food is not going to be well tolerated.

In addition to this, a glance in the mouth provides insight into toxic exposures, particularly to mercury and fluoride. Despite the commonly held belief that both are safe, these are well-known and well-researched toxic substances.

Bleeding Gums

Sign

The gums bleed when brushed

Significance

Bleeding gums may indicate blood sugar problems, bacterial infection in the mouth, allergy, or deficiency of the nutrients essential for construction of connective tissue, the most significant being vitamin C and flavonoids.

Discussion

The gums should be pink and tight around the teeth, a condition that is difficult to maintain without adequate vitamin C and flavonoids in the diet. Swollen, bleeding gums are characteristic of scurvy, as are fatigue, swollen joints, hardening of skin around the hair follicles, corkscrew-shaped hairs, muscular aches and pains, and emotional changes.[1] Many of the signs of scurvy are a consequence of weakening of connective tissue. Vitamin C is the critical linchpin in the cement that holds the cells and tissues of the body together. Deficiency of this vitamin weakens blood vessel walls, increasing the chances of bruising or bleeding of the gums when they are brushed. Vitamin B3 has proven helpful when vitamin C is ineffective for bleeding gums.[2] Niacin improves circulation and provides energy for the cells.

Red and inflamed gums are often caused by bacterial infection of weakened or unhealthy tissues. Hal Huggins, a well-known alternative dentist, along with others, closely links the bacteria-causing gum disease with the long-term well-being of the heart.[3] Sugar loading, which enhances growth of bacteria, causes a decline in the vitality of the gums paralleled by worsening in heart function.[4] A number of bacterial and viral entities have been implicated in heart disease. In the future, advanced heart disease may be treated by a combination of nutrition and medical procedures to combat these infectious organisms.

Vitamin C is the critical linchpin in the cement that holds the cells and tissues of the body together.

One category of nutrients that can restore the vitality of the gums is calcium and its co-workers vitamin D and magnesium. Underlying a good deal of gum disease is erosion of bone, often ensuing from low calcium intake.[5] Supplementing with bone-building nutrients stops and can reverse this loss of bone, improving the health of the gums.

A second category of nutrients necessary for restoration of gum health is the antioxidants. Levels of these important nutrients are often depressed in serious gum disease due to bacterial activity in the mouth.[6] Topical applications of two nutrients with antioxidant properties, folic acid and coenzyme Q10, are sometimes useful for gum problems.[7, 8]

Mercury poisoning may trigger not only bleeding gums, but also bad breath, grinding of the teeth, gum disease, and a metallic taste in the mouth. Don't overlook this possibility if there are many "silver" fillings in the mouth.[9]

RELATED TOPICS

MERCURY AMALGAMS

TARTAR ON THE TEETH

SUGGESTIONS

- Avoid highly refined carbohydrates.
- Eat fresh, raw foods rich in antioxidants and fiber.
- Practice oral hygiene with regular brushing and flossing.
- Receive proper dental care.
- Supplement with vitamin C and flavonoids.
- Topical application of folic acid or CoQ10 may be helpful.
- Use biocompatible composites rather than mercury for fillings.

Canker Sores

SIGN

Painful sores on the lips or inside the mouth
(Scientific term: aphtha)

SIGNIFICANCE

Canker sores are often precipitated by allergy, viral infection, and/or nutrient deficiencies.

DISCUSSION

Most of those who suffer with recurrent canker sores within the mouth will find avoidance of specific foods to which they are intolerant constructive. Gluten intolerance is one of the most frequent agents responsible for mouth sores. Gluten intolerance is associated with specific genetic markers. Dr. James Braly, author of *Dangerous Grains*, discusses 187 different health problems connected with gluten-containing grains, one of which is canker sores. Approximately 25 percent of those with celiac disease, a severe form of gluten intolerance, have a history of oral ulcerations.[10] Intolerance to other foods such as nuts, citrus, or berries may also cause canker sores.[11]

Very tiny quantities of a troublesome food can initiate severe damage in the delicate tissues of the mouth or digestive tract. One study of a 32-year-old woman with celiac disease found that many of her health problems improved by avoiding gluten. She insisted on taking a communion wafer daily, which contained only 1 mg of gluten. Examination of the lining of her digestive tract showed that this tiny exposure to gluten prevented complete healing of the digestive tract for two years. She also continued to have elevated numbers of white blood cells indicative of allergic responses taking place in the digestive tract.[12] Gluten is found in wheat, rye, oats, barley, spelt, tritacale, and kamut. A tiny bit of "cheating" may prevent or slow improvement when intensely allergic to gluten or other foods.

Nutritional deficiencies of vitamins and minerals may also attend canker sores. In one study over half the sufferers were lacking in vitamin B1, while other studies have shown deficiencies of iron, folic acid, vitamin B2, and vitamin B6. Flavonoids can significantly reduce length of outbreaks. [13] Low zinc levels may depress immune function, and supplementation with this mineral sometimes reduces frequency of canker sores.

There is a viral component to some canker sore infections as well. Lysine, abundant in fish and milk products, may help prevent canker sores and resist herpes infections. Herpes viruses require the amino acid arginine, found in chocolate and nuts, for reproduction. Combining a high-lysine, low-arginine diet makes it more difficult for these viruses to reproduce. This approach does not obviate the need to identify and remove from the diet poorly tolerated foods.[14]

Non-food items can also precipitate canker sores. Avoidance of toothpastes with sodium lauryl sulfate reduced mouth ulcers 64% in one study.[15] Canker

Approximately 25 percent of those with celiac disease, a severe form of gluten intolerance, have a history of oral ulcerations.

A tiny bit of "cheating" may prevent or slow improvement when intensely allergic to gluten or other foods.

sores are a puzzle to many who do not consider the wide range of possible allergic triggers for this symptom.

SUGGESTIONS

■ Don't put anything in the mouth, including toothpaste, that irritates the oral tissues.

■ Identify and avoid allergy triggers for canker sores.

■ Prevent nutritional deficiencies.

■ Test a diet rich in lysine and low in arginine or try supplementing with lysine.

Cavitations (Extraction of Wisdom Teeth)

SIGN

A pocket of infected bone

SIGNIFICANCE

Cavitations sometimes develop when wisdom or other teeth are extracted and the ligament that fastens the tooth to the jawbone is not removed. Incomplete healing will then take place, potentially leaving a site for bacteria to take up residence, multiply, and release toxins into the body.

DISCUSSION

Dr. Christopher Hussar, an oral surgeon, wrote, "The concept that a patient's health problems could be caused by hidden dental problems is…generally dismissed out of hand by most dentists and doctors…Nevertheless, there is overwhelming evidence that a great many of today's health problems have their origin in the mouth, stemming from the effects of toxic dental materials and/or the disease conditions resulting from the standard practices of root canal fillings and tooth extractions." Dr. Hussar reported, "I have been privileged to be able to remove small areas of infected dead bone from people's jaws, resulting in the cure of such diverse conditions as headaches, blindness, migratory arthritis, autoimmune disease, tinnitus, fibromyalgia, ear pain, neck pain, and many others."[16] Dr. Hussar wrote the forward to a book by Susan Stockton entitled *Beyond Amalgam: The Hidden Health Hazard Posed by Jawbone Cavitations*. In

RELATED TOPIC

NUMBNESS OF THE HANDS OR FEET

"A great many of today's health problems have their origin in the mouth."

Christopher Hussar, DDS, DO

this book Stockton explains how cavitations damaged her health for many years until they were removed through seven hours of exhausting surgery.

SUGGESTIONS

- Maintain optimal immune function by avoiding sweets and eating a healthy diet.
- Realize hidden infection in the jawbone can exist.
- Seek out someone who specializes in this kind of work if you suspect a problem. Many dentists do not have equipment to detect cavitations effectively.

RELATED TOPIC
ROOT CANALS

Cracks at the Corner of the Mouth

SIGN

"A condition characterized by the presence of fissures and other lesions on the lips and at the angles of the mouth."[17]
(Scientific term: cheilosis)

SIGNIFICANCE

Cracks at the corner of the mouth are characteristic of nutrient deficiency, especially vitamin B2 or riboflavin. Deficiency of vitamin B3 can also cause this symptom.

DISCUSSION

Cheilosis lesions resulting from riboflavin deficiency can extend into the mucous membranes in the mouth. The cracks would normally appear raw, but can become yellowish if they become infected. Painful cracks can also appear on the upper and lower lips.

Other signs of deficiency of riboflavin may be magenta tongue, scrotal dermatitis which is very itchy, growth of blood vessels into the white of the eye, and sensitivity to bright light. Vitamin B2 deficiency may also cause plugging of the pores around the nose, mouth, ears, and eyes.[18]

Mouth breathers are prone to develop cracks around the mouth owing to dehydration of the lips.[19] Bodily dehydration is a side effect of a number of medications and a consequence of not drinking enough water. Older people often lose their sense of thirst and become seriously dried out.

RELATED TOPICS
CARPAL TUNNEL SYNDROME
MIGRAINE
YELLOW URINE

Chapter 6 – Mouth and Teeth

SUGGESTIONS

- Drink sufficient water to prevent dehydration.
- Obtain adequate B complex vitamins.

Crimson Crescents in the Throat

SIGN

Bright crimson crescents near the back molars on both sides of the throat

SIGNIFICANCE

Chronic fatigue patients will often exhibit crimson crescents in the throat.

DISCUSSION

Dr. Burke A. Cunha, chief of the infectious disease division at Winthrop-University Hospital in New York has discovered crimson crescents in the throats of 80% of those with chronic fatigue. These crescents are on both sides of the throat, are near the back molars, and are often very bright. Physicians have missed this sign for years because they are trained to look further back in the throat. The edges of the crescent become less distinct when the tonsils are removed. The crescents will fade when the disease goes into remission and return when the disease worsens. A small number of normal people may have the sign.

Dr. Cunha suspects the cause is viral. He finds evidence of infection with coxsackie B and Human Herpes Virus-6 (HHV). Dr. Cunha believes adults pick up HHV from children. Those with chronic fatigue often have depressed natural killer cells as well.[20]

Poor functioning of the glandular system, particularly with regard to the adrenal glands and thyroid, can result in fatigue. These glands play an important role in immune competence. Support for endocrine function is often highly beneficial for those who suffer with chronic fatigue.

Many cases of chronic fatigue improve dramatically with supplementation and avoidance of foods that are not tolerated. This may be due to the fact that the immune system, unburdened of allergens and reinforced with nutrients, deals more effectively with whatever other barriers to good health remain. We have an army of defenders against viruses within us, but an army that is not fed

RELATED TOPICS
DIZZINESS UPON RISING

FLUOROSIS

JOINT AND MUSCLE PAIN

SENSITIVITY TO BRIGHT LIGHT

UNDERARM TEMPERATURE TEST

cannot fight. Superior nutrition is essential if we are to hope to have an efficiently functioning immune system.

My own experience and a considerable amount of research suggest that chronic fatigue often responds to nutritional support for the functioning of the nerves and endocrine glands. The high-quality oils, including phospholipids and phytosterols, are essential to the support of these tissues. My own mother suffered many years of fatigue, despite the use of vitamin and mineral supplementation, until these quality oils were added to her diet.[21, 22]

SUGGESTIONS

■ Don't skimp on sleep. Many people with chronic fatigue attempt to function without adequate rest.

■ Eat an optimal diet low in sugars and high in protein, fruits, and vegetables.

■ Eliminate allergy-evoking foods.

■ Supplement with all essential nutrients, especially the antioxidants.

■ Support brain, nerve, and glandular function with quality fats, including omega-3 oils, phospholipids, and phytosterols.

Fissured or Geographic Tongue

SIGN

The tongue looks like a map with denuded patches or cracks on the surface

SIGNIFICANCE

Fissured or geographic tongue may reflect deficiency of the B complex vitamins, especially vitamin B3. Changes in the appearance of the tongue may also result from allergic responses to foods and from infection.

DISCUSSION

Dr. Alan Pressman, Chair of the Department of Clinical Nutrition of New York Chiropractic College, suggested that niacin deficiency should be considered when cracks appear on the surface of the tongue. Other B vitamin deficiencies can influence the appearance of the tongue as well. A smooth, pale and slick tongue may be associated with deficiencies of folic acid, vitamin B2, iron, or vitamin B12. Vitamin B2 deficiency can make the tongue appear beefy and purplish red.[23] Dr. William Kauffman found that a tongue that looks like a bald tire reflects deficiency of the B vitamins.[24] An article published in *Lancet*, the British medical journal, in 1975 suggested that when the tongue is reddened and smooth there is an 80% probability of a deficiency of vitamins B2 or B3.[25]

Vitamin B3 or niacin is a highly significant vitamin. Symptoms of niacin deficiency or pellagra include the "4 D's": diarrhea, photosensitive dermatitis, dementia, and death (usually in this order). Pellagra is an Italian word meaning "rough skin." Interestingly, it is generally acknowledged that deficiency in niacin causes black tongue in dogs, lending credence to the idea that deficiency might also alter the appearance of the human tongue. Niacin deficiency also changes the appearance of the skin and changes in the appearance of the tongue are known to be associated with skin disorders such as psoriasis.

Dr. Jonathan Wright suggested that geographic tongue normalizes with supplementation with folate, vitamin B12, and zinc. He wrote, "…liver from organically raised animals is a good source of all three." Liver is a treasure trove of nutrition, and nutrients besides the ones mentioned could improve the appearance of the tongue as well. Supplementation should continue until the tongue normalizes. He observed that these nutrients almost always improved a geographic tongue although this phenomena is sometimes genetic.[26]

SUGGESTIONS

- Consider the possibility that allergy or infection may be involved.
- Supplement with omega-3 oils.
- Supplement with desiccated liver or vitamin B complex and zinc for a prolonged period of time.

Fluorosis

SIGN

White chalky spots or brown staining and pitting on the teeth

SIGNIFICANCE

Fluorosis shows that an individual is being or has been exposed to excessive fluoride, which can be quite toxic. Mild excess results in

RELATED TOPICS
OSTEOARTHRITIS
SCHIZOPHRENIA
SENSE OF HUMOR
UP AND DOWN,
SIDE TO SIDE EYE
MOVEMENT

chalky spots on the teeth, while considerable excess causes brown stain, and pitting of the teeth. Extreme fluorosis is quite unsightly and damaged teeth result in decreased self-confidence and self-esteem.

DISCUSSION

Fluoride is probably the most widely promoted measure for prevention of tooth decay—more so than avoiding sweets. The American Dental Association admits that when fluoride is added to the water supply 10% of the population will develop fluorosis.[27]

Water is only one source of fluoride exposure. Fluoride is also found in substantive amounts in toothpaste, mouthwashes, fluoride gels and rinses, foods processed in fluoridated areas, and tea. This sign is increasing rapidly as total fluoride use increases.[28] The fact that fluorosis can ruin the teeth is evidenced by a "goodwill" payment of 1000 pounds a toothpaste manufacturer made in 1996 to a family in London with a child whose teeth were ruined by fluoridated toothpaste.[29]

Toothpastes now carry warnings that young children should not swallow them due to fluoride's toxicity. An example of such a warning follows:

"Warnings: Keep out of the reach of children under 6 years of age. If you accidentally swallow more than used for brushing, seek professional help or contact a poison control center immediately."[30]

I have known several mothers with children who were extremely hyperactive. Discussion with these women often finds that they have taken every measure they can to make sure that their children get "lots" of fluoride to prevent tooth decay.

Recent studies on the neurotoxicity of fluoride are disturbing. Rats exposed to levels of fluoride comparable to human exposure when using fluoridated toothpaste manifested attention and cognitive deficits and hyperactivity. These injuries appeared more frequently in male animals just as attention deficit does in male children. Fluoride may be contributing to these behavioral problems. You will find more detail on this subject in the section discussing ADHD.[31]

Fluoride's capacity to do damage goes beyond its influence on the brain. Fluoride has a high bonding affinity for hydrogen, and hydrogen bonds hold DNA together.[32] Excessive fluoride may speed the aging process by tearing apart the DNA of the cells and overworking repair enzymes.

RELATED TOPICS

ATTENTION DEFICIT HYPERACTIVITY DISORDER

TOOTH DECAY

Rats exposed to levels of fluoride comparable to human exposure when using fluoridated toothpaste manifested attention and cognitive deficits and hyperactivity.

Suggestions

- Avoid excessive exposure to fluoride.

- Avoid sugar and refined carbohydrates to reduce tooth decay.

- Fluoride is most toxic to the portion of the population suffering the greatest degree of malnutrition.

Mercury Amalgams

Sign

"Silver" (actually silver-mercury amalgam) fillings in the mouth

Significance

Mercury has been described as the second most toxic natural element on earth after uranium. Mixtures of gold and mercury in the mouth can increase the rate at which the mercury amalgams deteriorate, increasing overall exposure to this highly toxic metal. Amalgams also release mercury every time an individual with amalgams in the mouth chews food.

Potential toxic effects of mercury include loss of self-control, irritability, shyness, memory problems, depression, bleeding gums, bad breath and digestive problems, nervous symptoms, including heartbeat irregularities, tremors, dizziness, ringing in the ears, hormone disturbances, immune problems, and kidney damage, which can result in high blood pressure.[33]

Discussion

A number of years ago I lost one of the crowns in my mouth. One of the pioneers in removal of mercury amalgams lived in the California seaside community where this took place. I contacted him and asked if he could repair the damage.

This great dentist told me that he had a chair in his home and would be delighted to provide a temporary solution. When he looked in my mouth, he noted the many mercury amalgams and suggested that they be removed. He pointed out that mercury is toxic and gradually releases in the body. It also weakens the structure of the teeth, while the newer composites tend to bond the teeth together.

I consented to the removal of the mercury amalgams, which took place over several months. When the last of the amalgams were removed, I was overcome by extreme drowsiness for a couple of days. Little red dots broke out around my mouth. I am convinced that these phenomena were an effort on the part of my body to unload the metal after the last of the amalgams were removed. I have never regretted the expenditure involved in having this work done. Subtle improvements in my health have shown themselves over time. The more I learn about mercury toxicity, the happier I am to have reduced my exposure many years ago. "Silver" fillings contain up to 70% mercury, which is highly toxic to brain and nerve tissue.

I am often asked why the American Dental Association would permit mercury amalgams if they are hazardous to health. This requires a little historical perspective. The first dental society in the United States was the American Society of Dental Surgeons. This association was firmly committed to using only gold and silver for fillings. Those who joined the organization were required to sign a pledge stating that they would not use amalgam fillings. So many members were removed from the society for violations that the organization lost its power and disintegrated.

Ousted members formed their own organization called the American Dental Association, which has maintained an official position that mercury is made virtually harmless when it combines with other metals to produce amalgam. Repeated scientific studies have shown this to be false, but traditional ways of thinking are difficult to change. It is an unfortunate fact that modern medicine is so specialized that the practicing dentist is often incompletely aware of the toxic nature of mercury, a risk that is obvious to the toxicologist. The result is that most of us have been exposed to mercury fillings and need to inform ourselves on appropriate means of protecting our bodies from this toxic substance.

The importance of selenium as a protector against mercury toxicity is illustrated by an experiment conducted by H. E. Ganther in which Japanese quail were fed toxic methyl mercury. Only 7% of the quail died when fed methyl mercury along with mercury-contaminated tuna, while 52% of the animals given an equivalent amount of methyl mercury died. Research revealed that the tuna contained large quantities of the trace mineral selenium, which was protecting the quail from the full toxicity of the mercury.[34] Selenium is absolutely essential in small quantities, but can be highly toxic in excess. Reasonable selenium supplementation is one of the best means of protecting ourselves from highly toxic mercury compounds.

A glance at the periodic table of elements reveals why selenium protects from mercury toxicity. Selenium and sulfur occupy the same column in the periodic table of elements. Both have a strong affinity for mercury. Selenium has the ability to replace sulfur in chemical bonding—mercury is usually found in sulfur bonds in the human body. The displaced mercury is then free to be excreted.[35] Vitamin C also supports the glutathione antioxidant system and is an important tool for counteracting mercury toxicity.

Sulfur-containing foods assist in reducing mercury exposure and toxicity. Mercury is attracted to sulfur and appropriate sulfur compounds can escort mercury out of the body or dilute its effect on the tissues. Helpful sources of sulfur include amino acids composed of sulfur, cilantro, cruciferous vegetables, garlic, and onion.

SUGGESTIONS

- Eat sulfur-containing foods.
- Removal of amalgams should be performed by a knowledgeable dentist, aware of the toxic risks this metal poses.
- Supplement with B complex vitamins and betaine.
- Supplement with a multiple vitamin that contains selenium.

Root Canals

SIGN

Removal of the infected center of a tooth and replacement with a packing material.

SIGNIFICANCE

Almost all materials used to fill the tooth after a root canal shrink. Bacteria can grow in the miles of tubules in the dentin of the teeth. These bacteria may then travel to other parts of the body or release toxins that can damage remote sites.

Selenium has the ability to replace sulfur in chemical bonding—mercury is usually found in sulfur bonds in the human body.

DISCUSSION

I found it necessary to have a root canal at one point in my forties. Shortly afterwards, I read Dr. George Meinig's *Root Canal Cover-Up*. This is a rather disturbing book for anyone who has received a root canal.

Meinig uncovered 4,000 pages of research by Dr. Westin Price, which demonstrated that teeth with root canals may harbor pathogenic bacteria that can precipitate arthritis and other illnesses. Price observed that when infected teeth were removed from patients, illnesses often cleared up. When infected teeth were implanted beneath the skin of rabbits, they developed the same health problems the people with the root canals had experienced. Meinig pointed out that root canal bacteria most often affected the heart, but other tissues could be harmed.[36]

I called Dr. Meinig and told him that I found his book a little disturbing in view of the fact that I had just experienced a root canal. His response was something like, "If you think you feel bad, I was one of the founders of the practice of root canals." Thanks to Dr. Meinig's work many dentists are now aware of the potential problem root canals may create.

The best way to deal with root canals is to prevent them. This involves adequate nutrition to prevent tooth decay. Due to the fact that up to 75% of a tooth may be ground away when a crown is placed, crowns may so decrease the vitality of a tooth that a root canal becomes necessary. The American Dental Association admits that one in five crowned teeth dies. The consequence is an extraction or a root canal. Dr. Frank Jerome, a brilliant alternative dentist, discussed alternatives to crowns such as inlays and onlays in his excellent book *Tooth Truth*.[37]

Options are limited when the root canal becomes diseased. The tooth can be extracted and the associated ligament that attaches the tooth to the jaw removed or a root canal may be performed. An improved packing material, calcium hydroxide, that does not shrink is available for filling the root canal, although little information is available on its effectiveness in preventing bacterial growth in the tubules in the dentin. Unfortunately, calcium hydroxide also expands when placed in the tooth, which can result in a crack in the tooth.

SUGGESTIONS

■ Check teeth with root canals regularly for infection.

The American Dental Association admits that one in five crowned teeth dies. The consequence is an extraction or a root canal.

RELATED TOPICS

CAVITATIONS

MERCURY AMALGAMS

TOOTH DECAY

Chapter 6 – Mouth and Teeth

- If root canals exist already, reducing sugar intake may inhibit bacterial growth.
- Investigate the possibility of an inlay or onlay rather than a crown.
- Prevent tooth decay in the first place.

Scalloped Tongue

SIGN

The tongue has indentations on the edges

SIGNIFICANCE

A scalloped tongue may indicate allergy or adrenal weakness. Allergic response causes fluid retention, creating this sign.

DISCUSSION

Dr. Jonathan Wright links a scalloped appearance to the edges of the tongue with allergies (which might reflect adrenal weakness). The indentations appear due to fluid retention in the tissue accompanying allergic response.[38] Endocrinologist John Tintera identified weakness of the adrenal gland as a root cause of affliction with allergies. He found it difficult to think of improving an allergy condition without also improving adrenal functioning.[39]

Allergies are best dealt with not only by avoiding offending substances, but also by improving the ability of the body to tolerate potential triggers. Support the adrenal gland with a diet low in sugar and refined carbohydrates. Fresh, raw foods improve adrenal function. Dr. Francis M. Pottenger, Jr., found the adrenal glands of cattle fed green grass were far healthier and more valuable therapeutically for treating allergy and asthma than adrenals of cattle fed dry feed.[40] Fresh, healthy foods are essential for building the strength of these glands that enable us to cope with stress.

A number of dietary supplements may also improve adrenal function. Supplement with the amino acid tyrosine (a precursor to adrenal hormones), vitamin B complex, vitamin C, adequate protein, antioxidants and digestive aids that minimize allergic responses to foods. Phospholipids and phytosterols from grains and legumes also appear to be supportive of adrenal function.

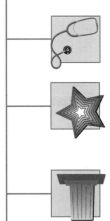

RELATED TOPICS

ALLERGIC SALUTE

CRAVING FOR SALT

DIZZINESS UPON RISING

PUFFY, DARK, INFLAMED, OR WRINKLED UNDER THE EYES

RUNNY NOSE

SENSITIVITY TO BRIGHT LIGHT

SUGGESTIONS

- Avoid sugar, caffeine, and refined carbohydrates.

- Avoid allergens.

- Build health to improve tolerance to allergens.

- Supplement or eat foods rich with vitamin B complex, antioxidants, amino acids, and essential fatty acids.

Tartar on the Teeth

SIGN

Periodontal disease begins with the buildup of sticky plaque on the teeth. This is followed by the development of tartar or hard mineral deposits at the gum line.

SIGNIFICANCE

Bacteria accumulate in these deposits, irritating and inflaming the gums. Tartar may indicate inability to properly digest fats or a deficiency of essential fatty acids.

DISCUSSION

Plaque can be removed by brushing. Tartar is difficult to remove and requires scraping. Many dental professionals do not have nutritional suggestions for reducing tartar buildup, but there is at least one suggestion that may work.

Dr. John Waters was a dentist who lived in the early 1900s. He perceived that at least 90% of his patients with mineral deposits on the teeth did not like the taste of fatty meats. (He lived before the modern fear of fat.) Dr. Waters surmised that these individuals with dislike for sausages, fatty meats, and bacon were low in bile. Bile salts act much like soap, helping to break down fats into small particles for proper absorption. He felt that fats helped the kidneys to remove acid from the body, and when fats were not properly handled, the blood remained excessively acid, allowing solids to precipitate on the teeth.

The best fats for neutralizing acids were beef, mutton, poultry, and cold-water mammals. Waters tested his theory by giving his patients supplemental ox bile and these foods. He found he was able to completely eliminate calculus or tartar formation.[41]

The foods Waters felt helpful all tended to be good sources of omega-3 oils when he lived and did his work. Beef and poultry are commonly grain-fed today and no longer provide a reliable source of omega-3 oils. Improvement in the quality and quantity of fats in the diet could account for some of the benefits Waters observed.

Relatively modest intake of vitamin E (50 I.U.) appears to reduce tartar formation as well.[42] Vitamin E prevents quality oils from oxidizing in the body. Protection of these oils is one way in which vitamin E can boost immune function throughout the body, including the mouth.

Fresh fruits and vegetables are rich in minerals that promote a normal alkaline pH of the blood. These foods should reduce tartar deposits. Refined sugar is highly acid and also feeds bacteria, which may contribute to tartar buildup and tooth decay.

Newly discovered "nanobacteria" have been implicated in creation of calcium deposits in the body in a number of diseases and may contribute to tartar as well. Tartar is composed of calcium phosphate in the chemical structure called "apatite." This chemical structure is what one would expect if nanobacteria were a causative factor in tartar formation. Endocrinologist Dr. R. Paul St. Amand found that tartar formation was often accompanied by fingernails that break easily, fibromyalgia, and tendency to develop osteoarthritis.[43] All of these conditions may be accompanied by overgrowth of nanobacteria.

If nanobacteria are proven to be involved with tartar formation Dr. Waters' insights regarding the importance of pH balance of the blood may provide a clue to a novel nutritional approach for coping with them. Nanobacteria may prove to be opportunistic organisms that thrive when certain conditions such as abnormal saliva or blood pH exist in the human body.

Nanobacteria may also be a factor in the calcification of the arteries in atherosclerosis. Prior to 1900, atherosclerosis and heart disease were virtually unheard of, while today they are major killers. The question that must be asked is, "Are nanobacterial problems more common because of increased infection from the organisms or is our state of resistance to infection eroded because of the quality of the food we eat?" Carlton Fredericks, an early pioneer in nutrition education, once wrote that the average American's idea of health is the ability to stand upright when the wind is blowing in the right direction. This kind of health makes a population susceptible to a wide variety of infectious organisms.

RELATED TOPICS

ARTHRITIS
(OSTEOARTHRITIS)

BRITTLE NAILS

JOINT AND MUSCLE PAIN

KIDNEY STONES

TOOTH DECAY

Endocrinologist Dr. R. Paul St. Amand found that tartar formation was often accompanied by fingernails that break easily, fibromyalgia, and tendency to develop osteoarthritis.

SUGGESTIONS

- ■ Avoid sugar and refined carbohydrates.
- ■ Eat generous quantities of fresh fruits and vegetables.
- ■ Supplement with vitamin E and bile acids, observing if tartar formation is reduced.

Tooth Decay

SIGN

An infection of the tooth that results in erosion, more commonly known as a cavity.

SIGNIFICANCE

One of the most common body signs in the United States is tooth decay. It provides evidence of the widespread malnutrition of the American population. Infections in the teeth can release toxins throughout the body if not treated. This condition is probably more common than any other except the common cold.

DISCUSSION

Dr. Weston Price, wrote, "…human teeth and the human mouth have become…the foci of infections that undermine the entire bodily health…"[44] The primary cause of tooth decay is poor nutrition, including lack of trace minerals and vitamins and excessive intake of refined sugars, which promotes bacterial growth in the mouth, resulting in acid formation that eats away at teeth.

Primitive peoples and those who eat unrefined foods have very little tooth decay. Price recorded that "…caries is a comparatively modern disease and …no skull showing this condition can be regarded as ancient." He believed the source of tooth decay was obvious: "It is store food which has given us store teeth."[44]

A number of years ago I had the opportunity to hear a brilliant presentation by Dr. Ralph Steinman. This outstanding dentist conducted work that demonstrated that there is a natural flow of fluids from the *inside* of the tooth to the *outside*. This natural flow nourishes the teeth, aids in repair, and flushes out bacteria. Unfortunately, a high intake of refined sugar reverses this natural flow, leading to the movement of acids from the outside of the tooth to the inside. This contributes greatly to tooth decay. Steinman demonstrated that sugar placed directly into the stomach (bypassing the teeth) could cause tooth decay in animals.[45]

Some sugars such as xylitol actually inhibit bacterial growth and tooth decay. Xylitol gums are available and studies indicate that they can significantly reduce tooth decay. The more frequently the gum is chewed, the greater the reduction in tooth decay. Xylitol coats the surface of bacteria, preventing them from adhering to the teeth.

Proper nutrition with adequate intake of whole foods, minerals and B complex vitamins can significantly reduce the risk of tooth decay. Dr. Roger Williams emphasized the importance of the B complex vitamins in prevention of tooth decay by noting an experiment in which tooth decay was reduced by 40% among children supplemented with 3 milligrams of vitamin B6 a day.[46]

Calcium, phosphate, and vitamin D are important nutrients for constructing healthy teeth. John Ott, who was granted an honorary doctorate for his pioneering work with light, founded the science of photobiology while doing time lapse photography for Walt Disney. He discovered that light regulates the endocrine system in its use of calcium and other nutrients involved in the building of healthy teeth. He wrote, "Recent experimental studies have indicated that abnormal growth responses develop when any part of the natural sunlight spectral energy is blocked from entering the eyes, and these include dental caries and tooth decay in both laboratory animals and schoolchildren."

In one study, 27 of 53 children under normal Cool-White fluorescent bulbs developed cavities over a one-year period of time. Only 10 of 46 children under fluorescents that duplicate normal sunlight developed cavities. Healthy light exposure is an important consideration in tooth decay, normal calcium and phosphorus metabolism, and also healthy bone development.[47]

Dr. Ott was one of the first to emphasize the benefits of light beyond the formation of vitamin D on the skin. Light entering the eye has a profound effect upon brain and glandular function.

Fluoride is a questionable means of reducing tooth decay due to its inherent toxicity.

SUGGESTIONS
- Avoid sugar and refined carbohydrates.
- Expose the body and eyes to modest amounts of sunlight.

■ Obtain "chain of life" nutrition, including cod liver oil, B complex vitamins, and the entire spectrum of minerals.

Food for Thought

One of my friends, a prominent dentist, once said, "Look in your patient's mouth. If a dentist has been there you have found the source of his problems!" This man believed strongly that mercury and fluoride were major health issues. What are your thoughts on these issues after reading the discussions provided here? Why do you think the dental profession has been so slow and resistant to acknowledge the toxicity of mercury and fluoride?

What changes have you noted in your health, good or bad, after having dental work performed?

The mouth is the first point of contact a food has with the human digestive tract and the immune system that protects it. Have you noted any changes in the oral tissues after eating certain foods?

Neck and Shoulders: *Pedestal for the Head*

I was sitting in traffic waiting for the light to change when I absently glanced in my rearview mirror. I did a doubletake when I saw an SUV behind me, approaching too rapidly. I knew that it would be a matter of seconds before the driver hit me. I had nowhere to go and only enough time to slide down in the seat to cushion my neck from the coming blow. The SUV slammed into me and pushed me into the car in front. This accident left me reeling for days—it could have left me suffering with pain for the rest of my life. If you've been through anything similar to this you know how delicate the neck can be.

One would not expect to see nutritional indicators in the neck and shoulders, however several factors make this part of the anatomy unique. The neck supports the head all day long. This can test the strength of muscles in the neck and shoulders as well as the resilience and integrity of the spinal column. Mineral deficiencies often result in deterioration of the bones in the neck and also affect the muscles in neck and shoulders which are under tension most of the day due to the weight of the head.

The thyroid gland is found in the neck. This important gland plays a large part in the amount of energy we enjoy. It has the ability to swell dramatically when it is not receiving enough iodine. Prior to adding iodine to salt this swelling was common in parts of the United States that contained little iodine in the soil. This chapter provides important insights on disorders of thyroid function, which are fairly common. The role of iodine in promoting health extends beyond support for thyroid function. This mineral enhances immune activity against viruses and bacteria and regulates cholesterol metabolism.

Deficiency of vitamin B12, which is essential for health of nerve tissue, may be indicated by a shooting pain in the neck. This nutrient is not as readily avail-

The thyroid gland is found in the neck. This important gland plays a large part in the amount of energy we enjoy.

able in the food supply as it once was. Older individuals are especially prone to develop deficiency of vitamin B12.

Finally, the neck is not covered by clothing, revealing how bare skin responds to exposure to sunlight. One of the most dread diseases of all time, pellagra, was often diagnosed by excessively heavy and persistent pigmentation of the neck and shoulders. Pellagra results from deficiency of vitamin B3. This nutrient has a proven ability to benefit schizophrenics, lower cholesterol levels, and reverse some of the ravages of osteoarthritis.

Electric Shock Sensation in the Neck

SIGN

A sensation of electric shock running down the spinal cord when the neck is bent is called Lhermitte's syndrome.

SIGNIFICANCE

This syndrome can be caused by deficiency of vitamin B12.[1] Multiple sclerosis or other nerve problems may also be indicated.[2]

DISCUSSION

Absorption of vitamin B12 is complex and difficult, requiring adequate stomach acid, two vitamin B12–binding proteins and a secretion of the stomach lining called intrinsic factor. Decreased production of intrinsic factor, or low stomach acid may result in vitamin B12 deficiency, particularly as we age. Intrinsic factor will not function properly in the absence of stomach acid.

Since vitamin B12 is essential for normal maturation of red blood cells, deficiency results in a severe anemia called pernicious anemia which may afflict as many as 1 out of 50 of those over 60 years of age. Dr. Jonathan Wright felt there was such a strong relationship between vitamin B12 deficiency and low stomach acid that he wrote, "One hundred percent of individuals suffering from pernicious anemia have *achlorhydria* (no stomach acid at all), which is the worst form of *hypochlorhydria* (a low stomach acid level)."[3]

Nitrous oxide anesthesia can antagonize vitamin B12 within the body. Serious vitamin B12 deficiency may result in Lhermitte's sign, irreversible deterioration of the nervous system and even death. Symptoms of depleted vitamin B12 include not only this sign, but also fatigue, numbness, abnormal sensations like burning or insects crawling on the skin, difficulty walking, urinary retention, difficulty thinking, and mild confusion.[4]

Vitamin B12 injections have been successfully used to treat bursitis. This is a condition in which inflammation develops at sites where sac-like cavities filled with fluid are situated to prevent friction in the body. Individuals with bursitis almost always suffer from indigestion and low stomach acid, indicating that vitamin B12 is not being absorbed. Use of antacids may contribute to low stomach acid and poor vitamin B12 absorption.[5]

Russell Jaffe, M.D., Ph.D., and Patrick Donovan have identified what they call "the great B12 robbery." They observed that the amount of vitamin B12 found in foods has declined dramatically in the time period from 1960 to 1990. For instance, the amount of B12 in beef liver declined from 122 mcg per 100 grams in 1960 to no detectable B12 in 100 grams of liver in 1990.

There are many possible reasons for this decline. One potential contributor is decline in soil cobalt essential for B12 synthesis as a result of use of artificial fertilizers. Widespread use of antibiotics and insecticides is also a factor, since vitamin B12 is synthesized by bacteria. The bacteria *P. Shermanii* which synthesizes B12 in cattle has adapted to antibiotics and other pollutants, but no longer synthesizes vitamin B12. Many common pollutants such as sulfur dioxide, mercury salts, and nitrous oxide are also vitamin B12 antagonists.[6]

SUGGESTIONS

- A sublingual vitamin B12 may be helpful if intrinsic factor is not functioning properly.

- Physicians can give injections of vitamin B12 in cases of serious deficiency.

- Supplement with a vitamin B complex to assure a reliable dietary source of vitamin B12.

- Support stomach acid if necessary.

Heavily Pigmented Neck (Casal's Necklace)

SIGN

Areas of the face, neck, or upper chest exposed to light become excessively pigmented or red. The skin may also be rough.

Use of antacids may contribute to low stomach acid and poor vitamin B12 absorption.

SIGNIFICANCE

This sign is the most often diagnosed characteristic of pellagra or vitamin B3 deficiency.

DISCUSSION

In Caucasians the skin lesions characteristic of pellagra often look like sunburn. In those with darker skin there is the appearance of excessive pigmentation of the skin. If deficiency continues, the skin becomes dry, scaly, and cracked and may peel off. The skin often cracks or blisters. When an open-neck shirt is worn, the condition affects the neck and upper chest and is called Casal's necklace.

An early indicator of pellagra is stomach pain and/or diarrhea. The tongue (and perhaps the rest of the digestive tract) can become sensitive and burn. The earliest diagnostic sign of pellagra is a tongue that looks smooth and red. The tongue can swell. The tip of the tongue and margins can become red and shiny. This has been referred to as the "strawberry tip" tongue.[7] These early signs of niacin deficiency can be accompanied by a darkening of the pigmentation on the backs of the hands and on the neck and shoulders.

SUGGESTION

■ Obtain adequate B complex, especially niacin, and omega-3 oils.

Sore Neck and Shoulders

SIGN

Tightness or stiffness in the neck and shoulders

SIGNIFICANCE

Sore neck and shoulders may result from allergy or deficiencies of calcium or magnesium.

DISCUSSION

Tightness in the neck and shoulders is sometimes a symptom of allergic response.[8] Avoiding the appropriate foods will eliminate symptoms under this circumstance.

Deficiencies in calcium or magnesium are more common causes of inability of the muscles of the neck and shoulders to relax. I remember one case of a woman who was seeing a therapist for sore neck and shoulders. Supplementation with an easily absorbable calcium and magnesium combination resolved the woman's pain and discomfort within a short period of time. Consumption of diuretics or high-phosphate beverages such as soda or coffee causes magnesium loss—a frequent cause of muscle stiffness and tightness.

SUGGESTIONS

- Try a high-quality calcium and magnesium supplement.
- If the problem persists, consider the possibility of allergic response.
- Lack of other nutrients may contribute to muscle problems as discussed in RELATED TOPICS.

Goiter or Swelling of the Neck

SIGN

A swelling of the thyroid gland

SIGNIFICANCE

A swelling of the thyroid may have several causes, including Hashimoto's thyroiditis, multinodular goiter, Graves disease, or iodine deficiency.

DISCUSSION

The thyroid is a small butterfly-shaped gland located in the neck just below the Adam's apple. A swelling of the neck may be more noticeable if the head is tilted back and water is swallowed while looking into a mirror. This is a procedure recommended on the website of the American Association of Clinical Endocrinologists.[9, 10]

Historically, the most common cause of goiter has been iodine deficiency. The incidence of this problem has decreased due to the addition of iodine to salt in the diet. The thyroid hormone thyroxine is 64% iodine. If this important trace mineral is lacking, the gland will swell as it overworks to try to produce the hormone thyroxine.

Thyroiditis, an inflammation of the thyroid gland, is caused by the body's attack against its own thyroid. This is eight times more common among women than men, suggesting that sex hormones may play a role in the development of the condition. Thyroiditis is often accompanied by a poorly functioning set of adrenal glands—a factor that may contribute to inflammation. The adrenals produce cortisone, an anti-inflammatory hormone.

Proper thyroid function is essential for normal cholesterol metabolism.

Increase in the size of a gland or muscle when it is overworked is not uncommon. This is called hypertrophy. The arm of a righthanded tennis player will become larger and stronger than the left due to greater use. The pancreas also appears to increase in size when animals are fed cooked foods as opposed to raw foods, which are rich in enzymes. Consider the possibility that a tissue is being overworked if informed that it is increasing in size. The thyroid is particularly susceptible to hypertrophy. Some areas of the world have very low iodine levels in the soil, which can predispose those living in these areas to goiter.

Some foods increase the risk of goiter by interfering with thyroid function. These foods include cabbage, kale, turnips, and soy. Reasonable intake of these foods should not pose problems unless iodine intake is inadequate.

There is a mass of clinical and experimental data that shows that the thyroid is intimately associated with cholesterol metabolism and that it has a controlling influence on the level of cholesterol in the blood plasma.

Proper thyroid function is essential for normal cholesterol metabolism. Dr. John Myers wrote, "The thyroid hormone, thyroxin, is the only hormone that stimulates the excretory function of the Kupffer cells of the liver. There is a mass of clinical and experimental data that shows that the thyroid is intimately associated with cholesterol metabolism and that it has a controlling influence on the level of cholesterol in the blood plasma."

A faulty thyroid gland may lead to cholesterol accumulation and increase the risk of heart disease. Dr. Myers described the normalizing effects of the Kupffer cells, "In the normal man and animal, the cholesterol ingested with the food, along with the excess of cholesterol synthesized by the tissues, is rapidly absorbed from the bloodstream by the Kupffer cells of the liver and excreted into the bile. The cholesterol level in the circulation remains constant by this regulator action."[10] Thyroid function should be examined prior to the use of medications to lower cholesterol levels.

Myers found that infectious mononucleosis responded remarkably to iodine supplementation. This may be explained by the fact that iodine and the thyroid are important for healthy immune function. Without proper thyroid function the immune system may not provide the body sufficient energy to effectively deal with viral infections.

Thyroid & cholesterol

Iodine has been used to treat other viral diseases such as polio and herpes zoster as well as mononucleosis. Dr. J. F. Edward suggested that many viral diseases that cause neurolgic symptoms such as polio often occur during warm summer months when thyroid function is at its lowest.[11]

Iodine has been used for a wide variety of other purposes. Dr. Richard Kunin, a pioneering nutritionally oriented physician, found topical application of saturated solution of potassium iodide (SSKI), a particularly safe form of the mineral, useful for removing bulky scar tissue called a keloid. He has also used topical iodine for sebaceous cysts, finding it helps soften and dissolve accumulating oils as well as acting as an antibiotic to kill bacteria. Dr. Kunin used this antibiotic property of iodine to treat bladder infections in women.[12]

Some people have used what is called the iodine patch test to determine if iodine intake is adequate. This involves painting a one-to-two inch square of iodine (2% or Lugol's solution) on the skin of the abdomen, upper arm, or leg. Let the iodine dry before allowing it to come into contact with clothing as it will stain. Repeated applications at the same location may cause a burning sensation.

If the patch disappears within 24 hours iodine may be deficient and a low thyroid condition may exist. Iodine status is normal if the patch lasts longer than 24 hours. The patch should be checked every hour. This test has probably fallen into disuse because other measures of thyroid function are available and some people react to iodine with strong allergic responses. Elemental iodine is much more toxic and likely to create problems than the SSKI mentioned above— similar to the difference between highly toxic chlorine gas and the chlorine in salt.

Overactive thyroid or hyperthyroidism, which can be caused by excessive iodine, is often associated with especially prominent, even bulging eyes.

SUGGESTIONS

- Excess iodine intake may cause hyperthyroidism and should be avoided.

- Avoid iodine antagonists such as fluoride.

- Make an attempt to consume foods that have a natural source of iodine such as kelp and seafoods, unless one is reactive to iodine or allergic to seafoods.

- Healthy thyroid function, promoted by adequate iodine intake, may be particularly important for those fighting viral infections or wrestling with elevated cholesterol.

Kunin

RELATED TOPICS
BREAST LUMPS
FLUOROSIS

Low thyroid function is considered by some to be epidemic among the American population despite the addition of iodine to salt. This may be due to the presence of fluoride in food, water, tea, toothpaste, and mouthwashes. How many sources of fluoride are you exposed to?

Some suggest that vitamin B12 has become almost impossible to obtain in the food supply. What is the source of vitamin B12 in your diet? How reliable is this source?

Do you find the neck and shoulders highly stressed parts of your body?

The Skin: *Our Birthday Suit*

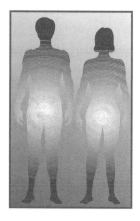

R on sported a deep rich tan he had obtained working as a missionary with one of the tribal peoples of what was then New Guinea. The attention of our small group was riveted as he showed slides and told stories to convey what life was like in his corner of the world—a cobra in the bedroom, falling into a river with a man-eating crocodile, watching natives battle to the death on one's doorstep—the kinds of experiences one never thinks about when preparing to go to a far-off place.

I have changed his name.

Two observations I made that day are pertinent to a discussion of the skin. Firstly, I observed that the slides showed this man as appearing rather pale and unhealthy, while the narrator in front of the group was a vibrant, well-tanned individual. I could not help feeling that the exposure to sunshine and a new diet appeared to have improved the man's health remarkably.

Secondly, Ron spoke of the unusual thickness of the skin of the people with whom he worked. He injected them with a hypodermic with great difficulty because their skin was so tough that needles would bend when he attempted to introduce medications.

The skin is thick or thin, rough or dry, with large pores or small. These things are undoubtedly influenced by heredity, the diet we eat, and environmental exposures. The skin is particularly reflective of oxidative damage resulting from exposure to the sun. Excessive exposure, particularly when accompanied by inadequate intake of antioxidants, can lead to toughening, wrinkling, premature aging and even skin cancer.

Durk Pearson and Sandy Shaw in their book *Life Extension: A Practical Scientific Approach* suggest the "pinch" test to gage the physiological age of the skin: "Place the wrist and hand palm down on a flat surface with the fingers stretched as widely as possible. Take a pinch of skin on the back of the hand between your thumb and forefinger and pull it up as far as you comfortably can. Hold the pinched skin for five seconds and suddenly release it. The skin will snap back very rapidly in a healthy teenager. In an 80-year-old, the pinched skin may still form a visible ridge five minutes later."[1]

The skin has remarkable elasticity. As we age, not only the elasticity of the skin changes, but we also lose flexibility of other tissues as well. This is a result of damage to protein and fat molecules.

Proteins have a three-dimensional shape that confers elasticity. The structure and function of these proteins is dependent upon the links or hooks that hold the protein together. Free-radical damage as we age alters protein links. This makes skin "tough, hard, inelastic, brittle, and wrinkled." The process is similar to "the tanning of a soft cattle skin into hard, tough leather."[1] Loss of elasticity can give us a measure of our physiological age—telling us if we are prematurely aging or aging more slowly than the norm.

Looking at the importance of nutrition at the cellular level can provide a better understanding of the significance of nutrition for the skin. An excess of artificial or altered fats in the cell membrane causes loss of water and dehydration. This altered cell wall, inhibits absorption of nutrients, allows unwanted substances into the cell, and provides a barrier to excretion of wastes. High-quality oils and the antioxidants that protect them build a healthy cell wall, which prevents dehydration while permitting absorption of essential nutrients and efficient elimination of waste products.

The skin, like that cell wall, becomes visibly rough and blotchy when fats of inferior quality are consumed. The skin begins to harden, dry, and flake. Allergic responses become more likely as the skin becomes less capable of coping with potentially harmful environmental exposures. The skin is the body's largest organ of elimination. This avenue of excretion for toxins can become blocked when the skin is poorly nourished.

Numerous people have shared with me over the years that improved nutrition has resulted in profuse sweating and even black secretions from the skin for a period of time. These people had experienced a buildup of toxic wastes the body was incapable of eliminating until supplementation improved the health of the skin.

The skin and the cell wall are alike in another aspect. Both are subject to free-radical damage due to their high fat content. These fats can oxidize,

The skin has remarkable elasticity. As we age, not only the elasticity of the skin changes, but we also lose flexibility of other tissues as well.

The skin, like that cell wall, becomes visibly rough and blotchy when fats of inferior quality are consumed.

Chapter 8 – The Skin

producing the same results as if poor-quality oils were consumed. A number of years ago I spoke with the owner of a large research corporation after a seminar. This man wished to share his research on vitamin E and lead poisoning. He explained that when red blood cells are exposed to lead, the cell walls harden in a process called "tanning". This impairs their ability to filter through small capillaries to nourish and oxygenate the tissues of the body and makes red blood cells more easily destroyed, resulting in anemia. Vitamin E prevented this tanning process, even in the presence of high levels of lead.[2]

The principle here is important for the skin. The rate at which the skin ages can be slowed considerably by taking measures to assure that antioxidant intake is continuously adequate to counteract any free-radical exposure that takes place, whether from diet or exposure to sunlight. The condition of the skin reflects the adequacy of intake of protein and fat from which it is constructed as well as the sufficiency of intake of antioxidants to protect the tissues that are built from these raw materials. Next time you pick up a food with partially hydrogenated oils or overcooked protein ask yourself, "Am I going to regret this next time I look in the mirror?"

The rate at which the skin ages can be slowed considerably by taking measures to assure that antioxidant intake is continuously adequate to counteract any free-radical exposure that takes place, whether from diet or exposure to sunlight.

Bumps on the Skin

SIGN

A thickening of the skin around the hair follicle (Scientific terms: perifollicular hyperkeratosis, hyperkeratosis follicularis or phrynoderma)

SIGNIFICANCE

Bumps on the skin are associated with deficiencies of vitamins A and C, zinc and essential fatty acids. This sign may be an indicator of diabetic risk.

DISCUSSION

Dr. Mark Altschule, President of the Boston Medical Library and Visiting Professor of Medicine at Harvard Medical School, linked bumps on the skin with inadequate intake of vitamin A—especially when it is conjoined with callusing.[3] Vitamin A is the most important nutrient for removing these hardened bumps around hair follicles.

Vitamin A plays an important role in controlling the growth of cells and keeping them young. Pregnant women are advised not to consume high levels of vitamin A because of the powerful effect this nutrient has on developing cells. Large quantities of vitamin A may harm a fetus.[4]

Bumps on the extremities are frequent on the skin of diabetics. Dr. Altschule observed that in adult onset diabetes "very high serum carotene levels occur frequently, and some of the patients show readily visible signs of vitamin A deficiency in the form of perifollicular hyperkeratosis over the trunk and proximal (or outer) parts of the extremities and also very thick and resistant calluses on the feet and elbows." The suggestion here is that diabetics cannot convert carotenoids to vitamin A, which explains both the high levels of carotenoids in the blood and the explicit signs of vitamin A deficiency.[3]

Altschule emphasized that zinc is necessary for removal of vitamin A from liver storage and its delivery to the tissues. This mineral is often deficient in the diet when large amounts of processed foods are consumed—another road block to the diabetic's efficient utilization of vitamin A.[5] Zinc is also essential for regulation of blood sugar, and often a benefit for the diabetic.

Deficiency of vitamin C can produce a condition of the hair follicle very similar to inadequate vitamin A intake. Around 1940 a surgeon named Crandon put himself on a diet deficient in vitamin C. The vitamin became undetectable in the blood 41 days later and by the 120th day skin cells were piling up around the hair follicles. Bleeding and other symptoms of scurvy developed after 160 days of deficient dietary intake. This sign can be an early indicator of vitamin C deficiency long before the more recognized symptoms of scurvy are visible.[6]

SUGGESTIONS

- Supplement with vitamin A or cod liver oil.
- Vitamins C and B complex, zinc, and essential fatty acids may also be helpful.

Butterfly Rash

SIGN

A butterfly-shaped rash bridges the nose and covers the cheeks.

Thickening of the skin around the hair follicles can be an early indicator of vitamin C deficiency long before the more recognized symptoms of scurvy are visible.

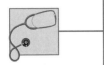

Butterfly Rash – Lupus

SIGNIFICANCE

This sign is a characteristic of Lupus erythematosus, a serious autoimmune disorder.

DISCUSSION

Lupus is a Latin word meaning "wolf" while erythematosus means "reddening". The distinctive red rash covering the nose and cheeks that characterizes lupus gives the sufferer the appearance of a wolf.[7] Dr. Vincent Marinkovitch, an allergist in Redwood City, has suggested that the rash affecting uncovered areas of the skin is caused by immune complexes, often resulting from allergic response.[8]

One of my clients was informed by her physician she required chemotherapy to treat her severe lupus, which had affected her to the point that she could not walk up or down the stairs of her home. She decided to see what nutrition could do for her first. She avoided sugar, wheat, milk and nightshade plants such as tomato, potato, eggplant, and peppers. She began a heavy supplement program with generous intake of vitamin C, grain and legume oil extracts, vitamins and minerals, and salmon oil. She had quite a few mercury amalgam fillings in her mouth and began working with a dentist to have these removed. Within a few months, the lupus was in remission, and at the end of a year she no longer had the blood measurements characteristic of the disease. Lupus is not a hopeless diagnosis.

Dr. Chris Reading, a practicing physician in Australia and author of *Your Family Tree Connection*, has treated many patients with lupus successfully by addressing allergy issues.[9, 10] He has documented frequent gluten intolerance, which he finds to be a genetic trait passed down the family tree. Other allergies may contribute to lupus as well. Dr. James Braly, a physician who specializes in food allergy and gluten sensitivity, agrees with Dr. Reading that gluten intolerance is a genetically linked trait that can cause lupus.[11]

Omega-3 oils provide tremendous benefit in many inflammatory, autoimmune, and food allergy situations. These oils reduce kidney damage in an animal model of lupus. After noting that other approaches are not very practical, researchers suggested that "…dietary enrichment with EPA (the anti-inflammatory oil in the omega-3 family of fats) may offer a novel and nontoxic approach to the treatment of renal diseases in systemic lupus."[12] Concurrent use of vitamin E with fish oils prevents oxidation of these oils within the body.

Omega-3 oils provide tremendous benefit in many inflammatory, autoimmune, and food allergy situations. These oils reduce kidney damage in an animal model of lupus.

The body does not turn on itself without a reason. One of the challenges of autoimmune disease is to determine why the immune system is malfunctioning. Common triggers for autoimmune disease include hormone imbalances, overgrowth of bacteria, heavy metal poisoning, high blood sugar, low-grade viral infections or allergic responses to foods.

Ninety percent of the patients who suffer with lupus are women. This kind of sexual disparity in a health condition suggests that estrogen may be a contributing factor. Estrogens switch on the immune system in autoimmune disorders such as lupus, rheumatoid arthritis, myasthenia gravis, and Hashimoto's disease. Male hormones tend to turn the immune system off. Male mice given estrogens develop significantly more lupus-like disease, while female animals dosed with male hormones have a dramatically lower incidence and severity of lupus-like disease.[13]   Try DHEA

The story of Goldilocks and the three bears contains a little episode in which three bowls of porridge are tasted. One is too hot, one too cold, and the other just right. The immune system can be too hot, too cold, or just right. Excessive activity of the immune system can trigger allergy and autoimmune conditions. An unresponsive immune system permits cancer to grow or increases the chances of developing infections. Neither of these conditions is desirable. The immune system tends to become overactive when the system is overloaded with estrogen or omega-6 fats. Malnutrition or excess sugar intake can turn the immune system off. Adequate intake of omega-3 oils powerfully contributes to an immune system that functions properly.

Dr. John Lee confirms that estrogen may be a central problem in autoimmune disorders. He wrote, "Hashimoto's thyroiditis, Sjogren's disease, Graves' disease (toxic goiter), and lupus erythematosus are all not only more common in women, but appear to be related to estrogen supplementation or estrogen dominance. Recent studies have shown that women who use hormone replacement therapy containing estrogen are more likely to get lupus."

Dr. Lee recommended use of progesterone to counteract estrogen dominance in women. He observed, "Many of my patients with autoimmune disease who began using natural progesterone to relieve menopausal symptoms reported that their disease symptoms also gradually abated."[14] Nutritional supports for proper glandular function and for optimal immune function tend to help both men and women with autoimmune conditions.

RELATED TOPIC

ROSACEA

Nutritional supports for proper glandular function and for optimal immune function tend to help both men and women with autoimmune conditions.

Chapter 8 – The Skin

SUGGESTIONS

for heat

- Avoid gluten and other foods to which one is allergic.
- Avoid refined sugar.
- Balance hormone chemistry and eliminate estrogen dominance.
- Minimize heavy metal exposure. *(mercury)*
- Supplement with omega-3 fish oils, grains, and legume extracts.
- Supplement with antioxidants and other essential nutrients.

but not wheat

(1) natural progesterone
(2) DHEA - to up testosterone

Calluses

SIGN

Hardening and thickening of the skin on the bottom of the feet or other parts of the body.

SIGNIFICANCE

Calluses may indicate deficiencies of vitamin B3 or vitamin A.

DISCUSSION

Many years ago a middle-aged woman shared a frustrating problem with calluses on her feet which she found necessary to repeatedly grind down with a pumice stone—only to have them re-grow. She found aloe ointment helped soften them. Those heavy calluses were probably reflective of deeper nutritional needs.

Calluses develop in response to pressure on the skin. For example, school-children form calluses where they hold a pencil, and a guitarist will form them on the fingertips. The thickness of calluses varies not only with the frequency and strength of the stimulus, but also with nutritional intake. Deficiencies of vitamin A or vitamin B3 can cause calluses to thicken uncomfortably, especially on the bottom of the feet where they often splinter and form needle-like pieces of skin.

Dr. Mark Altschule found that patients deficient in vitamin A "…develop thick stubborn calluses on the feet and sometimes on the elbows." Deficiencies of zinc, essential fatty acids, or protein may interfere with proper vitamin A utilization, in effect creating a deficiency.[3]

Dr. William Kauffman discovered that vitamin B3 deficiency caused the growth of a slightly different kind of callus, often pigmented yellow to brown. His research established that "excessive callusing with or without pigmentation

RELATED TOPICS

BUMPS ON THE SKIN

FISSURED OR GEOGRAPHIC TONGUE

ROUGH ELBOWS

took three to six months to resolve" after adequate amounts of the nutrient were provided. One of his papers contains a photograph of a woman who developed marked pigmented callusing on her rump as a result of the minor pressure of sitting in a secretary's chair. This callusing disappeared when vitamin B3 in the form of niacinamide was added to her diet.[15]

SUGGESTIONS

- Massage an aloe ointment into the skin.
- Supplement with preformed vitamin A and essential fatty acids.
- Supplement with vitamin B complex.

Contact Dermatitis

SIGN

The skin breaks out with blisters or cracks after physical contact with some substance

SIGNIFICANCE

Contact dermatitis is a consequence of an allergic response or a toxic exposure.

DISCUSSION

A number of years ago I developed clear fluid sacks on my skin. A visit to the doctor provided little help as to the cause. The physician said he simply did not have a clue as to what could have caused the blisters. The following day, a conversation with a family member enlightened me. She said, "I know what those blisters are—our dog runs around in poison oak and when you pet him you get the oils on your skin and then spread them over your body." Many people unnecessarily suffer constant skin irritation due to inability to identify the cause of the problem.

The skin can react to almost anything, including metals. Nickel is a common initiator of skin problems. Nickel sensitivity was first observed in 1889 in the nickel-plating industry. It has become a common problem among women due to nickel-plated accessories, buttons, and costume jewelry. Ear piercing with nickel-plated ear pins can further sensitize the body. In the United States and

Western Europe between 8 and 14% of the female population demonstrates contact sensitization to nickel, while only 1 to 3% of males are sensitized.[16, 17]

In view of the fact that nickel can create skin problems, it is of interest that dermatologist Steven Smith of Tulsa, Oklahoma, found that nickel combined with bromide and fumaric acid can often result in dramatic improvement of psoriasis. Dr. Smith found that 90% of a group of 300 patients with psoriasis improved moderately or markedly with this approach. A truly effective therapy for this problem should incorporate avoidance of sugar, alcohol, and refined food, elimination of allergens from the diet, and support for the digestive process.[18] Use if nickel may pose a risk of toxicity.

Many medical professionals have developed dermatitis as a result of wearing latex gloves. I have spoken with some of these people who faced the dilemma of needing to use protective gloves that triggered a powerful allergic response. Fortunately, a zinc cream is being developed to reduce or eliminate this predicament. Zinc binds with latex allergens and renders them incapable of triggering an allergic response. Alternatives to latex have also become available.[19]

The pigments used in the process of tattooing can be responsible for severe contact dermatitis. Beware of this risk before making the decision to acquire a tattoo.[20] Another risk of puncturing the skin is infection—my office manager's husband contracted hepatitis C as a result of the use of a contaminated needle in creation of a tattoo.

Allergic response to sunscreen lotions is common. The poorer the quality, and the greater the amount of non-sunscreen ingredients, the greater the risk of allergy.[21]

Australian dermatologists report contact dermatitis from tea tree oil. This product is becoming increasingly popular in the United States. Users should be aware of the possibility of contact dermatitis.[22]

Studies at the Mayo Clinic found that 3% of those who used corticosteriods developed contact dermatitis. This is a greater degree of reaction than that to formaldehyde. Exercise caution when using any cream containing corticosteroids.[23]

Contact irritation is not limited to the outside of the body. Foods and chemicals put in the mouth can create considerable irritation. Toothpastes contain fluoride, detergents, and flavorings to which an individual may be sensitive, resulting in irritation of the lips and the inside of the mouth.[24]

In the United States and Western Europe between 8 and 14% of the female population demonstrates contact sensitization to nickel, while only 1 to 3% of males are sensitized.

RELATED TOPICS

ALLERGIC SHINERS

CANKER SORES

PUFFY, DARK, INFLAMED, OR WRINKLED UNDER THE EYES

Studies at the Mayo Clinic found that 3% of those who used corticosteriods developed contact dermatitis.

SUGGESTIONS

■ Consume a diet rich in quality oils and antioxidants to build healthy skin more resistant to allergic response.

■ Make an attempt to identify any substance that irritates the skin and avoid it.

Fluid Retention (Edema)

SIGN

Fluid retention under the skin (most noticeable under the eyes or in the ankles)

SIGNIFICANCE

Many factors, including kidney damage, can cause fluid retention. Edema or swelling of the legs and ankles is a common characteristic of inadequate intake of vitamin B1 or thiamine.

DISCUSSION

My mother suffered with fluid retention, heart palpitations, and profound fatigue for many years. Doctors experimented with all manner of strange treatments, none of which provided any relief. No one suggested she might be deficient in the B complex vitamins despite a regular consumption of coffee and a lifelong history of consumption of large amounts of sweets—she grew up in a candy store. All of these health problems disappeared after she began supplementing with a multiple that contained a generous amount of the B complex vitamins in a natural brewer's yeast form. I believe she was deficient in vitamin B1, which is necessary for proper metabolism of carbohydrates and production of energy in the body.

The deficiency disease resulting from lack of vitamin B1 or thiamine is known as beriberi. Two forms of beriberi are generally recognized. Dry beriberi is characterized by damage to the nerves, resulting in fatigue, numbness, paralysis, or weakness of the legs, which can make it difficult to rise from a squatting position.[25] Wet beriberi manifests as damage to the circulatory system with symptoms that include fluid retention, palpitations of the heart, limbs that feel heavy and weak, chest pain, or a rapid and irregular heartbeat.

Mild deficiency of thiamine is not rare, particularly among alcoholics and those who consume large quantities of sugar or caffeine-containing beverages. Symptoms of mild deficiency can include loss of appetite, weakness, pain in the extremities, fluid retention, low blood pressure, and low body temperature.[26]

Fluid retention can also result from damage to the kidney caused by diabetes or exposure to heavy metals such as mercury, cadmium, or lead. Sometimes protein or trace mineral supplementation will reduce fluid retention. High protein intake is not suggested where kidney damage exists.

SUGGESTIONS

- Allergic responses cause fluid retention. Identify and eliminate allergic exposures.

- Mercury, cadmium, and lead can damage kidney function. Consider this possibility.

- Supplement with trace minerals and quality protein.

- Try a natural vitamin B complex (especially important are vitamins B1 and B6).

Heavily Pigmented Skin

SIGN

Darkening of the skin or retaining a suntan long after it should have disappeared. Pigmentation of the skin often begins on the back of the hands.

SIGNIFICANCE

Prolonged retention of a suntan can indicate deficiency of vitamin B3 or niacin. This should be distinguished from carotenoid buildup in the skin which provides a "glow of health" and the appearance of a generalized tan to the skin.

DISCUSSION

William Kaufman, M.D., Ph.D., noted "prolonged retention of suntan" as a prominent characteristic of niacin deficiency. This excessive pigmentation took several weeks to disappear after adequate vitamin B3 was added to the diet.[15] Darkening of the skin results from photosensitivity and occurs only in parts of the body exposed to sunlight.

Sometimes the skin will have a tanned appearance even on parts of the body not exposed to sunlight. This is usually caused by accumulation of carotenoids in the fat of the skin. Carotenoids are fat-soluble yellow, orange, and red coloring pigments found in fruits and vegetables.

A simple test for the presence of carotenoids in the skin is to squeeze the hand tightly into a fist. Release it suddenly and see if the skin has a slight yellow color. This slight yellow color usually indicates that the skin contains a substantial quantity of carotenoids. A pasty white color to the skin is undesirable and probably indicates deficiency of carotenoids in the diet and increased risk of oxidative diseases, including cancer. Length of life has been linked to carotenoid and vitamin E levels in the blood by gerontologists.

Yellow skin can also result from a pigment called bilirubin—a result of the death and reprocessing of old red blood cells. This yellow coloration of the skin results from liver damage or inability to carry bilirubin out of the body. This yellowing of the skin is called jaundice and can turn not only the skin, but also mucous membranes and the white of the eye yellow.

SUGGESTIONS

■ Obtain adequate carotenoids in the diet to give the skin a slight "tanned" appearance.

■ See a physician if jaundice develops.

■ Supplement with the entire B complex.

Old-Age Pigmentation

SIGN

Dark or brown spots on the skin, often called "age spots" or "liver spots." Durk Pearson, author of *Life Extension*, refers to them as "those telltale brown spots."

SIGNIFICANCE

These brown spots are caused by free-radical damage to structures within cells and the accumulation of wastes. Age pigments are particularly abundant in fatty tissues such as the skin. The function of cells is hindered by waste accumulation.

DISCUSSION

Free-radical production in the body accelerates with age, causing formation of old-age pigments. The older we become, the more important it is to increase our antioxidant intake to minimize an ever-increasing generation of free radicals within the body. The pigments produced by these free radicals have the potential to kill cells by interfering with normal function. A nerve cell can accumulate up to 70% of its volume as age pigment before the cell dies. These pigments can build up in both skin cells and also the brain where they interfere with brain function, leading to mental deterioration.[27] Accumulation of pigment in the skin may provide a clue to what is happening in the brain.

Vitamin E and acetyl-l-carnitine have been shown to help prevent accumulation of aging pigments, as well as slowing the road to senility in animals.[28] Buildup of one form of pigment, ceroid, has been associated with deficiency of selenium.[29] Supplementation with other antioxidants, especially the fat-soluble ones, also helps prevent these "telltale brown spots."

Diabetics are especially prone to accumulation of aging pigments.[30] Free-radical production goes into overdrive when blood sugar is high. In diabetic animals, reduced vitamin E speeds the development of aging pigments. Both elevated blood sugar and obesity tend to decrease vitamin E levels in tissue. Diabetics often notice that they feel much better when they supplement with the fat-soluble antioxidants including vitamins E, D, and A. Vitamin D has recently been shown to be a powerful antioxidant.

SUGGESTIONS

- Avoid junk fats, sugar, and stale foods.
- Eat a diet rich in antioxidants.
- Reduce elevated blood sugar levels.
- Supplement with antioxidants, including vitamins A, C, D, E, selenium, and carotenoids.

RELATED TOPICS

DUPUYTREN'S CONTRACTURE

PREMATURE WRINKLING

SKIN TAGS

UPPER BODY WEIGHT GAIN

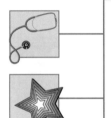

Premature Wrinkling

SIGN

The skin wrinkles and takes on the appearance of age before one would expect to see such wrinkling.

SIGNIFICANCE

Wrinkling is caused by oxidative damage to the skin and deterioration of connective tissue.

DISCUSSION

Fats and protein structures in the skin are prone to oxidation, resulting in wrinkling and sagging. Smoking, drinking, and excessive exposure to ultraviolet light can prematurely age the skin by causing wrinkling, brown age spots, and loss of elasticity.

RELATED TOPIC

OLD-AGE
PIGMENTATION

The research of Dr. Harry Daniell of Redding, California, revealed that in every age group those who smoke have more wrinkling and yellowing of the skin than those who do not. He attributed the aging to decreased circulation in the skin—a result of nicotine intake and damage to the circulatory system from the chemicals released into the body by smoking. The healthy pink color of the skin is an outcome of blood circulating under the skin's surface. Less blood flow produces a yellow and sallow-looking skin.

A history of more than 50,000 hours of sun exposure increases the risk of wrinkling more than three-fold—a level of damage comparable to what is experienced by a heavy smoker. Both smokers and sunbathers should supplement with a wide range of antioxidants, including vitamins A, C, E, and carotenoids to reduce damage to the skin.[31, 32, 33]

Diet plays an important role in wrinkling, as well as exposure to sun and smoking. One study found that diets high in vegetables, legumes, olive oil, and fish reduced wrinkling. Prunes, apples, and tea played a major role in reducing wrinkling. Diets high in meat, dairy, and butter increased wrinkling.[34]

SUGGESTIONS

■ Avoid excessive time in the sun and severe sunburn.

■ Do not smoke.

- Eat a diet high in antioxidants and quality oils.
- Supplement with antioxidants.

Purple Spots on the Skin

SIGN

Purple spots on the skin (Scientific term: petechiae)

SIGNIFICANCE

This may be a sign of outright scurvy or vitamin C deficiency.

DISCUSSION

Vitamin C is often deficient in junk-food diets eaten by many Americans, especially young people.[35] This nutrient is essential for the formation of the collagen or tissue cement that holds the cells of the body together. We literally begin to come unglued when vitamin C levels are inadequate. This is observed as rupture of tiny capillaries in the skin, bruising, or bleeding gums.

The tendency to bruise easily will often disappear when vitamin C and flavonoids have been added to the diet. The addition of vitamin K to the diet may work if vitamin C complex fails to eliminate bruising. Vitamin K regulates blood clotting and may help eliminate menstrual clotting as well as easy bruising.[36]

RELATED TOPIC

SUDDEN INFANT
DEATH SYNDROME
(SIDS)

Vitamin C is often deficient in junk-food diets eaten by many Americans, especially young people.

SUGGESTIONS

- Eat at least 5 to 9 servings of fruits and vegetables rich in vitamin C each day.
- Supplement with vitamin C on a regular basis.

Red Cheeks (Rosacea)

SIGN

The cheeks appear red or pink (Scientific term: rosacea)

SIGNIFICANCE

Cheeks can become red as a result of allergic response or vitamin B2 deficiency. Low hydrochloric acid may be a factor in rosacea.

DISCUSSION

Rosacea is a condition in which the cheeks become red and flushed. H. W. Ryle noted a common incidence of low stomach acid in acne rosacea as long ago as 1920.[37] Dr. Jonathan Wright also found rosacea and low stomach acid occurred together. Rosacea has been associated with spices, alcohol, hot beverages, and allergies. Poor stomach function increases the likelihood that allergens will not be well tolerated because they cannot be completely digested. Low stomach acid also increases the intensity of allergic response.

Vincent Marinkovitch suggested that reddening of the cheeks is caused by immune complexes. These immune complexes settle in areas where the skin temperature is below 37° Celsius (98.6° Fahrenheit), such as the skin on the nose and cheeks.[7]

On a more benign note, redness of the cheeks can be associated with a deficiency of vitamin B2. Tiny blood vessels will normally be visible in the skin if red cheeks are caused by lack of this vitamin.[38] Redness of the cheeks associated with allergy will come and go unless the allergic response is very strong and the food or foods causing the problem are consumed frequently.

RELATED TOPIC
BUTTERFLY RASH

Recent research suggests that H. pylori *infection may cause rosacea and low stomach acid.*[61]

SUGGESTIONS

■ Avoid foods that trigger reddening of the cheeks.

■ Consider the possibility of *H. Pylori* infection.

Rough Elbows

SIGN

Elbows or skin that is as rough as sandpaper

SIGNIFICANCE

This sign may reflect deficiencies of essential fatty acids, and vitamins A and B complex.

DISCUSSION

Drying and flaking of the skin, most evident on the elbows and knees, may be caused by deficiencies of essential fatty acids and vitamin A.[3] Lack of these nutrients makes cells dehydrate. Dr. Jonathan Wright suggested supplementing with cod liver oil for omega-3 fats and a source of omega-6 such as sunflower, sesame, or safflower oil. Supplementation should continue for 6 to 8 weeks and be accompanied by a quality supplement of vitamin E.[39] Dr. Abram Hoffer emphasized that a number of nutrients are essential for normal function of essential fatty acids, including zinc, calcium, magnesium, biotin, and vitamins B3, B6, and C. Any of these nutrients can potentially affect the appearance of the skin.[40]

The deficiency disease associated with lack of vitamin B3 or niacin is called pellagra. The word pellagra means "rough skin" in Italian vernacular. Skin cells can peel off the elbow in severe deficiency of vitamin B3, resulting in redness.[41] Less severe vitamin B3 deficiency may be characterized by callusing and rough skin.

RELATED TOPICS

CASAL'S NECKLACE

OSTEOARTHRITIS

CALLUSES

SUGGESTIONS

- Avoid alcohol and refined carbohydrates.
- Drink plenty of water.
- Supplement with essential fatty acids, and vitamins A and B complex.

Skin Tags

SIGN

Little folds of skin often found on the neck, shoulder, and underarm

SIGNIFICANCE

This body sign has been associated with increased risk of diabetes and blood sugar disorders.

DISCUSSION

Dr. Jack Margolis, of the Veteran's Hospital in Big Spring, Texas, found that 72% of the patients he examined with skin tags were diabetic. Some of his patients who did not have diabetes developed it several years later.[42] In a separate report Margolis wrote, "Of the 47 patients with skin tags, 34 had diabetes mellitus as noted by repeat fasting blood sugar of 130 mg per 100 ml or higher and two-hour postprandial (after the meal) sugar of over 150 mg per 100 ml....One can almost predict that a male patient will have diabetes if the lesions are multiple, large, hyperpigmented (dark colored) and bilateral (on both sides of the body)."[43]

Dr. Keith Lowell of Houston once emphatically told me that "All diabetics are liars and cheats…against themselves." He said this because they often know they should avoid refined carbohydrates, but they rarely do. An excellent discussion of the importance of control of carbohydrate intake in diabetes can be found in Dr. Richard K. Bernstein's *Diabetes Solution*. Bernstein himself suffered with juvenile diabetes for over fifty years—successfully avoiding complications by controlling his carbohydrate intake. Dr. Bernstein was forced to attend medical school and obtain a medical degree before other diabetics would listen to his suggestions for controlling blood sugar.[44]

The important role of digestive aids for the diabetic will be found in *Victory Over Diabetes* by Dr. William Philpott, who found that food allergy could cause high blood sugar. Digestive support would often prevent allergy-caused rises in blood sugar. Philpott also discusses the importance of vitamin C, a nutrient of particular importance for the diabetic.[45]

SUGGESTIONS

■ Control intake of carbohydrates, especially sugars.

■ Don't overeat.

■ Use digestive aids if necessary.

■ Supplement with a good multiple vitamin and with antioxidants.

Stretch Marks (Striae)

SIGN

The skin of the breasts, thighs, hips and especially the abdomen breaks or tears, leaving scars

SIGNIFICANCE

Stretch marks are a clue to imperfect formation of elastin, one of the two major components of connective tissue. Deficiencies of zinc, copper, or vitamin C may be indicated. Weakened elastin in arteries increases risk of heart disease.

DISCUSSION

Dr. Carl Pfeiffer, a leading nutrition researcher, noted that stretch marks can occur among diabetics, those with high cortisone secretion, at puberty, and commonly during pregnancy. These are all situations where rapid growth or potential nutritional deficiencies may exist.

Connective tissue is made from collagen and elastin. Stretch marks are associated with defective elastin. Nutrients necessary to build healthy elastin fibers include lysine, an amino acid, vitamin C, vitamin B6, and the trace minerals zinc and copper. Dr. Pfeiffer suggested that the most frequent deficiencies associated with imperfect elastin are zinc and vitamin B6. Stretching imperfectly made elastin causes tears which we identify as stretch marks.[46]

Elastin is built during rapid growth. Once built, it lasts for life. Prevention of stretch marks is dependent upon adequate supply of the key nutrients involved in elastin formation during rapid growth spurts. Periods of nutrient deficiency result in formation of weakened elastin. This weakened elastin will be at risk of tearing later on when it is stretched, as during pregnancy.

RELATED TOPIC
QUICK EARLY
WARNING SIGN
(QEW TEST)

SUGGESTIONS

■ Avoid deficiency of key nutrients involved in elastin formation during periods of rapid growth: vitamin C, zinc, copper, lysine, and vitamin B6.

Thickening of the Skin

SIGN

Scleroderma is a hardening or thickening of the skin from increasing accumulation of collagen. (Scientific terms: fibrotic disorders, scleroderma)

SIGNIFICANCE

Scleroderma is believed to result from chronic immune activation.

DISCUSSION

Thomas Brown, whose work is discussed under the topic of rheumatoid arthritis, felt that fibrotic disorders resulted from bacterial infection. You should read the discussion found there.

Exposure to environmental pollutants that cause immune activation appears to be a potential causative factor in scleroderma. Silica dust and exposure to paint thinners have been implicated as triggers for this disease.[47, 48]

A nutrient that offers promise for fibrotic disorders is para-amino-benzoic acid (PABA). A prescription form of this nutrient called POTABA is mentioned in the *Physician's Desk Reference* as a treatment for fibrotic disorders such as scleroderma. The suggested mechanism of action is increasing oxygenation of tissue.[49] Dramatic improvements have been reported with 6 grams per day for a child and 12 grams per day for an adult.[50] Double-blind studies have shown the benefit of PABA for fibrotic disorders.[51] Dr. Jonathan Wright observed that iodine in the form of SSKI and vitamin E mixed with DMSO for improved absorption through the skin provided additional benefit in fibrotic disorders.[52]

A number of other nutritional approaches are available. Intake of vitamin E, which improves oxygenation of tissue, at a level of 800 to 1200 I.U. has been shown to be beneficial for scleroderma.[53] The amino acids tyrosine and phenylalanine are involved in collagen formation and restricting them sometimes results in improvement of lupus and scleroderma.[54] Quality oils have been used to treat scleroderma with success.[55] Research suggests that disorders of fat metabolism are involved with scleroderma. Vitamin C and zinc supplementation, along with avoiding red meat and eggs, may restore proper metabolism of essential fats. [56]

SUGGESTIONS

- Avoid intake of extra phenylalanine (found in Nutrasweet) and tyrosine.
- Make a trial of vitamins E, C, and zinc.
- Supplement with essential fatty acids.
- Try POTABA under the guidance of a physician.

Underarm Temperature Test

SIGN

Take the temperature under the armpit upon waking and before getting out of bed. Leave the thermometer under the arm for ten minutes. Women should take the test on the second or third day after menstrual flow starts.

SIGNIFICANCE

A normal temperature under the arm will be between 97.8° and 98.2° Fahrenheit. Dr. Broda Barnes was a physician specializing in thyroid disorders. He told patients "A temperature below 97.8 indicated hypothyroidism; one above 98.2, hyperthyroidism." Infections can cause an elevation of underarm temperature.

DISCUSSION

Dr. Barnes found that undiagnosed abnormal thyroid function is a contributor to many health conditions. Barnes assessed metabolic rate and functioning of the thyroid gland by measuring the temperature under the arm.[57] He wrote that "hypothyroidism of the mild to moderate kind…can be and very often is responsible for a wide range of health problems and hazards, and its recognition and proper treatment can have profoundly beneficial consequences."

Most common indications of low thyroid according to Dr. Broda Barnes:

- Fatigue
- Migraine headache
- Emotional and behavioral problems
- Susceptibility to infectious diseases
- Skin problems
- Menstrual disorders
- High blood pressure
- Heart attacks
- Arthritis
- Diabetes
- Hypoglycemia
- Obesity
- Autoimmune diseases

Low thyroid increases blood pressure because of the circulatory damage resulting from depressed thyroid function.

Additional indications of low thyroid observed by others:

- A hoarse or gravelly voice
- Depression
- Low blood pressure

RELATED TOPICS
BREAST LUMPS
FLUOROSIS
GOITER

- ▸ Swollen eyelids and face
- ▸ Water retention
- ▸ Thinning or loss of the outer third of the eyebrow
- ▸ Lump in the throat and difficulty swallowing
- ▸ Slowed mental or physical functioning[58]

Excessive fluoride ingestion may suppress thyroid function, particularly if iodine intake is marginal. Refer to the discussion under the topic of FLUOROSIS.

SUGGESTIONS

- ■ Avoid excess fluoride ingestion.
- ■ Obtain adequate iodine, zinc, copper, selenium, and manganese— all essential for thyroid function.
- ■ Supplement with essential fatty acids, including omega-3 oils.

Vitiligo

SIGN

Loss of natural pigment in the skin

SIGNIFICANCE

Vitiligo is associated with deficiencies of stomach acid, vitamin C, vitamin B12, and folic acid.

DISCUSSION

Dr. Leopoldo Montes, M.D., examined vitiligo patients in Buenos Aires and found that 11 of 15 patients had low blood folic acid levels, vitamin B12 was low in five, and vitamin C low in four. Eight of these patients received treatment with folic acid and vitamin C twice a day. Vitamin C is known to be involved in folic acid utilization and is also involved in the synthesis of melatonin. Vitamin B12 injections were given every two weeks. All eight patients steadily improved over a two-year period. Improvement was apparent after about three months. It appeared that folic acid alone would have been effective, but the addition of the other nutrients helped speed the process. Six of the

Deficiencies of hydrochloric acid, folic acid, vitamins B12 and C may be involved with vitiligo.

eight patients had complete repigmentation after two years and the other two had 80% repigmentation.[59]

The government limits the amount of folic acid allowed in supplements because it can mask a deficiency of vitamin B12. Extra folic acid may be necessary. Folic acid is naturally found in fresh green foods and liver. This vitamin is unstable in the presence of heat and light.

Deficiencies in hydrochloric acid production should also be considered in vitiligo. Stomach acid is necessary for absorption of vitamin B12 and has been suggested as an important nutritional consideration for this condition.[60]

SUGGESTION

■ Regular intake of folic acid, vitamin C, and vitamin B12. Older people are often deficient in stomach acid production.

Food for Thought

 What clues would you look for in the skin to guess a person's age? What clues would you look for to indicate someone was aging too rapidly?

 Why do you think the skin is such a good guide to allergic phenomena?

 What clues would you look for in the skin to better understand an individual's nutritional status?

Hands and Fingers: *Remote Sensing Devices*

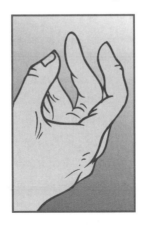

One of the most famous paintings in the world is commonly known as "The Praying Hands" by Albrecht Durer. The story is told that these are the hands of Albrecht's brother, Albert, who labored four years in the mines so his sibling could study art. After completing his education and establishing his career, Albrecht wished to pay his brother's expenses to the art academy, but his brother held up broken and mangled hands riddled with arthritis and said such a task was now impossible as a result of years of difficult and dangerous work in the mines. Durer chose to paint those hands in the act of prayer as a memorial to the sacrifice of his brother which made his own career as an artist possible.

The precise details of this story are not known, but we know with certainty that the hands reflect the nutritional world in which they exist. They will become swollen if vitamin B6 is lacking in the diet. Allergy can turn the fingers ice cold or make them stiff. Arthritis can lead to swollen and deformed joints.

Nails can provide an early warning system of impending difficulties. The fingernails grow about one-eighth inch a month and take almost six months to grow out from the nail bed. They are like a history book. Pinhead-sized depressions in the fingernails can indicate psoriasis. The absence of moons at the base of the nail may indicate low thyroid function, while a depressed area or white lines on the nail may result from viral infections or zinc deficiency. Spoon-shaped nails may indicate iron deficiency.

The fingernails speak volumes by their strength, the rate at which they grow, whether they tear or chip easily, the presence or absence of inflammation at the nail bed, and whether they are chewed down or allowed to grow long. The chewing of the nails may indicate nervousness, which can result from poor diet and excessive sugar intake. Weak nails with thin hair and fatigue may indi-

The fingernails grow about one-eighth inch a month and take almost six months to grow out from the nail bed. They are like a history book.

The chewing of the nails may indicate nervousness, which can result from poor diet and excessive sugar intake.

cate a weak thyroid gland. Poor nail condition along with bloating and burping may be a clue to digestive problems.

Even the fingerprints have been coerced into testifying about an individual's health. Researchers at the University of Pennsylvania have been able to predict the existence of diabetes with an 81% success rate by examining the number of loops on the index finger. This is an aspect of diagnosis called dermatoglyphics, which is too technical for inclusion in this volume.[1]

The crippling effects of arthritis are perhaps the most common and certainly the most debilitating readily visible sign in the hands. Arthritis is a disease characterized by changes in health, ranging from muscle stiffness to crippling disability and pain. Sufferers often have little hope other than powerful medications that can themselves create serious side effects.

Nightshade plants contain powerful cholinesterase inhibitors, which Childers found could induce arthritis.

An older woman once made her way into my office on crutches with obvious pain and great difficulty. She told me that she had visited numerous physicians for eight years but no one had been able to help her. Her diet diary showed that she was eating large quantities of tomatoes daily so I suggested she avoid them. She became intensely angry at my suggestion that she give up her "favorite" food. I explained that people usually develop intolerance to the foods they enjoy most frequently. In addition to this, Dr. Norman Childers, Ph.D., a professor of horticulture, spent years documenting the ability of nightshade plants, including tomatoes, potatoes, eggplant, tobacco, and red and green peppers to cause arthritic symptoms in some people.

The woman, with great reluctance, decided to avoid tomatoes. Two weeks later she was pain-free for the first time in eight years. She was convinced that this was a spontaneous remission so she ate two bites of tomato—which crippled her for two days.

Cholinesterase inhibitors are commonly used as pesticides.

Her dramatic improvement was much faster than the several months discussed by Childers; however, improvement in less than a week is common with food sensitivities. Childers found after 25 years of research that 72% of arthritics improved by avoiding nightshade plants and following his other suggestions. Nightshade plants contain powerful cholinesterase inhibitors, which Childers found could induce arthritis: "Cholinesterase is an enzyme in the body that affords agility of movement of the muscles. This may account for the stiffness and slow movement of some people susceptible to this inhibition."[2]

Cholinesterase inhibitors are commonly used as pesticides. As a matter of fact, both nicotine in tobacco and the water in which green potatoes have been boiled have been used as pesticides. The fact that foods that contain cholinesterase inhibitors may induce arthritic symptoms suggests that pesticides which function in a similar manner may also contribute to arthritic symptoms in a susceptible segment of the population.

Childers realized that other dietary changes besides avoiding nightshades could improve arthritic symptoms. He observed that avoiding milk and eggs was often helpful and recorded that vitamins A and D offered considerable benefit. (See the discussion on Joint and Muscle Pain.)

I find that many who suffer with arthritis are not even familiar with the basic nature of their condition. An understanding of the different forms of arthritis opens the door to comprehension of the way in which modern lifestyles are involved in induction of inflammatory and degenerative disorders that affect every part of the body, including the hands. An understanding of the cause and nature of a problem is the first step toward its solution.

Arthritis (Osteoarthritis)

Sign

Osteoarthritis is characterized by bony lumps on the outermost joints of the fingers (Heberden's nodes) or excessive wear and tear of the joints.

Significance

Osteoarthritis is a "wear and tear" disease—joints deteriorate more rapidly than repair can take place. Infection or physical injury may play a role in damaging the repair process.

Discussion

Osteoarthritis develops gradually and most often begins with the joints on one side of the body. Redness, warmth, and swelling of joints are unusual, a key difference between osteoarthritis and rheumatoid arthritis. Osteoarthritis commonly affects knees, hands, hips, feet, and the spine. There is no overall feeling of sickness as with rheumatoid arthritis.[3]

A notable sign of osteoarthritis is the formation of bony lumps (Heberden's nodes) on the outermost finger joints. William Heberden, Jr., wrote a book in which he described these bony lumps: "What are those little hard knobs, about the size of a small pea, which are frequently seen upon the

The fact that foods that contain cholinesterase inhibitors may induce arthritic symptoms suggests that pesticides which function in a similar manner may also contribute to arthritic symptoms in a susceptible segment of the population.

fingers, particularly a little below the top near the joint? ... they continue for life: and being hardly ever attended with pain, or disposed to become sore, are rather unsightly than inconvenient, though they must be some little hindrance to the free use of the fingers."[4]

Bony lumps can also form on the middle finger joints (Bouchard's nodes) in osteoarthritis. This more often strikes middle-aged women. Middle-aged men are more likely to develop a firm, tender mass on the back of the hand covering the affected joints in the wrist (carpal boss). The most common tissues affected by osteoarthritis are the spine (number one), the hips (number two), and the knees (number three).[5]

Wear and tear on the joints is part of day-to-day living, but poor nutrition can make repair of this damage difficult or impossible. Those with this wear-and-tear disease must make every effort to obtain the complete spectrum of nutrients necessary for a timely and complete repair of daily damage to joint tissues. Research indicates some nutrients are particularly important.

In 1949 Dr. William Kaufman, a physician who specialized in joint diseases, reported that niacinamide can step up the repair process of the joints, improving the range of joint movement and improving the overall condition of those with osteoarthritis.[5] Kaufman observed that "Even persons subsisting on 'good' or 'adequate' diets of today lack sufficiently potent reparative mechanisms to offset for any prolonged period of time the retrograde influences of the deteriorative process in joints. However, with supplementation of the average 'good' or 'adequate' diet of today with adequate amounts of niacinamide (vitamin B3), the articular reparative process becomes sufficiently powerful to overcome the retrograde changes in articular tissues produced by the deteriorative process, and in time permits improvement in the functional status of joints."[6] In everyday language Kaufman is saying that given sufficient time, vitamin B3 supplementation can improve joint function in osteoarthritis by speeding the repair process.

Vitamin B3 is sold in two forms: niacin and niacinamide. Niacinamide is a buffered form and does not cause flushing. Niacin is unbuffered and can cause a dramatic flushing in which the skin turns red. Many years ago I took a generous amount of niacin just prior to the return of a roommate. I was beet red with a livid flush when he walked through the door. In a panic he noted that I had obtained far too much sun that day and was suffering extreme sunburn. He was amazed when I informed him that I had simply taken a vitamin. Those who doubt the powerful impact of nutrients upon physiology

"Even persons subsisting on 'good' or 'adequate' diets of today lack sufficiently potent reparative mechanisms to offset for any prolonged period of time the retrograde influences of the deteriorative process in joints."
William Kaufman, M. D.

should permit themselves to experience a good niacin flush. Kaufman used niacinamide, the form of vitamin B3 that does not cause a flush.

Vitamin B3 functions more efficiently with omega-3 oils. Donald Rudin observed that omega-3 oils decreased the amount of niacin necessary to create a flush tenfold. [7] Research shows that omega-3 oils, even apart from vitamin B3, decrease both wear and tear and inflammation of osteoarthritic joints.[8] Nutrients often work together and the combination of vitamin B complex, omega-3 oils, calcium and magnesium, and vitamin C are a wonderful blend for the joints.

Vitamin C is essential for prevention of excessive wear and tear of joints. Guinea pigs on diets low in vitamin C developed every indication of advanced osteoarthritis. When generous amounts of vitamin C were added to the diets, there was much less cartilage erosion. The preventive dose of vitamin C was 150 mg for a tiny guinea pig. This is more than the recommended intake for a human being by the U.S. government at this time. A human who weighed 110 pounds would need to take 7,500 milligrams or 7.5 grams of vitamin C to get the equivalent amount of vitamin C with which the guinea pigs were dosed to prevent osteoarthritis! (A guinea pig weighs about 2.2 pounds). [9] High doses of vitamin C should be used under the supervision of a knowledgeable professional. Vitamin C is most effective taken in multiple doses or in a form that releases gradually to achieve consistent blood levels of the nutrient—large doses of vitamin C simply wash out of the body unless intake is spread through the day.

Cartilage repair is only as good as the synthesis of glucosamine and chondroitin, two of the major building blocks of joint tissue.[10] A number of medical trials indicate that these nutrients can reduce pain and improve mobility in osteoarthritis with none of the side effects of common medications used to treat the disease. I have seen this nutrient benefit a number of arthritis sufferers.[11]

I feel that a good multiple should be used to assure all repair nutrients are present in addition to the specific nutrients mentioned here. The health and functioning of the cells involved in joint repair is dependent upon all the nutrients essential for life or what Roger Williams called the "chain of life." Lack of even one key nutrient can impair crucial life processes such as repair.

Osteoarthritis has been traditionally viewed as a wear-and-tear disease. This is certainly a contributing factor to the deterioration of joints as discussed above. The recent discovery of tiny microorganisms that have the ability to cause calcification may open a door to a new understanding of a possible infectious contributor to this condition.

> *Research shows that omega-3 oils, even apart from vitamin B3, decrease both wear and tear and inflammation of osteoarthritic joints.*

> *Vitamin C is most effective taken in multiple doses or in a form that releases gradually to achieve consistent blood levels of the nutrient.*

SUGGESTIONS

- ■ Avoid sugar and junk fats.

- ■ Eat a nutrient-rich diet.

- ■ Keep weight down to avoid excessive wear and tear on the joints.

- ■ Supplement with vitamin B complex (especially vitamin B3), vitamins C, E, A, and D. Calcium, magnesium, glucosamine, and chondroitin may also prove beneficial.

- ■ Obtain essential fatty acids derived from fish, grains, and legumes, which are essential for repair and immune processes.

RELATED TOPICS

JOINT AND MUSCLE
PAIN

KIDNEY STONES

Arthritis (Rheumatoid)

SIGN

Rheumatoid arthritis is characterized by an almost universal redness, warmth, and swelling of the joints on both sides of the body. The disease is accompanied by a feeling of sickness and fatigue.[3]

Rheumatoid arthritis is very different from osteoarthritis. Dr. James Balch, recorded that "Joints afflicted with rheumatoid arthritis tend to make a sound like crinkling cellophane, whereas osteoarthritic joints make popping, clicking, and banging noises."[12]

SIGNIFICANCE

Rheumatoid arthritis is one of humanity's oldest, most common, and debilitating diseases. Costs due to both treatment and loss of ability to work are extensive. Rheumatoid arthritis has been associated with allergic responses to foods, autoimmune activity, and infections.

DISCUSSION

One of our family friends was so crippled with rheumatoid arthritis in the late 1950s that she could not turn over in bed. Her husband who worked at a condiment factory had to come home on his lunch hour and turn her over. This woman had tried every kind of medical treatment and had a kitchen cupboard full of vitamins—yet nothing had alleviated the grinding pain. She began using a multiple vitamin with grain and legume extracts containing phospholipids and phytosterols. Eight months later she was in remission. Subsequent addition of other nutrients such as vitamin C, flavonoids, fish oils, and amino acids provided further benefit. As of the date of this publication almost fifty years later she has had no recurrence and her doctors tell her she no longer has rheumatoid factor in her blood. This story shows the powerful and long-term benefits nutrition can offer the arthritic. In this particular situation the addition of quality oils to the diet made the difference between disease and health. Commonly consumed oils in the American diet are often poor quality and major contributors to poor health.

Symptoms of rheumatoid arthritis come and go without warning. Attacks may be triggered by stress, poor nutrition, illness, or the intake of foods to which one is allergic. One thing is certain. Nutrition plays an important role in this condition.

Over three decades ago Dr. Thomas Brown suggested that rheumatoid arthritis is a "bacterial allergy, leading to collagen vascular disturbances."[13] Dr. Brown saw over 10,000 patients with rheumatoid arthritis and successfully treated about 80% of these with the tetracycline family of antibiotics. His success rate was far higher than that of his fellow rheumatologists. The key to Dr. Brown's treatment was his understanding that rheumatoid arthritis could be caused by an infection with an allergic and autoimmune component.

The body responds to infection with inflammation. It is nature's way of limiting damage from bacteria or allergens. Physicians often give patients anti-inflammatory medications to treat rheumatoid arthritis. Dr. Brown described the result of the use of these medications on arthritic patients who are suffering with an infection with an unforgettable analogy: "When any such medicine removes the inflammatory barrier from around the source of the antigen, it is like removing the coolant from a nuclear power core, and the eventual result is a meltdown. The inflammation is nature's way of holding the reaction in check; it happens to be a painful method, but it is the only means by which the spread of the source of the antigen is contained."[13]

Brown felt bacterial infection caused rheumatoid arthritis—the best model for the condition being Lyme disease—and a good candidate for the causative agent being streptococcal or mycoplasma bacteria whose toxins have an affinity for joint tissue. He noted that many of his patients had severe troubles with the sinuses, tonsils, or ears prior to developing rheumatoid arthritis. Others had suffered with rheumatic or scarlet fever. Brown's successful treatment involved long-term therapy with the tetracycline family of antibiotics which are the most effective against mycoplasma bacteria.[14]

Substantial research suggests that quality oils, particularly the fish oils, improve arthritic symptoms.

Fish, grain, and legume oil extracts can perform the twofold function of simultaneously acting as natural anti-inflammatory substances and enhancing immune function.

Pioneering oral surgeon George Meinig recorded that a Dr. Billings published findings in 1933 that rheumatoid arthritis was often due to streptococcal infection that came from the tonsils, teeth, or sinuses. Dr. Meinig wrote that root canals could provide an opportunity for streptococcal bacteria to take up residence in the roots of teeth and damage not only joints, but also the heart, digestive tract, and other tissues.[15]

The idea that microbes could be causative agents of rheumatoid arthritis (and possibly osteoarthritis) has recently been revived with the discovery that very tiny organisms that lack cell walls (one of which has been labeled *Nanobacterium sanguineum*) are involved in a number of diseases that were not previously thought to be infectious. These nanobacteria exhibit many of the properties discussed by Dr. Brown, including sensitivity to the tetracycline family of antibiotics—and resistance to other antibiotics that are effective only against bacteria with cell walls. As we learn more about nanobacteria we may find they are common causative agents in a variety of diseases characterized by calcification and inflammation.[16] The *Merk Manual of Diagnosis and Therapy* has observed that "crystals occur in snowball-like clumps in rheumatic conditions." This description accurately describes recently identified calcium-coated nanobacteria and suggests they may be part of the disease process.[17]

One nasty but little-understood aspect of infection by some organisms without cell walls is their ability to borrow material from cell membranes or even from blood fats with which they cloak or hide themselves from the immune system. This behavior appears to be one of the mechanisms involved in development of autoimmune syndromes.

Not all fats provide ideal cloaking material for these organisms, which may explain why some types of fat worsen arthritic symptoms while other types of fats result in improvement. [18] Substantial research suggests that quality oils, particularly the fish oils, improve arthritic symptoms. A prospective, double-blind, controlled study gave patients 1.8 g of EPA for 12 weeks: "Results favored the experimental group at 12 weeks for morning stiffness and number of tender joints. On follow-up evaluation 1 to 2 months after stopping the diet, the experimental group had deteriorated significantly in patient and physician global evaluation of disease activity, pain assessment, and number of tender joints."[19]

Fish, grain, and legume oil extracts can perform the twofold function of simultaneously acting as natural anti-inflammatory substances and enhancing immune function. In this they are quite different from pharmaceutically produced anti-inflammatory drugs, which tend to suppress immune function.

Fish oil supplements are best taken before bed or in the middle of a meal. Refrigerating or freezing the capsules may also help to prevent "burping."

Antioxidants play an important role in both preventing fats within the body from oxidizing as well as supporting a vigorous immune defense. The immune system attacks and destroys infections with powerful free-radical substances similar to chlorine and hydrogen peroxide. Deficiency of antioxidants permits a spillover of these immune cell–manufactured free radicals, damaging immune cells and other tissues as well.

I use the illustration of trying to do welding with a blow torch or a flame thrower. A flame thrower will destroy everything in its path and is very difficult to control. This is a picture of the immune system without a sufficient supply of antioxidants. A blow torch can be easily controlled to accomplish the user's purpose. This illustrates a healthy immune system adequately supplied with antioxidants. The fires the body creates to destroy invaders work much more efficiently when adequate antioxidants are supplied.

A vegan diet (free of all meats, eggs, and milk) with no gluten has been documented to improve as many as half of all rheumatoid arthritics. This may be due to increased antioxidant intake, decreased dietary intake of inflammatory fats, and removal of foods to which the arthritic is allergic.[20]

Those who suffer from conditions of an infectious nature should understand that a particularly effective treatment against infectious organisms may result in a Herxheimer reaction. This is a sudden turn for the worse, resulting from the dieoff of large numbers of disease-causing organisms. This phenomena usually accompanies antibiotic use, but may also be elicited by use of some nutritional approaches. The sufferer should realize that sometimes a condition worsens for a period of time before it improves and a brief "healing crisis" is not a cause for discouragement.[21]

SUGGESTIONS

- Avoid sugar.
- Avoid suspected allergens.
- Consume a vegetable-based diet.
- Consume or supplement with only the highest-quality oils, including olive, macademia, fish, grain, and legume oils.
- Supplement with all essential nutrients, including antioxidants.

Antioxidants play an important role in both preventing fats within the body from oxidizing as well as supporting a vigorous immune defense.

The fires the body creates to destroy invaders work much more efficiently when adequate antioxidants are supplied.

RELATED TOPICS

CAVITATIONS

JOINT AND MUSCLE PAIN

KIDNEY STONES

QUICK EARLY WARNING SIGN (QEW TEST)

ROOT CANALS

TARTAR ON THE TEETH

■ Vitamin B complex, especially vitamin B6, can be helpful in rheumatoid arthritis. (See QUICK EARLY WARNING SIGN.)

Brittle Nails

SIGN

Thin, brittle nails that break easily

SIGNIFICANCE

Poor-quality nails can indicate digestive problems, protein or biotin deficiency.

DISCUSSION

Far more women than men complain that their fingernails crack and split. Fingernails swell when they become wet then shrink as they dry out. Women constantly expose their nails to water, soaps, and harsh chemicals that can damage the nails and make them fragile and brittle. Wearing gloves when cleaning can eliminate many cases of brittle nails.

Brittle nails linked to protein deficiency will be accompanied by thin, brittle hair and loss of muscle. Poor digestion is a major contributor to protein deficiency.[22] Poor digestion may also lead to poor absorption of trace minerals, which can weaken the nails.

Dr. Alan Gaby, a pioneer in the identification of nutrient deficiencies, reported that up to 20% of the American population (primarily women) suffers from brittle nails. Veterinarians have used biotin to strengthen and harden the hooves of horses and pigs. A study of biotin at levels of 2,500 mcg/day resulted in improvement in the nails of 63% of 35 patients who had tried a variety of other treatments without success.

Biotin deficiency is a distinct possibility. The major sources of supply in the diet are egg yolk, kidney, liver, and some cheeses. Bacteria in the gut manufacture most of the biotin we absorb from the digestive tract. Use of antibiotics can lead to biotin deficiency because it kills these bacteria. Avoiding egg yolks in the diet may also contribute to deficiency. Dr. Gaby observed that he has also had success in strengthening and reducing the brittleness of nails with calcium, trace minerals, essential fatty acids, and hydrochloric acid supplementation.[23, 24, 25, 26] Dr. Jonathan Wright found through very careful testing that over 90% of his patients with poor-quality nails were deficient in hydrochloric acid.

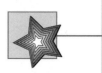

RELATED TOPICS

BLOATING, BURPING AND BAD BREATH

JOINT AND MUSCLE PAIN

OSTEOPOROSIS

STOMACH ACID SELF-TEST

FOREHEAD FURROWS OR WRINKLES

Dr. Jonathan Wright found through very careful testing that over 90% of his patients with poor-quality nails were deficient in hydrochloric acid.

Horrible fingernails are a very good indicator of low hydrochloric acid, the stomach's major protein-digesting enzyme.[25]

Insufficient iron may also cause brittle nails. A study of five women with iron deficiency in England found that all had brittle nails. After the anemia was treated, the women no longer had the brittle nails.[27]

A discussion of brittle nails associated with fibromyalgia will be found under the topic of JOINT AND MUSCLE PAIN.

A study of five women with iron deficiency in England found that all had brittle nails.

SUGGESTIONS

- Consume eggs if well tolerated.

- Supplement with beneficial microflora to supply bacteria that synthesize biotin in the digestive tract.

- Supplement with protein, essential fats, trace minerals, and biotin if necessary.

- Use digestive aids if needed.

Carpal Tunnel Syndrome

SIGN

The fingers develop a burning sensation or tingle. The thumb, index, and middle fingers are more frequently involved. Carpal tunnel syndrome may make it difficult to grip objects or make a fist. Symptoms usually begin at night, perhaps due to decreased circulation.

SIGNIFICANCE

Carpal tunnel results from inflammation of tendons and ligaments in close proximity to the carpal tunnel which encloses nerve tissue in the wrist. Pregnancy, diabetes, and obesity may aggravate or induce the condition. Vitamin B6, a natural diuretic, may be an important preventative.

DISCUSSION

A young, good-looking, muscular man sat in front of me with both hands in braces. Despite every appearance of strength he suffered from carpal tunnel

"Biochemistry allowed us to discover that subjects with the carpal tunnel syndrome, male or female, teenagers to oldsters, have a severe deficiency of vitamin B6."

The benefits of good nutrition are accomplished through use of adequate quantities of appropriate nutrients for a sufficient period of time.

syndrome to such a degree that he was having difficulty performing his job—threatening his ability to support his family.

He gained hope as we talked about the importance of good nutrition for his condition, despite the fact that his physician had previously informed him that nutrition offered little promise. The alternatives he had been given were rest for the wrists and surgery to provide relief—neither of which appealed to him.

As we talked, it became obvious that he had some bad nutritional habits. He was accustomed to drinking several pots of coffee each day. I explained that coffee has diuretic properties, tending to wash vitamin B complex out of the body. Coffee can also cause loss of calcium and magnesium.

I encouraged him to reduce or eliminate the coffee and to supplement his diet with a multiple containing generous amounts of vitamin B complex, chelated calcium-magnesium, and salmon oil for its high omega-3 content.

He followed my suggestions and within a period of three months, his wrists improved so dramatically that he could function normally. He was enabled to continue his job and also undertake vigorous athletic activities.

Subsequent to his improvement he revealed that he had also suffered from a bad back and breathing difficulties. These improved as he pursued his nutritional regimen. This apparently healthy young man had obviously been suffering from a number of nutritional deficiencies as a result of his poor dietary habits. How did I know that nutrition might be involved with carpal tunnel? What vital information did I share with this young man?

Dr. Karl Folkers is a legendary nutrition pioneer who clarified the structure of vitamin B6 and worked on synthesis of the vitamin. Folkers discovered that carpal tunnel syndrome was often associated with inadequate vitamin B6 (or pyridoxine) intake. He wrote: "Biochemistry allowed us to discover that subjects with the carpal tunnel syndrome, male or female, teenagers to oldsters, have a severe deficiency of vitamin B6. The majority of people on no daily vitamin supplement may have subclinical deficiencies of vitamin B6…"

Folkers found that prolonged use of vitamin B6 was necessary for improvement of carpal tunnel syndrome. A six-week double-blind trial of vitamin B6 proved a total failure while a 12-week trial was a success. I mention this because many people fail to understand that the benefits of good nutrition are accomplished through use of *adequate quantities of appropriate nutrients for a sufficient period of time.*

Folkers found that vitamin B6 did not do its work alone. Vitamin B2, essential for conversion of vitamin B6 to its biologically active form, was also essential. Folkers wrote, "While we were doing the biochemistry of B6 in the blood of patients with the carpal tunnel syndrome, we also did some assays for the presence of a deficiency of vitamin B2 or riboflavin, and, indeed, we discovered that this deficiency is also present."[28]

An important nutritional point is revealed in this research. Those with degenerative conditions often have multiple deficiencies due to genetic weaknesses, poor diets, or faulty health habits. In addition to this, lack of one nutrient can alter the ability to utilize other nutrients. A number of years ago Drs. Harte and Chow reviewed over 200 scientific papers dealing with dietary interrelationships. *"Their findings reveal that the shortage of a single essential vitamin, mineral element, amino acid, or fatty acid will create a shock wave that spreads to affect the utilization and/or function of every other essential nutrient."*[29] The common assumption that nutritional adequacy is easily maintained on a diet of highly refined foods is naive.

This research is one of the reasons why I tell those who seek my nutritional advice that they should supplement with a good-quality multiple derived from food sources as much as possible. It is also essential to eat the best diet possible. Dr. Roger Williams described the basket of nutrients essential for life and health as the "nutritional chain of life." He wrote, "The chain representation is used to emphasize the fact that all links are needed; if even one link is missing or weak, the whole chain is weak and the favorable environment disappears."[30] Through years of study in the field of nutrition I have learned that results of supplementation are far better if a few extra nutrients are provided than if one key nutrient is overlooked. The value of nutrients derived from foods is that they provide thousands of accessory factors that are not recognized as being essential, but which facilitate and improve the utilization of essential nutrients.

Dr. Folkers described the symptoms associated with vitamin B6 deficiency as follows:

▶ Morning stiffness of fingers

▶ Impaired sensation in fingers and impaired finger flexion

▶ Pain in hands, weakness of hand grip and dropping of objects

▶ Nocturnal paralysis of arm and hand

▶ Rheumatism and arthritis

"…the shortage of a single essential vitamin, mineral element, amino acid, or fatty acid will create a shock wave that spreads to affect the utilization and/or function of every other essential nutrient."
E. Cheraskin

The value of nutrients derived from foods is that they provide thousands of accessory factors which are not recognized as being essential, but which facilitate and improve the utilization of essential nutrients.

► Painful and stiff shoulders, elbows, and/or knees

► Fluid retention in the hands, feet, and/or ankles[28]

These symptoms may be an everyday part of your life that could be eliminated by the addition of a few essential nutrients to the diet.

SUGGESTIONS

■ Avoid drinking excessive coffee.

■ Avoid substances to which you are allergic.

■ Allow at least three months for supplementation to work.

■ Supplement with vitamin B complex obtaining at least 50 mg of vitamin B6 for at least 12 weeks.

■ Supplement with omega-3 oils, calcium, and magnesium.

Dupuytren's Contracture

SIGN

The skin shrinks and hardens in the center of the hand, forming a nodule or lump near the small or ring finger

SIGNIFICANCE

Dupuytren's contracture is a risk indicator for diabetes. Over time the fingers will be pulled toward the palm—in severe cases this can interfere with the normal activities of daily living.

DISCUSSION

Dupuytren's contracture derives its name from Baron Dupuytren, a French physician who described the condition in one of his lectures. His students widely disseminated his notes, resulting in the adoption of his name for the condition.

Dr. Maxwell Spring and Dr. Berton Cohen, diabetes researchers at the New York Medical College and the Bronx-Lebanon Hospital Center, found more than a 90% incidence of glucose intolerance in patients who have Dupuytren's contracture. Not all these patients show full clinical diabetes mellitus, but the abnormal glucose tolerance suggests that they may be in the incipient or beginning stages of the disease.[31]

The development of Dupuytren's may provide a clue that insufficient attention has been given to control of blood sugar. Refined sugar, excess fats, and excess carbohydrates should be avoided. A sedentary lifestyle also predisposes to diabetes. Dupuytren's has been improved by supplementation with vitamin E and zinc, antioxidants that are known to protect against diabetes. Other antioxidants that benefit diabetes may be beneficial for Dupuytren's.[32, 33]

Dupuytren's is more common in those with seizure disorders, alcohol-induced liver disease, and those who smoke.

SUGGESTIONS

- Avoid sugar and refined carbohydrates.

- Be aware of increased diabetic risk.

- Supplement with antioxidants, including vitamin E and zinc.

Flattened or Spoon-shaped Nails

SIGN

The nails become flattened or spoon-shaped

SIGNIFICANCE

This sign often reflects iron deficiency or excess. Nails can also flatten for other reasons, including Raynaud's disease and other anemias such as those caused by vitamin B12 deficiency.[34]

DISCUSSION

Spooning of the nail is common in iron deficiency, although it can sometimes appear in hemachromatosis—a genetic disorder associated with iron excess. Deficiency of iron is believed to be the most prevalent worldwide deficiency and the most frequent cause of anemia.[35] Iron deficiency is common for a number of reasons. It is found on a regular basis among children who do not eat meat or other iron-containing foods. Menstruating women lose iron monthly with blood loss. Older people become low in hydrochloric acid, which can make it quite difficult to absorb iron.[36] Iron is not abundant in plant foods and is more difficult to absorb from vegetable sources—vegetarians are at considerable risk for developing iron deficiency.

Symptoms of iron deficiency, aside from spoon-shaped nails, include inflammation of the tongue, inflammation of the corners of the mouth, a pale complexion, and fatigue.[37] Iron deficiency can cause a craving for ice and pink urine after eating beets.

Many of the symptoms of iron deficiency are a consequence of poor ability to deliver oxygen to the tissues and the inability to produce energy. Extreme fatigue and mental retardation are common with severe iron deficiency. Even a slight deficiency of iron can seriously impair energy production. The elderly may develop restless leg syndrome when they become iron deficient.[38]

Supplementation with a poor quality of iron may cause nausea, flatulence, diarrhea, and black stool. Iron is quite toxic in excess, particularly for the individual who has a genetic disorder called hemachromatosis which results in accumulation of iron. Children can also be poisoned if they ingest an excessive amount of iron.[39]

Excess iron in the body acts as a free-radical and also tends to encourage bacterial growth. One should supplement with large amounts of iron only when guided to do so by a physician who is knowledgeable in the field of nutrition and aware of the dangers of iron excess as well as the problems associated with deficiency of the mineral. Iron in the form of an amino acid chelate tends to produce less digestive difficulty when iron supplementation is necessary and is also more readily absorbed than the forms of iron often recommended. This form of iron is bonded with amino acids to decrease free-radical activity and improve absorption.

SUGGESTIONS

- Be wary of excess iron intake.

- Support stomach acid if it is low and contributing to anemia.

- Supplement with chelated iron if deficient.

- Vitamin C improves iron absorption.

Moons on the Nails

SIGN

The presence or absence of moons at the base of the nail

Supplementation with a poor quality of iron may cause nausea, flatulence, diarrhea, and black stool.

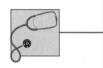

SIGNIFICANCE

The presence or absence of the moons at the base of the nails may reflect thyroid function.

DISCUSSION

Moonless nails when accompanied by a broad, spongy hand with sausage-shaped fingers and a tapered little finger may reflect lower thyroid function. By contrast, long, narrow, shiny nails with large moons may indicate active thyroid.[40]

Thyroid activity varies from individual to individual. Thyroid can be suppressed by excessive exposure to fluoride or by a deficiency of the nutrients essential for thyroid function—zinc, copper, selenium, iron, tyrosine, and essential fatty acids.

RELATED TOPICS

FLUOROSIS

SWELLING OF THE
NECK (GOITRE)

SUGGESTIONS

- Avoid sugar and caffeine-containing foods and beverages.

- Minimize fluoride use.

- Obtain nutrients essential for healthy thyroid function.

Pitted Fingernails

SIGN

Pinhead-sized depressions in the fingernails

SIGNIFICANCE

This sign is characteristic of psoriasis.

DISCUSSION

Dr. Norman Levine, a physician who specializes in the study of the fingernails, noted that "Psoriasis is one of the most common causes of fingernail deformity." Pinhead-sized depressions may be irregular or form a grid-like pattern. In psoriasis the nail plate can also separate from the underlying bed. The nails often thicken and take on a red or yellow-brown discoloration. A clue to the cause of these nail changes would be to look for evidence of psoriasis elsewhere.[41]

RELATED TOPIC

CONTACT
DERMATITIS

Those allergic to gluten who suffer from psoriasis may improve dramatically when gluten-containing foods are removed from the diet.[42] Foods such as carrots, tomatoes, and fresh fruits rich in caroteonids and other antioxidants reduce the severity of psoriasis—possibly by halting inflammation characteristic of the disease.[43] Fish and fish oils, also anti-inflammatory, decrease the severity of psoriasis lesions.[44] Those with psoriasis may suffer from deficiencies of selenium[45], vitamin D[46], glucosamine[47], and folic acid.[48]

Infection may also play a role in this skin condition. Those with psoriasis are more prone to nail fungus and improve with antifungal therapy.[49] Dr. Robert Giller observed that those with psoriasis often do not tolerate yeast.[50]

Those allergic or sensitive to mold or fungi face a daunting challenge. A wide range of foods frequently contain fungi, including aged cheese, mushrooms, overripe fruits and vegetables, tomato products, most alcoholic beverages, processed meats, aged meats including hamburger, soy sauce, black tea, commercial fruit juices, yeast and malt-containing products, and chocolate. Skin tests that look for IgE antibodies will not usually detect mold sensitivity. Most physicians are not taught a great deal about mold problems.

Molds are quite opportunistic and can grow in any tissue which is damaged or compromised nutritionally. Molds can cause dandruff, athlete's foot, toenail fungus, and vaginal yeast infections. Antibiotics kill bacteria, but may open the door for fungus infections.

SUGGESTIONS

- Consider the possibility of fungus problems.

- Identify and remove allergens from the diet.

- Obtain a generous intake of antioxidants from foods and supplements.

- Supplement with fish oils, acidophilus, and garlic.

Quick Early Warning Sign (QEW Test)

SIGN

Inability to flatten the fingers against the palm with the wrist unbent

SIGNIFICANCE

This sign provides an early warning of vitamin B6 deficiency.

DISCUSSION

Have you experienced tingling of the arms and hands? Do you eat a high-fat and highly refined diet? You could have a deficiency of vitamin B6, according to Dr. John Ellis, a physician who studied this nutrient his entire medical career. Dr. Ellis developed a simple test which he used to confirm deficiency of this vitamin.

Dr. Ellis grew up and practiced medicine in Mt. Pleasant, Texas. This gave him an advantage because he came to intimately know the dairymen, the cattlemen, the swine growers, and others he treated in his daily practice.

Dr. Ellis became interested in nutrition when an oilfield worker from the Talco oil field came to him with tingling in his hands and arms. This man also suffered with cramps in his legs at night. There was nothing unusual about his hands and fingers except that the "coloring in the creases across the backs of the hands was slightly redder than normal."

This patient's breakfast was the same every day, consisting of bacon, eggs, and coffee. Dr. Ellis put him on a low-fat diet, which resulted in transient pain in the elbows and shoulders followed by a startling improvement. The man lost eight pounds and three inches around his waistline.[51]

One day a bachelor in his sixties came to Dr. Ellis and explained that pain in his knees and stiffness and swelling of his fingers improved when he added 12 pecans a day and peanut oil to his diet. Dr. Ellis added pecans and peanuts to the low-fat diet and noted improvements in the stiffness of the fingers and tingling of the hands in an elderly diabetic woman. He deduced that his dietary changes must be addressing some basic nutritional need of his patients, and when he began giving injections of the vitamin B complex his patients reported even more improvements than with the changes in diet alone.[52]

Dr. Ellis asked himself, "Which vitamin is making the difference?" He was familiar with deficiency symptoms of many of the B vitamins. Vitamin B1 deficiency usually caused tremors of the tongue. Vitamin B2 deficiency caused cracks at the corner of the mouth. Vitamin B3 caused skin lesions on the hands and legs. None of these fit the symptoms he saw in his patients.

No deficiency symptoms had ever been associated with vitamin B6, but he chose to try this vitamin alone. The first patient to receive an injection of

Vitamin B1 deficiency usually caused tremors of the tongue. Vitamin B2 deficiency caused cracks at the corner of the mouth. Vitamin B3 caused skin lesions on the hands and legs.

vitamin B6 was a 37-year-old pregnant woman. She had tingling in her hands and numbness in her elbows as well as swelling of hands and feet. His first injection was on May 26, 1962, and the woman's swelling, numbness, and tingling began to disappear within four days.[53]

Dr. Ellis learned that high-fat diets and coffee could deplete vitamin B6 in his patients, which resulted in this swelling in the hands and feet, tingling of the extremities, and arthritic symptoms. He discovered inability to completely flex the fingers, often diagnosed as arthritis, was readily resolved by the addition of generous amounts of vitamin B6, or pyridoxine, to the diet.

Dr. Ellis developed a simple test for vitamin B6 deficiency: the Quick Early Warning (QEW) test. He wrote, "Early in my treatment of patients with crippled hands I devised a test to determine the extent of their disability. Eventually I came to use the test with all of my patients as a clinical method of screening them for a long-standing need for B6." The test is simple: "Hold the hands out with the palms up. Flatten the palms and fingers and keep the wrists straight. This should leave a straight line from the tip of the longest finger to the elbow. Now flex the fingers at the two outer (distal and proximal interphalangeal) joints only, leaving the knuckle (metacarpophalangeal) joints straight with the wrist. By flexing the two outer joints, bring the fingers firmly down to the palms at the metacarpophalangeal crease, to use the anatomical description. The knuckle joint that connects the finger bones to the hand bone must remain straight and unflexed during this test."[54]

In other words, attempt to bring the tips of the fingers flat with the hand with no bending any lower than the first joint in the finger—only two joints are bent or flexed. Lack of the ability to bend any joint (barring previous injury or disability) indicates a need for additional vitamin B6 in the diet, according to Ellis.

Dr. Ellis described the symptoms he often found in women deficient in vitamin B6 as being "...characterized by a 'pins and needles' tingling or numbness, as if the hands were asleep, and by swelling about the finger joints, and there was frequent complaint of pain upon movement of the fingers, particularly upon waking in the morning. A complaint of stiffness of fingers was all too common, and wedding rings were tight—in fact, in some cases, could only be removed with extreme difficulty; indeed, movement of the fingers was incomplete, and to shake hands in even the mildest of greetings caused intense pain when the fingers were squeezed."[55]

Dr. Ellis learned that high-fat diets and coffee could deplete vitamin B6 in his patients, which resulted in this swelling in the hands and feet, tingling of the extremities, and arthritic symptoms. He discovered inability to completely flex the fingers, often diagnosed as arthritis, was readily resolved by the addition of generous amounts of vitamin B6, or pyridoxine, to the diet.

Dr. Alan Gaby, a noted vitamin B6 researcher, has documented that pyridoxine deficiency plays a role in hyperactivity, premenstrual tension and swelling, kidney stones, autism, depression, heart disease, lupus, diabetes, cancer, carpal tunnel syndrome, arthritis, tooth decay, asthma, and Chinese restaurant syndrome.[56] Vitamin B6 deficiency may also be indicated by "trigger finger" where a joint gets stuck in a flexed or semiflexed position and can only be released with extra force.[57]

Deficiency of this vitamin is common because we live in the midst of a flood of vitamin B6 antagonists that either destroy the vitamin or block the ability of the body to properly use it. One of these antagonists, a hydrazine molecule, binds to a vitamin B6 receptor site one hundred times more strongly than the vitamin itself! Hydrazines are present in rocket and military aircraft fuel, tobacco smoke, and in a growth inhibitor used on potatoes and onions. Some people consume more maleic hydrazide from potato chips in a day than they consume vitamin B6 itself.

Other B6 antagonists include a ripening agent sprayed on fruits and vegetables, FD&C Yellow No. 5, the birth control pill, PCBs, overheated oils, and caramel color. Even common foods contain substances that block vitamin B6 utilization, including linatine found in flaxseed meal, agaritine found in button mushrooms, and L-canaline found in alfalfa sprouts. (Monkeys fed large amounts of dried alfalfa sprouts have developed a disease similar to lupus.)[56]

I once asked Dr. Arthur Furst, one of the world's leading toxicologists, how we could be expected to survive with pesticides laced throughout the food supply. He commented that he did not know how people managed without regular vitamin B complex supplementation since these nutrients are necessary to detoxify pesticides. The same advice would apply to vitamin B6 antagonists in the environment—we must obtain enough pyridoxine to compensate for the fact that our world is flooded with antagonists to this essential vitamin. Inadequate intake of vitamin B6 contributes to a wide spectrum of health problems.

SUGGESTIONS

■ Avoid as many vitamin B6 antagonists as possible.

■ Supplement with B complex vitamins.

■ Test yourself with the QEW test to see if there are indications you might be deficient in vitamin B6.

Deficiency of this vitamin is common because we live in the midst of a flood of vitamin B6 antagonists that either destroy the vitamin or block the ability of the body to properly use it.

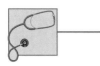

White Spots or Bands on the Fingernails

SIGN

White spots or bands appear on the fingernails

SIGNIFICANCE

White lines, spots, or bands on the nail may indicate deficiencies of protein, zinc, or vitamin B6.[58]

DISCUSSION

My fingernails as a youngster were often covered with white clouds, a sign that often indicates deficiencies of protein or zinc. The fact that these nutrients are important for immune function may explain the constant infections of my early years.

Seventy percent of the zinc in the human body is bound to a protein called albumin. For this reason, low albumin levels often result in zinc deficiency. Observations substantiate that albumin deficiency by itself can result in white spots on the fingernails.

Dr. Carl Pfeiffer founded the Princeton Bio Center, where the mentally ill are treated with nutritional modalities. His careful observation of the nutritional status of his patients revealed that white spots on the fingernails could be caused by zinc deficiency alone or in combination with deficiency of vitamin B6.[59]

His careful observation of the nutritional status of his patients revealed that white spots on the finger-nails could be caused by zinc deficiency alone or in combination with deficiency of vitamin B6.

Dr. Pfeiffer identified a number of patterns on the nails, depending upon the cause of the zinc deficiency:

■ An isolated white spot resulting from a short period of fasting or altered diet deficient in zinc or protein.

■ Frequent small white spots on the fingernails resulting from a prolonged deficiency of zinc or protein, usually accompanied by a compromised immune system.

Many women developed white bands on the fingernails prior to menstruation when estrogen drops zinc levels, often resulting in depression.

■ Many women developed white bands on the fingernails prior to menstruation when estrogen drops zinc levels, often resulting in depression.[60]

■ A horizontal depression in the nail called a Beau's line, resulting from an infection due to altered metabolic rate during the illness.

It takes about 160 days for the nail to grow out, making it possible to estimate when an infection has taken place. Lack of a white line at the point of the depression indicates zinc is probably adequate even under the stress of an illness.[61, 62]

■ Mee's lines where a white line crosses the nail horizontally.[61] Dr. Pfeiffer wrote, "When the body is sharply deficient in zinc white spots show up on the fingernails. Because a virus infection tends to cause a radical loss of zinc from the body, it often follows that white spots indicate the timing of an infection."[60]

■ A consistent white opacity in the entire nail can be caused by a simultaneous deficiency in both zinc and vitamin B6.[59]

Zinc is essential for a healthy immune system. Zinc deficiency of mice in the womb resulted in offspring with deficient immune systems throughout life, even when sufficient zinc was added to the diet later in life.[63]

Dr. James Balch reported that white lines on the nail can indicate other health problems, including heart disease, high fever, arsenic poisoning, or liver disease.[64]

SUGGESTIONS

■ Build the immune system if illness is causing white lines.

■ Increase protein and zinc in the diet, if deficient.

■ If the sign continues, consider checking other possibilities.

RELATED TOPICS

ANOREXIA

BINGING

QEW TEST

Zinc deficiency of mice in the womb resulted in offspring with deficient immune systems throughout life, even when sufficient zinc was added to the diet later in life.

Food for Thought

Have you ever attempted to relate joint pains to dietary habits?

Vitamin B6 is an excellent example of an important nutrient with many nutritional antagonists. Does the concept of a nutritional antagonist make sense to you? Have you ever consumed or been exposed to any vitamin B6 antagonists?

Iron is a two-edged sword. Deficiency can impair thinking and immune function, while excess can contribute to free-radical damage and overgrowth of harmful bacteria. How does this speak to the need for a balanced nutritional intake?

Why do you think people chew their nails? What thoughts run through your head when you look at fingernails?

Back and Legs: *Our Locomotive Devices*

At the age of 43 my mother was attempting to close the door of her automobile when she slipped on wet pavement and landed with a resounding thud on the street. She thought nothing about the fall until her arm began to throb, but by the end of the day she was in excruciating pain. She persuaded my father to rush her to the hospital. Her physician X-rayed the arm, developed the film, and then called her into his office. He smiled and said, "You broke your arm like a little old lady!"

The doctor may have been smiling, but my mother was not. She had been present when her grandmother suffered a broken hip as a result of a similar fall. Due to complications resulting from osteoporosis she died. My mother, realizing her bones were in a condition similar to that of her grandmother's in her old age, became motivated to undertake a dietary and supplement program to improve her health and the strength of her bones.

In a remarkable case of serendipity a friend shared the benefits of whole food–based supplements with my mother the very day she experienced her fall. This woman's timing proved to be impeccable. My parents drove to this woman's home after her arm had been set in a cast. She purchased a wide range of supplements and began to take them faithfully.

Her recovery was remarkable. The bone healed in half the time the doctor was expecting. He had never seen such rapid healing of such a severe break, and he asked my mother if she could acquire some of the supplements for his nurse and himself. She did and found herself in the supplement business.

My mother suffered an accident at the age of 79. Realizing her risk for osteoporosis, due to her condition at the age of 43, she asked the doctor to check the density of her bones. His examination revealed that she had healthy bones for a woman of her age.

My own mother's experience convinced me that bones are a living tissue. Like every other tissue in the body, bones require nutrients. The more complete and consistent the supply of essential nutrients, and the more efficiently these nutrients are used, the healthier and denser the bones are going to be.

Wear and tear of bones and joints usually begins in the spine and legs, which must carry body weight day after day. Poor diet not only weakens these tissues but can also promote weight gain, which places undue stress on back, hips, and knees. Treatment for painful backs and repair of damaged hip and knee joints is a multibillion-dollar expense in the United States every year.

The muscles in the legs are the largest in the human body. Nutrient deficiencies which affect these muscles will often be indicated by cramping, pain, or weakness of the legs.

The ability to move is one of life's greatest gifts. Learn to cherish the ability to exercise and do it frequently to preserve optimal health. Combine your exercise program with some of the tips in this chapter for keeping the back and legs healthy and capable of performing their functions.

Back Pain

SIGN

Pain in the lower back

SIGNIFICANCE

Back pain is a leading cause of visits to health professionals and also a major factor involved in inability to work.

DISCUSSION

Donald E. Pickett, founder of the Neo-Life Company, shared the story of his own struggle with lower back pain in 1978. He injured his back in 1946. The back began to deteriorate rapidly despite treatments by chiropractors, osteopaths, and medial doctors. He was informed that the cartilage or discs in his back had totally deteriorated and fusion of the spine was strongly recommended. Instead he chose to wear a large steel structure called a "chair brace." He wore this apparatus every day for six years.

Mr. Pickett met Dr. Dean Conrad of Urbana, Ohio, one day. Dr. Conrad observed and felt the brace and then asked, "Would you like to get rid of that brace?" Mr. Pickett responded with an emphatic "Yes!"

Dr. Conrad suggested taking 1 tablespoon of cod liver oil with 2 ounces of hot milk just before bedtime every day. Mr. Pickett, almost from desperation, began the regimen immediately. Ten days later he woke one morning without his familiar and constant lower back pain. He felt brave enough to take the back brace off a week later and never wore it again. Many years later examination of his back found none of the spinal abnormalities that had been observed years earlier.[1]

Many years ago my father suffered with severe back pain. Mr. Pickett shared this story with him and then gave him a bottle of cod liver oil capsules from his own supply. The supplement worked so well for my father that my mother suggested Mr. Pickett make the cod liver oil available as a supplement through his nutrition company, which he did.

The magic ability of cod liver oil to alleviate many cases of back pain was greeted with a good deal of disbelief even by Mr. Pickett. Our greater understanding of nutrition today enables us to understand that cod liver oil is a rich source of vitamins A and D, both of which are necessary for healthy bones. Cod liver oil also contains anti-inflammatory omega-3 oils.

Back pain may be caused by weakening of the bones and muscles of the back or by putting excessive strain on them. A common cause of excessive stress on the bones and muscles of the lower back is unreasonable weight gain. The obvious solution here is to lose weight, but a weight loss program that does not supply the nutrients necessary to build and maintain healthy bones can result in increased back pain, even if weight loss does take place. Bones starved of good nutrition become weaker.

The natural tendency when one suffers with back pain is to avoid exercise and movement when the back hurts. Proper exercise will often reduce pain.[2] A good physical therapist is able to provide competent guidance regarding the proper exercises for lower back pain. Chiropractic treatments and massage are sometimes helpful for those who suffer from chronic back pain as well.

Several factors contribute to weakening of the bones or bone loss. A diet that contains highly acid foods and beverages weakens bones. The body uses minerals from the bones to buffer and excrete excess acids in the diet. Alkaline foods such as fruits and vegetables are generally high in bone-building and sustaining minerals. Acid foods such as meats, grains, sugar, and sodas provide little in the way of beneficial minerals, but considerable acid that must be buffered and excreted. Eating more alkaline foods or supplementing with alkaline minerals has been demonstrated to reduce the symptoms of lower back pain.[3]

SUGGESTIONS

■ Consume adequate water to prevent dehydration.

■ Increase fruits and vegetables in the diet.

■ Supplement with alkaline minerals, including calcium and magnesium.

■ Supplement with salmon oil or eat salmon.

■ Take a tablespoon or equivalent in capsule form of cod liver oil with warm milk before bed. Capsules make this more pleasant and protect oils from oxidation.

Bowed Legs (Rickets)

SIGN

The legs are bowed or bent. Bones and muscles are weak and a "pigeon chest" is common.

SIGNIFICANCE

Bowed legs are a classic sign of rickets or vitamin D deficiency.

DISCUSSION

The United States is experiencing a tidal wave of vitamin D deficiency as children and adults consume less vitamin D-fortified foods and spend less time outdoors where vitamin D is formed with exposure of the skin to sunlight. Many people today spend most of their time indoors watching television or involved with computers or video games. The use of sunscreen has been so effectively marketed that many people never go outdoors without it. Vitamin D deficiency has serious implications for normal development of children, loss of bone and muscle strength among the elderly, deterioration of blood sugar control for the diabetic, and increased risk for developing a number of cancers.[4]

Infants and children are at greatest risk for vitamin D deficiency. This nutrient is absolutely essential for normal development, yet deficiency can take place in infants who nurse at the mother's breast, if the mother is not consuming foods with sufficient vitamin D or not exposing the skin to sunlight. A mother is not able to pass along to her infant nutrients she does not possess.

Americans have become increasingly intolerant to sunlight. They rapidly develop sunburn when outdoors, for at least two reasons. First, they are not outdoors sufficiently to gradually develop a tan. Second, insufficient intake of antioxidants, particularly the photoprotective, fat-soluble, coloring pigments in fruits and vegetables called carotenoids, increases the probability of burning rather than tanning. Lack of antioxidants also increases the risk for developing skin cancer with prolonged exposure to sunlight.

Spending considerable time outdoors is no guarantee that one will obtain adequate vitamin D. Studies indicate that very little vitamin D is formed within the skin of those who live in the northern hemisphere north of San Francisco during the wintertime. There is simply not enough direct sunlight available for substantial vitamin D formation.

Infants with vitamin D deficiency look plump and wellfed, but the muscles are flabby, development is impaired, digestive upsets are common, and excessive sweating of the scalp is common. Vitamin D deficiency can also cause a pigeon-shaped chest and result in muscle tightness with the thumb being pulled to the palm. Dr. Joseph Hart found head sweating the most obvious and common early sign of vitamin D deficiency—he found this symptom in 66% of his patients who were vitamin D deficient. The symptom was often accompanied by pain when the hair was brushed or pulled gently. He noted that the sweating or dampness of the head will usually cease three or four weeks after adequate vitamin D is given. These signs are particularly common in children.[5]

A number of recent studies indicate that vitamin D is important not only for infants and children, but also for adults. Vitamin D has been shown to trigger an enzyme in the digestive tract that destroys a cancer-causing substance found in bile called lithocholic acid. In this manner, vitamin D decreases the risk of colon cancer.[6]

Vitamin D also decreases the risk of developing autoimmune disease in young and old. A study of nurses who obtained at least 400 IU of vitamin D daily demonstrated that they reduced their risk of developing multiple sclerosis by 60%. Immune cells forming where vitamin D is adequately supplied are less likely to engage in autoimmune activity or attack one's own body.

Infants with vitamin D deficiency look plump and wellfed, but the muscles are flabby, development is impaired, digestive upsets are common, and excessive sweating of the scalp is common.

Vitamin D has been shown to trigger an enzyme in the digestive tract that destroys a cancer-causing substance found in bile, called lithocholic acid.

Immune cells forming where adequate vitamin D is adequately supplied are less likely to engage in autoimmune activity or attack one's own body.

RELATED TOPICS

LONG FACE
SYNDROME

TOOTH DECAY

MERCURY
AMALGAMS

Improved immune function in the elderly resulting from adequate vitamin D may prevent loss of teeth. Inflammation of the gums often leads to tooth loss. Tooth loss is 25% higher when vitamin D intake is low, due to decreased ability of the immune system to respond to gum infections. Teeth that are sensitive or throb may indicate vitamin D deficiency.

Vitamin D also appears to reduce the risk of colon, breast, and prostate cancers. One important role the vitamin plays is support for differentiation. Differentiation is the process whereby a cell develops into a specific kind of tissue such as a breast cell, a prostate cell, or a colon cell. A key characteristic of cancer cells is that they do not differentiate properly. The less differentiation a cancer cell has, the more malignant it tends to be. Dr. Gerald Dermer, a life-long cancer researcher, observed that, "Pathologists around the world know that the risk of metastasis (spread of cancer) is inversely related to the level of tumor differentiation."[7] Vitamin D is essential for differentiation or the normal development and maturation of cells.[8]

Finally, vitamin D appears to be very helpful for those with diabetes. In one study, increasing blood measurements of vitamin D from 35 nmol/l to 75 nmol/l (or essentially doubling vitamin D blood levels) improved insulin sensitivity by 60% "which is a greater increase than many anti-diabetes drugs provide."[9] Vitamin D, or the sunshine vitamin, is an essential nutrient from the time we are in the womb until the time we depart this earth.

Researchers are now suggesting that optimal vitamin D intake may be between 800 and 1,000 IU for fair-skinned people and up to 2,000 IU for dark-skinned women. Cod liver oil is an excellent natural source of vitamin D. A reasonable amount of exposure to sunlight may also be an excellent means of meeting requirements for this vitamin.[9] Vitamin D is fat soluble and can be toxic when taken orally in great excess, though sunlight exposure poses no such risk.

Vitamin D also appears to reduce the risk of colon, breast, and prostate cancers.

Vitamin D appears to be very helpful for those with diabetes.

SUGGESTIONS

- Expose the skin to reasonable amounts of sunlight.

- Supplement with cod liver oil or a multiple with vitamin D.

Discoloration of the Skin of the Lower Leg

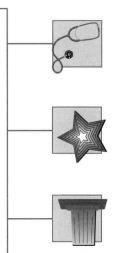

SIGN

This sign consists of "slowly spreading brownish-reddish (with occasional yellowish) discolorations on the skin of the lower legs."[10]

SIGNIFICANCE

This sign is often an early warning sign of the development of adult-onset diabetes.

DISCUSSION

Dr. Jonathan Wright observed that this sign is linked not only to a risk of diabetes, but also insulin resistance which often precedes the development of diabetes. The discoloration results from deterioration of the circulatory system, which accompanies blood sugar irregularities.[10] The circulatory system is damaged in those with blood sugar problems by glycosylation—a process in which sugars bond with protein in blood vessels, damaging their integrity.[11] High blood sugar also interferes with vitamin C utilization. Vitamin C is not only an antioxidant, but also a key component of connective tissue and plays an important role in the health of the blood vessels and skin.

The diabetic is at risk for ketone poisoning. Every diabetic should know the early signs of this condition.

Signs that mark early ketoacidosis:

▶ Sleepiness

▶ Fatigue

▶ Great thirst

▶ Frequent urination

▶ Dry skin and tongue

▶ Digestive difficulties, including nausea

▶ Leg cramps

▶ Fruity odor to the breath similar to nail polish remover, resulting from acetone.[12]

RELATED TOPICS

BOWED LEGS (RICKETS)

DUPUYTREN'S CONTRACTURE

OBESITY

SKIN TAGS

UPPER BODY WEIGHT GAIN

SUGGESTIONS

- Reduce the intake of refined carbohydrates.

- Supplement with antioxidants such as vitamins C, D, and E.

- Test for a possible diabetic condition.

Leg Cramps

SIGN

Cramping of the legs, bottom of the foot, or twitching of other muscles

SIGNIFICANCE

This sign may indicate deficiencies of calcium, magnesium, vitamin B complex, vitamin E, vitamin C, or omega-3 oils.

DISCUSSION

As a youngster, I was awakened many nights with the sound of my father hopping around on one foot in the middle of the night due to leg cramps. I was not spared the agony of this condition and remember many nights being wakened from a sound sleep by a painful cramp in the calf or foot. Many years later I learned that high intake of sugar could trigger my cramping while supplementing with calcium and magnesium would usually prevent it. Cramping stopped altogether after I removed most of the sugar from my diet.

A surprising number of nutrients are associated with leg or other muscle cramping. Any muscle cramping or twitching should receive proper attention. Remember that the heart is a muscle too, and if this muscle begins to cramp a health crisis exists!

Calcium and magnesium are primary nutrients in muscle function. Calcium enables muscles to contract, while magnesium is essential for muscle relaxation. Deficiency of both is common, although magnesium is a more frequent deficiency due to the fact that calcium is often supplemented.

Both minerals, but especially magnesium, frequently relieve muscle cramping. This mineral has been proven to alleviate leg cramps of pregnant women.[13] Research indicates that leg cramps may be caused by acute deficiencies of sodium or magnesium. Diuretics, pharmaceutical or dietary, such as

Any muscle cramping or twitching should receive proper attention. Remember that the heart is a muscle too, and if this muscle begins to cramp a health crisis exists!

caffeine, may contribute to depletion of both sodium and magnesium.[14] Phosphoric acid in sodas and phosphates in baking powders combine with magnesium in foods creating insoluble magnesium phosphate which cannot be absorbed. This contributes to deficiency of the mineral magnesium.

The Food and Nutrition Board of the National Academy of Science has recommended an intake of 1.5 grams of calcium a day for a population that consumes less than 300 milligrams of magnesium a day. Magnesium deficiency can actually be *induced or intensified by a high intake of calcium* when magnesium intake is low. Dr. Mildred Seelig, a physician who is considered a world expert on magnesium, suggested that calcium and magnesium should be consumed in a 2:1 ratio in supplements in order to prevent the development of magnesium deficiency. Unfortunately, many professionals have recommended high intakes of calcium without emphasizing the importance of also obtaining adequate magnesium to prevent deficiency of this critically important mineral.[15]

Dr. Seelig shared an anecdote of a woman suffering extreme magnesium deficiency at a meeting of the International and American Associations of Clinical Nutritionists. This story illustrates how central magnesium balance is to prevention of cramping. Dr. Seelig was summoned to a hospital to examine a woman who could barely move. She tested the woman's muscles, which resulted in convulsions of the entire body, indicative of severe magnesium deficiency. Dr. Seelig then injected the woman with magnesium.

This woman had not arisen from bed, taken a bath, or combed her hair for many weeks. Within a couple of hours, she did all of these things. Dr. Seelig was beckoned to the woman's bedside. The patient commented that the convulsion therapy she had been subjected to was most unusual, but she had never experienced such a powerful medical procedure in her life. Her energy was fully restored and she felt well again. The convulsions, of course, had nothing to do with the woman's improvement. She had been restored by an injection of magnesium, which addressed her severe deficiency of the mineral.

Signs of magnesium deficiency include irregular heartbeat, numbness and tingling, sweating, rapid heartbeat, mild to severe confusion, disorientation, hallucinations, and paranoia. Depletion may result from illness, diarrhea, high sugar or alcohol intake, or unbalanced diets.[16] One of my friends found himself in the hospital where the doctors found a life-threatening deficiency of magnesium. The cause—an unbalanced weight loss program. I once talked to a taxi driver who drank only sodas, never water. He developed such a severe dehydration and magnesium deficiency that he nearly died.

Magnesium deficiency can actually be induced or intensified by a high intake of calcium when magnesium intake is low.

Signs of magnesium deficiency include irregular heartbeat, numbness and tingling, sweating, rapid heartbeat, mild to severe confusion, disorientation, hallucinations, and paranoia.

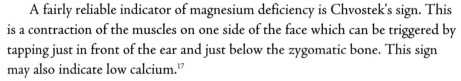

A fairly reliable indicator of magnesium deficiency is Chvostek's sign. This is a contraction of the muscles on one side of the face which can be triggered by tapping just in front of the ear and just below the zygomatic bone. This sign may also indicate low calcium.[17]

Related Topic
Restless Leg Syndrome

The elderly may require digestive support with hydrochloric acid for proper calcium and magnesium absorption. Stomach acid declines as we age. Use of antacids, which interferes with digestion, may contribute to deficiencies of these minerals.

In one study the severity of leg cramps improved in 86% of patients taking a high-potency vitamin B complex supplement.

Vitamin B complex plays a significant role in preventing muscle cramping. In one study the severity of leg cramps improved in 86% of patients taking a high-potency vitamin B complex supplement.[18] Other research found cramping of the legs of 16 patients at night dramatically improved with injections of 500 mcg of vitamin B12. Relief lasted for 4 to 6 weeks.[19] Vitamins B1 and B6 have been used successfully to treat muscle cramping during pregnancy. The benefit of vitamin B6 may be a consequence of the important part it plays in assuring proper metabolism of magnesium.[20]

Antioxidants have been shown to prevent leg cramping, perhaps by stabilizing cell membranes. A study of 125 patients with leg cramps found that most responded well to vitamin E. Levels of vitamin E used in this experiment were 400 to 800 I.U.[21] Patients who have cirrhosis often find relief from leg cramps with two other antioxidants—taurine and zinc.[22, 23]

Fluoride has been suggested by some doctors for leg cramps, but this is not a good idea.[24] Fluoride can suppress thyroid function. Muscle stiffness, pain, weakness and *cramping* may result from low thyroid function. [25]

Suggestions

- Avoid excess intake of sugar and phosphates.

- Essential fatty acids including omega-3 oils will sometimes alleviate cramping by improving utilization of other nutrients.

- Supplement with calcium, magnesium, and B complex vitamins.

- Supplement with antioxidants.

Numbness of the Hands or Feet

SIGN

A sensory loss in hands or feet, often with a distribution similar to what would be covered by wearing stockings or gloves.[26] Sensory loss may be accompanied by tingling or burning. (Scientific term: peripheral neuropathy)

SIGNIFICANCE

This sign is characteristic of nerve damage. Neuropathy often accompanies diabetes, heavy metal or pesticide poisoning. Neuropathy may also be caused by gluten intolerance.

DISCUSSION

It is little known among health professionals that neuropathy is the second most common symptom of gluten sensitivity.[27] Gluten intolerance is rarely diagnosed or even suspected. Carnegie Brown first associated gluten intolerance with peripheral neuropathy in 1908.[28] In 1966 a landmark paper was published that demonstrated gluten intolerance among ten patients suffering from peripheral neuropathy.[29] Neuropathy may predict Crohn's disease or other severe digestive problems when gluten is poorly tolerated.[30]

More than half of diabetic patients develop neuropathy, which results from oxidative damage to the nerves.[31] Attempts to control diabetic neuropathy should include not only control of blood sugar, but also the use of antioxidants to protect the nerves from oxidative damage. Alpha-lipoic acid is an important antioxidant for the diabetic, 600 mg or more a day having been used to successfully treat neuropathy.[32, 33]

Zinc and vitamin E, both of which play a role as antioxidants, have also been used successfully to treat this condition.[34, 35] Vitamin E protects the lipid membranes of nerve cells. Zinc aids in regulation of blood sugar and is essential for metabolism of fats—the major building block of nerve cells.

A number of B vitamins benefit neuropathy. They provide energy with which nerve cells can protect themselves and aid in the detoxification of substances that can damage the nerves.[36] Alcoholics are inclined to develop neuropathy, which may be prevented by vitamin B1 intake. The alcoholic is not necessarily deficient in the nutrient, but has a problem utilizing the vitamin.[37]

It is little known among health professionals that neuropathy is the second most common symptom of gluten sensitivity.

*Neuropathy often
follows exposure to
nerve toxins.*

*Because heavy
metals are heavy
they tend to migrate
to the lower parts of
the body, including
the hands and feet,
where they do
damage and create
symptoms.*

Common causes of neuropathy in the elderly who are not diabetics are deficiencies of vitamin B12 and folic acid.[38] Vitamin B12 deficiencies develop as a result of lowered hydrochloric acid production in the stomach as we age.

Nutrients that improve fat metabolism may also reduce symptoms of neuropathy. Animal studies have shown that myo-inositol may prevent diabetic neuropathy. This nutrient aids proper nerve function in the diabetic. Inositol, not considered an essential nutrient, can be found in lecithin.[39] Biotin has also been used successfully to treat diabetic neuropathy. Large amounts were given by injection.[40] This vitamin is normally synthesized by bacteria in the digestive tract. Use of antibiotics or poor diet may interfere with normal synthesis.

Nerves are built primarily of fat. The type of fat in the diet may alter symptoms of neuropathy, particularly for the diabetic. Gama-linolenic acid found in evening primrose, borage, or black currant oils has been identified as benefiting neuropathy in the diabetic literature.[41] The fat in these oils (GLA) is normally synthesized in the body, but diabetics are known to have a deranged fat metabolism.

Fish oils also benefit neuropathy. In one study 21 diabetics with neuropathy were given 600 mg EPA three times a day for 48 weeks. Indications of neuropathy began to improve significantly after 12 weeks. These diabetics also demonstrated improved blood flow to the feet and a significant improvement in kidney function. Deterioration in kidney function is generally considered difficult to prevent. Large amounts of fish oil may increase the diabetic's blood sugar, requiring careful monitoring as fish oils are added to the diet.[42]

Neuropathy often follows exposure to nerve toxins. Heavy metals such as lead, mercury, or cadmium have caused severe nerve degeneration for centuries.[43] Lead has been known to be a cause of neurologic problems, including neuropathy, since Roman times. "Mad as a hatter" refers to the insanity and brain damage caused in hat makers in England who worked with mercury. Because heavy metals are heavy they tend to migrate to the lower parts of the body, including the hands and feet, where they do damage and create symptoms.

Many industrial and agricultural chemicals are toxic enough to the nervous system that they also cause neuropathy.[44, 45] Included among these substances are widely used organophosphorus pesticides.[46] One of my friends led a normal life until he came home from work one day and lay on his lawn. He was unaware it had been sprayed with a now-banned pesticide (Dursban). This *single* exposure initiated a deterioration of nerve function that left him unable

Chapter 10 – Back and Legs

to care for himself. Those who carelessly use or expose themselves to toxic chemicals place their health at greater risk than they often know.

SUGGESTIONS

- Avoid gluten if sensitive to it.
- Avoid heavy metal, pesticide, and toxic chemical exposure.
- Eat fish or cautiously supplement with EPA (fish oils) and vitamin E.
- Keep blood sugar stable.
- Supplement with protein, B complex vitamins, and antioxidants.

Osteoporosis

SIGN

The skeletal structure becomes brittle and weak. Compression of the spinal column can lead to what has been called the "widow's hump" and loss of height.

SIGNIFICANCE

Fractures due to osteoporosis cost billions of dollars every year and can result in death.

DISCUSSION

The traditional medical approach to treating osteoporosis consists of large quantities of calcium and medications such as Fosamax®. Unfortunately, such medications create such digestive problems that almost half of the women who use them quit within ten months. These medications block the activity of cells called osteoclasts, which remove old bone so the body can replace it with new stronger bone. The result of using these medications is more bone mass, but it is weaker bone. After prolonged use of these medications, the fracture rate starts to rise to levels comparable to those of women who have never used the medication.[47]

One of the keys to prevention of osteoporosis is to build healthy bones when we are young.

One of the keys to prevention of osteoporosis is to build healthy bones when we are young. Those with greater bone mass at maturity have a lower risk of developing osteoporosis as they age. Unfortunately, the diets and exercise patterns of most young people are totally inadequate to produce healthy bones.

Many antacids contain aluminum which has been shown to speed the breakdown of bone and slow the formation of new bone.

Average intake of aluminum is 2 to 20 mg a day, but antacids may have 200 mg per tablet!

Our grandmothers gave their children cod liver oil, knowing that this promoted healthy bones. Vitamin D promotes early development of bone mass, as does vitamin K found in leafy greens.[48] Regular calcium and magnesium intake and exercise also promote strong bones at a young age.

Many of the elderly who suffer from bone loss experience mild to severe digestive difficulties. Supporting digestion with hydrochloric acid, if needed, improves calcium absorption. Unfortunately, many calcium supplements act as antacids, further depressing an already-low stomach acid secretion. Regular use of antacids, common in the elderly, impairs calcium absorption. My preference for calcium supplementation is an amino acid chelated form (calcium glycinate) which does not have the antacid properties of some other forms of calcium and also appears to be exceptionally well absorbed.

Many antacids contain aluminum, which has been shown to speed the breakdown of bone and slow the formation of new bone. Animals given aluminum develop osteoporosis and humans taking antacids containing aluminum have developed severe bone pain and softening of the bones. Average intake of aluminum is 2 to 20 mg a day, but antacids may have 200 mg per tablet! Significant amounts of aluminum are also found in beverages stored in aluminum cans, foods cooked in aluminum cookware, many processed foods, most baking powders, some salts, over-the-counter medications (including some buffered aspirins), and even many deodorants.[49]

Both progesterone and testosterone promote bone building and prevent bone loss. Dr. John Lee, a well-known expert on osteoporosis and female hormones, believed low progesterone was the primary cause of bone loss in women as they age.[50] I have observed that many of the women who have serious osteoporosis problems have undergone a hysterectomy many years previously. This common surgery (approximately 600,000 women a year undergo the procedure) may be one explanation for the widespread osteoporosis among older women in the United States.

Dr. Lee recommended moderate protein intake, a wide spectrum of minerals, vitamin B6, D, K, and C to prevent bone loss. Antibiotics destroy beneficial intestinal bacteria that produce vitamin K in the digestive tract— restoration of beneficial bacteria is helpful in correcting this imbalance. Dr. Lee also reported that overactive thyroid, fluoride, cortisone, and alcohol have negative effects on bone strength.[51] The trace mineral strontium appears to be a powerful stimulus for building healthy bone. Some women have reported benefit when this mineral was added to the supplement program.[52]

Chapter 10 – Back and Legs

SUGGESTIONS

- Don't eat a highly acid diet.

- Exercise regularly.

- Supplement with calcium, magnesium, and cod liver oil.

- Support stomach acid if it is deficient with betaine hydrochloride.

- Try to avoid using antacids.

- Use a good multiple vitamin along with quality oils.

Pain in the Big Toe (Gout)

SIGN

The joints become extremely painful and form lumps. Gout usually begins with severe pain in one of the big toes. A lump in the earlobe may be an early clue of uric acid buildup.[53]

SIGNIFICANCE

Uric acid crystals, a result of the breakdown of the amino acid purine, form in the joints of those suffering with gout. Gout is often found associated with low thyroid function, obesity, diabetes, heart disease, and high blood pressure. Those with gout have an increased probability of developing kidney stones.

DISCUSSION

Gout has been described as "a royal pain" because it was a common affliction of kings. This problem is much more common in men than in women, perhaps because men tend to eat high-purine foods, eat fewer vegetables, and consume more alcohol.

Gout is closely associated with excessive consumption of alcohol and foods high in purines, including glandular meats (liver, kidney, heart, and sweetbreads) and seafoods (herring and sardines). Other foods with uric acid include yeast, asparagus, peas, beans, and mushrooms.

Alcohol decreases uric acid excretion and increases uric acid production. Sugars, including fructose or fruit sugar, have been shown to aggravate gout.

High fructose corn syrup, hidden in many processed foods, is not recommended for an individual afflicted with gout.

Rich meats and other foods high in purines should also be avoided. One of the reasons meats may be a problem is due to poor digestion.[53] I was once told by a man who suffered greatly with gout that the use of hydrochloric acid and pancreatic enzymes greatly alleviated his suffering.

While meats make gout worse, a diet high in raw foods and vegetables is often beneficial. Vitamin C, abundantly supplied in these foods, has been shown to lower uric acid levels.

Dr. Jonathan Wright observed that a medication (Probenecid) used to treat gout works exactly like vitamin C, causing the body to dump uric acid. He treats gout with small amounts of lithium, which helps prevent uric acid from crystallizing and 1 to 2 grams of vitamin C three times daily. He found this often controls gout or reduces the amount of medication needed.[54] Lithium can produce a toxic reaction, which Dr. Wright has prevented with vitamin E and flax oil.[55]

In the 1950s Ludwig Blau, Ph.D. was suffering from gout. He ate a bowl of cherries and woke up with greatly diminished pain the next day. The active ingredient may have been a coloring pigment, keracyanin. Cherries are also a rich source of vitamin C and flavonoids, which may help lower uric acid levels. It should also be noted that cherries are high in sugar, which is why they might not work well for someone with blood sugar imbalances.[56]

Aspirin and other salicylates inhibit excretion of uric acid and should not be used to treat the excruciating pain of gout. A discussion of the association between salicylates and both gout and fibromyalgia will be found in R. Paul St. Amand's *What Your Doctor May Not Tell You About Fibromyalgia*.[57] Dr. Amand found that any treatment that benefited gout also tended to produce improvement in fibromyalgia. The discussion in this section may therefore have a double application.

Dr. Amand provided an important warning for those undergoing treatment for gout. He wrote, "We had always known that when we treat gout by lowering the blood uric acid, we precipitated attacks of gouty joints. As uric acid comes out of the joints, it seems to cause the same pains it did going in."

It is a tragic irony that often a treatment that is effective in the elimination of a problem often causes a "healing crisis." Several individuals suffering with arthritis over the years have described excruciating pain as an effective nutri-

Dr. Jonathan Wright observed that a medication (Probenecid) used to treat gout works exactly like vitamin C causing the body to dump uric acid.

Aspirin and other salicylates inhibit excretion of uric acid and should not be used to treat the excruciating pain of gout.

tional program led to disappearance of swollen and disfigured joints.[57] Fortunately, not everyone experiences this phenomena, because some people are not willing to go through this kind of pain to become well and there is always the nagging concern that the condition is worsening.

Some nutrients, in excess, can make gout worse. Be wary of using excessive quantities of vitamins A or B3 with this condition.[58]

SUGGESTIONS

- Avoid foods high in purines.

- Reduce intake of sugars, including fructose and alcohol.

- Improve digestion.

- Supplement with vitamin C.

- Try cherries.

Restless Legs Syndrome

SIGN

The legs are restless, jittery, or have a tendency to tighten up

SIGNIFICANCE

This sign may indicate excess caffeine intake or blood sugar problems. Restless legs may also be caused by lack of nutrients, including iron, magnesium, omega-3 oils, vitamin C, vitamin D, and vitamin E.

DISCUSSION

Restless legs syndrome is strongly linked with excessive caffeine intake. The restless legs phenomenon is frequently accompanied by insomnia, depression, or anxiety when caffeine is a causative factor. Caffeine is present in coffee, tea, chocolate, soft drinks, and many over-the-counter medications.[59]

Restless legs syndrome may be a sign of elevated insulin and a pre-diabetic or early diabetic condition.[60] Erratic blood sugar levels disturb the functioning of both muscles and nerves. Leg cramps may also indicate elevated insulin levels.

Restless legs syndrome is strongly linked with excessive caffeine intake.

Sugar and caffeine may be depressing magnesium levels in restless legs syndrome. Magnesium supplementation appears to decrease symptoms of both restless legs and also insomnia.[61]

Dr. Michael Murray observed that "Iron deficiency, with or without anemia, is an important contributor to the development of RLS (restless legs syndrome) in elderly patients, and iron supplements can produce a significant reduction in symptoms."[62] Stomach acid is necessary for absorption of iron. Low production by the stomach of hydrochloric acid should not be ruled out as a cause of iron deficiency and restless legs syndrome, particularly in the elderly, who often suffer from failing digestion.[63] Excess iron intake can be toxic and should be avoided.

Vitamin E sometimes provides substantial relief from restless legs. This vitamin stabilizes cell membranes.

SUGGESTIONS

- Avoid caffeinated beverages.

- Avoid sugar.

- Supplement with calcium and magnesium.

- Supplement with iron if deficient.

Stiffness

SIGN

Loss of flexibility and agility that is particularly noticeable in the arms, legs, and back

SIGNIFICANCE

Stiffness can be a sign of lack of physical fitness, particularly when we become stiff at a relatively young age. Inflammation is often indicated by stiffness.

DISCUSSION

One of the earliest results of lack of physical exercise is stiffness. This is probably caused by changes in connective tissue. Lack of physical fitness also contributes to fatigue, loss of coordination, aches, pains, and sensitivity. One of the best ways to avoid or reduce the stiffness we often associate with aging is to engage in regular exercise.[64] A combination of aerobic and weight-bearing exercises is helpful.

Dr. Ralph Paffenberger, Jr., a research epidemiologist at the University of California at Berkley, associated physical fitness with reduced risk of a number of diseases: "We know that being physically fit is a way of protecting yourself against coronary heart disease, hypertension and stroke, plus adult-onset diabetes, obesity, osteoporosis, probably colon cancer and maybe other cancers, and probably clinical depression. Exercise has an enormous impact on the quality of life."[65]

Stiffness may also be caused by allergic responses or intolerance to foods or chemicals, which result in inflammation and fluid retention. An example is the sensitivity to nightshades observed by Norman Childers. Nutrient deficiencies may also contribute to stiffness as evidenced by the work of William Kaufman with niacinamide, discussed under the topic of ARTHRITIS (OSTEOARTHRITIS). Deficiency of vitamin B6 often results in stiffness, as discussed under QUICK EARLY WARNING SIGN (QEW TEST).

Omega-3 oils often provide significant relief from stiffness due to their anti-inflammatory activity. An example of the ability of omega-3 oils to combat stiffness is provided under the topic ARTHRITIS (RHEUMATOID).

SUGGESTIONS

- Avoid allergens.

- Eat well.

- Exercise regularly.

- Obtain essential nutrients, including B complex vitamins, omega-3 oils, and antioxidants.

Varicose Veins

SIGN

The valves in the veins become damaged, causing blood to accumulate. The veins swell and can become inflamed or irritated.

RELATED TOPICS

ARTHRITIS
(OSTEOARTHRITIS)

ARTHRITIS
(RHEUMATOID)

OLD-AGE
PIGMENTATION

QUICK EARLY
WARNING SIGN

Omega-3 oils often provide significant relief from stiffness due to their anti-inflammatory activity.

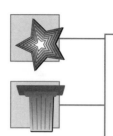

SIGNIFICANCE

Varicose veins are unsightly and can lead to deadly blood clots.

DISCUSSION

The body has a big job when it undertakes the task of returning blood from the feet to the heart. A mechanism known as the "muscle pump" squeezes the blood upward. Valves in the veins then hold the blood and prevent it from going backwards.

RELATED TOPICS

CONSTIPATION

STOOL BULK AND TRANSIT TIME

Constipation and straining at the stool, because of the high pressures developed, damage the valves in the veins. This results in varicose veins. Lack of exercise and poor muscle tone interfere with the functioning of the "muscle pump" and contribute to varicose veins as well. Physically active people in the world on a high-roughage diet have only 1 in 1,000 cases of varicose veins. The incidence in the United States is 1 in 10.

Varicose veins greatly increase the risk of blood clots. These can be quite painful (phlebitis) and can result in death (embolism). Adequate fiber intake and regular exercise reduce risk of a "potentially fatal barrage of blood clots to the lungs."[66]

SUGGESTIONS

- Consume adequate fiber in food or supplement form on a daily basis.

- Don't stand or sit without moving for long periods of time.

- Exercise to maintain proper muscle tone.

- Supplement with vitamin C and flavonoids, fish oils, and vitamin E.

Weakness in the Legs (Beriberi)

SIGN

Weakness in the legs

SIGNIFICANCE

Legs can become weak due to deficiency of vitamin B1 or vitamin D. Deficiency of thiamine (vitamin B1) may be indicated if the calf muscle is tender when squeezed.

DISCUSSION

Beriberi begins with weakness and loss of feeling in the legs. This is followed by swelling of the lower half of the body and can lead to heart failure and death.[67] Beriberi results from deficiency of thiamine or vitamin B1—a deficiency that cost many lives in the Orient after the introduction of white rice.

Prior to 1887 one-third of Japanese naval personnel were stricken with beriberi. There were no deaths in 1887 because consumption of white rice was reduced. The suffering resulting from refining of this one food was incalculable. Those who ate unrefined rice protected themselves from a horrifying death caused by deficiency of vitamin B1.

The elderly often develop weak legs due to deficiency of vitamin D. Senior citizens supplemented with 800 IU of vitamin D and calcium had half the falls of those who received only calcium. The vitamin D strengthened leg muscles. [68]

SUGGESTIONS

- Supplement with calcium, magnesium, B complex vitamins, and cod liver oil.

RELATED TOPICS

UP AND DOWN, SIDE TO SIDE EYE MOVEMENT

Food for Thought

How have living indoors and the development of the lightbulb altered man's way of life? <u>What are the results of decreased exposure to sunlight?</u>

How often do you experience muscle cramps? Have you ever noticed that certain foods like sugar, meat, or grains trigger tight muscles or cramping?

Introduction of malnutrition has followed closely behind man's alteration of his basic foods. What do you know about the results of refining or altering the following foods?

RICE   WHEAT   SUGAR CANE   SOY   CORN

Stiffness is a characteristic of aging and lack of exercise. How stiff are you compared to other people your age? How much exercise do you obtain on a weekly basis?

Elimination: *Our Sanitation System*

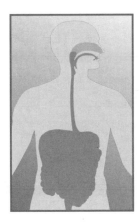

Elimination of waste products is one of the most vital functions of a living organism. This is illustrated by growth of cells in a tissue culture. The culture must be periodically cleansed of its waste products or the cells will die. Cells live longer without nutrients than they can live in accumulated waste products. Our health as human beings is dependent not only upon the intake of proper nutrients, but also the efficient elimination of waste.

Someone once said that it is better to have a good set of bowels than a good set of brains. The most brilliant individual does not escape incalculable misery if the simple precept that we require a given amount of fiber for normal elimination is neglected. Despite the critical importance of maintaining healthy elimination, highly intelligent people overlook this most essential building block of sound health.

Dr. David Reuben tells how his mind and heart were opened to an understanding of the importance of dietary fiber and proper elimination: "For five years I watched my father die slowly of cancer of the colon. I made sure he had the finest doctors in the country and the most advanced treatment available. It didn't make any difference because the slow-growing cancer relentlessly destroyed him. No one could tell me the cause of his malignancy, no one could tell me how it could have been prevented, and the best treatment modern medicine could offer was essentially the same as that used in 1900. The surgeons cut out the tumor and most of his large intestine; they relocated his anus in his lower abdomen, which caused him great emotional trauma. In spite of devoted doctors and massive medical costs, he died."

After years of researching the medical literature on fiber, Reuben came to a simple conclusion. "I am now convinced that not only could my father's life have

The most brilliant individual does not escape incalculable misery if the simple precept that we require a given amount of fiber for normal elimination is neglected. Despite the critical importance of maintaining healthy elimination, highly intelligent people overlook this most essential building block of sound health.

Problems with elimination cause a degree of suffering and discomfort unmatched by virtually anything else.

been saved, but millions of other cancer victims would be alive today if they had simply been able to add a few cents worth of vegetable fiber to their daily diet."[1]

Problems with elimination cause a degree of suffering and discomfort unmatched by virtually anything else. The tragedy is that most of this agony is avoidable with a few simple changes in diet or simple supplementation.

Elimination is such an important aspect of health that some laboratories devote considerable resources to collection and analysis of stool samples. Analytical examination of the stool indicates adequacy of digestion and the presence of undesirable parasites or microbes. Even without a laboratory at hand you should be able to perceive clues to digestive adequacy by careful observation of a few simple indicators discussed in this chapter.

Constipation

SIGN

Infrequent elimination and straining at the stool

SIGNIFICANCE

Constipation sets the stage for other health problems such as varicose veins, hiatus hernia, and diverticulosis.

DISCUSSION

Constipation is almost unheard of among primitive peoples on natural diets, yet it is one of the most frequent health complaints in the United States. Dr. David Reuben observed that "constipation has the dual distinction of simultaneously being the most common and the most neglected affliction of modern times." Nearly everyone eating refined foods experiences the problem at one time or another. Dr. Reuben reported that "even the most prestigious medical works underestimate the importance of the malfunction."[2]

"Constipation has the dual distinction of simultaneously being the most common and the most neglected affliction of modern times."
Dr. David Reuben

The most common cause of constipation is lack of fiber. The muscles of the small intestine and colon require bulk to act upon or squeeze in order to establish normal elimination. The average American and Briton consumes about 8 grams of fiber daily. By contrast, people on a high-roughage diet consume at least 25 grams a day, or three times as much fiber. Dr. Reuben observed that those few extra grams of fiber a day can "provide a million dollar's worth of life and health insurance."[3] Twenty-five grams of fiber is a small amount compared to what many people on a high-roughage diet consume.

Most people would find it depressing and disconcerting not to eliminate for days at a time, yet we were once able to help a woman who lived this way for years. She spent a period of time in a mental hospital for treatment of depression. She was fully convinced that the severe constipation she had endured for many years contributed to her mental problems. Supplementation with acidophilus restored her elimination to normal after all other measures had failed.

An often-overlooked factor in constipation (or chronic diarrhea) is lack of proper bacteria in the digestive tract. Approximately 2/3 of the stool volume is fiber and 1/3 consists of microorganisms. The bacteria in the digestive tract not only provide bulk, but they also break down fiber into butyrate, which is the primary nourishment for the cells that line the colon.

Other factors may cause constipation. Hydrochloric acid released by the stomach lining serves the role of initiating the worm-like motion of the digestive tract called peristalsis. This powerful substance also triggers normal secretions of the pancreas and the gallbladder. Insufficient secretion of stomach acid, which can be a consequence of the use of antacids, malnutrition, or aging, may contribute not only to constipation, but also a malfunctioning pancreas and gallbladder.[4]

Constipation may also result from lack of certain nutrients. B vitamins such as pantothenic acid and minerals like magnesium are necessary for the production of energy by the muscles of the digestive tract. Without these nutrients the muscles of the digestive tract lose their tone and can no longer contract efficiently, resulting in constipation. Many years ago I saw a study that demonstrated the total loss of muscle tone of the digestive tract of an experimental animal after it was deprived of vitamin B5.

Both magnesium and vitamin C are often excellent natural laxatives for those who are constipated. Large amounts of vitamin C create a "flush" of the digestive tract, which may be a little more in the way of elimination than most people would wish. Smaller amounts may aid normal elimination.

The muscle contractions of the intestines work most efficiently on a moist mass of material. Dehydration of the digestive tract tends to cause constipation. Two glasses of warm water does wonders in promoting normal elimination. A common mistake made when adding fiber to the diet is the failure to consume adequate water or fluids with it. The fiber then tends to constipate rather than to promote elimination because it will dry out the digestive tract. Squeezing a little lemon juice in water may provide additional stimulus to normal elimination.

B5

Wouldn't the same apply to all muscles?

Soluble fiber / No, all fiber is like a sponge

An often-overlooked factor in constipation (or chronic diarrhea) is lack of proper bacteria in the digestive tract.

Hydrochloric acid released by the stomach lining serves the role of initiating the worm-like motion of the digestive tract called peristalsis.

Dehydration of the digestive tract tends to cause constipation. Two glasses of warm water does wonders in promoting normal elimination.

insoluble fiber ? better see p. 181

Spread fiber intake through the day rather than consuming large quantities at one time.

An overly sedentary lifestyle contributes to constipation.

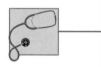

One of our family friends drank a large quantity of psyllium fiber without diluting it sufficiently with water while in Japan. He became ill and dehydrated as the fiber swelled in his stomach. As he drank more water the fiber swelled in his stomach, creating a good deal of pain. He became fearful he would have to go into the hospital and attempt to explain to a physician of another country where his language was not spoken that his crisis was not an anatomical problem, but consumption of an extremely hydrophyllic or water-loving fiber, without consuming sufficient water along with it. All ended well in this situation, but don't make the mistake of supplementing with fiber without also consuming sufficient water at the same time. Spread fiber intake through the day rather than consuming large quantities at one time.

Any kind of movement or exercise encourages transit of food though the digestive tract, while an overly sedentary lifestyle contributes to constipation. The movement of muscles and the force of gravity during exercise delicately massage the digestive tract, encouraging normal elimination.

Irregular bowel function exposes an individual to several risks. A slow transit of food through the body permits bacteria in the digestive tract to break down the bile acids. Some of these breakdown products, including apcholic acid and 3-methyl-cholanthrene, are among the most powerful natural carcinogens, increasing the risk of bowel cancer.[5] Americans have 13 times more colon cancer than inhabitants of Uganda, who eat a high-roughage diet.[6]

SUGGESTIONS

- Add fiber to the diet.

- Consider the possibility of low stomach acid.

- Drink adequate water.

- Use an acidophilus product periodically.

- Use a multiple vitamin and mineral product to obtain nutrients necessary for providing energy to the muscles lining the digestive tract.

Diverticulosis

SIGN

Diverticulosis is a condition in which small areas of the colon balloon out in pockets. These can become inflamed or infected, a condition called diverticulitis. Diverticulosis may be indicated by abdominal pain and sometimes tenderness in the lower left quadrant of the abdomen, although it can have no symptoms at all.

SIGNIFICANCE

Diverticulosis frequently progresses to diverticulitis, which can be life-threatening if the pockets in the colon rupture or become infected with bacteria.

DISCUSSION

Half the population over 60 years of age in the United States has diverticulosis and almost all of those over 80 are afflicted with this condition. Dr. Neil Painter found that the majority of his patients with diverticulosis who used a high-fiber diet regularly avoided complications associated with this condition. Dr. Painter gave his patients unprocessed wheat bran, finding that relief of symptoms took place in 62 of 70 patients.[7] Wheat bran is often effective for treating diverticulosis, although some individuals may experience allergic responses. Other sources of fiber should work as effectively as bran as long as a sufficient quantity is consumed. Avoid small seeds, which can lodge in the pockets and promote bacterial growth.

SUGGESTIONS

- Eat an unrefined diet or maintain a regular intake of fiber for prevention of this horrible condition.

Hemorrhoids

SIGN

The rectal and anal veins swell, become painful, and sometimes bleed

SIGNIFICANCE

Hemorrhoids can cause tremendous discomfort.

DISCUSSION

Some historians feel Napoleon lost the battle of Waterloo due to a painful hemorrhoid attack that clouded his thinking and delayed the battle, giving

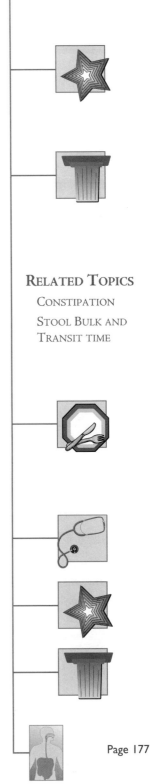

RELATED TOPICS

CONSTIPATION

STOOL BULK AND TRANSIT TIME

Wellington the opportunity to reform his ranks. Nearly half the population of the United States suffers from hemorrhoids, or "piles." Women often develop hemorrhoids during childbirth, although this condition most frequently results from straining at the stool as a result of constipation. Use of special preparations and suppositories does not address the underlying problem of constipation.

Straining at the stool increases pressure in the rectal and anal veins by 2 1/2 to 3 1/2 times. This weakens the blood vessel walls, resulting in or aggravating already existing hemorrhoids. Fiber supplementation relieves pressure on the veins by eliminating constipation. Regular consumption of fiber prevents not only development of hemorrhoids but also aggravation of an existing problem.[8]

SUGGESTIONS

- Avoid constipation.
- Increase dietary fiber.
- Supplement with vitamin C and magnesium.

Kidney Stones

SIGN

Small rocks or stones form in the kidney

SIGNIFICANCE

Kidney stones produce excruciating pain which has been compared with the pain of childbirth.

DISCUSSION

Kidney stones are more likely to form if deficiencies of vitamin B6 or magnesium exist.[9] Stones have repeatedly been produced in magnesium-deficient animals. Sugar is also a culprit in stone formation—possibly because it tends to deplete the body's reserves of magnesium and the B complex vitamins.

Even professionals jump to the conclusion that calcium should be avoided when someone suffers with kidney stones, although some research suggests that decreasing calcium intake may actually increase the risk of forming some types of stones.[10] The most common type of kidney stones are high oxalate. Oxalates increase the risk of kidney stones and are found in spinach, rhubarb, parsley,

RELATED TOPICS

CONSTIPATION

VARICOSE VEINS

STOOL BULK AND TRANSIT TIME

Avoiding calcium increases oxylate absorption and may increase the chances of developing this kind of stone.

instant coffee, tea, beans, chocolate, beets, and chard.[11] Avoiding calcium increases oxylate absorption and may increase the chances of developing this kind of stone.

Tiny, slow-growing infectious particles named nanobacteria were first isolated from kidney stones in 1998. Little is known about these organisms first observed in 1985 by Olavi Kajander. They are much smaller than bacteria and quite different in character. Nanobacteria are responsible for accumulation of mineral deposits, including calcium apatite, a major component of kidney stones.[12] Little is known about the conditions that would promote the growth of nanobacteria in the urinary tract. The pH of the urine might prove to be an important factor in nanobacterial growth and subsequent development of kidney stones.

Nanobacteria have been implicated in a number of conditions, including heart disease, where calcification is involved. The calcium deposits result from shells that nanobacteria build around themselves for protection from attack by the immune system. The antibiotic of choice to treat a nanobacterial infection has been tetracycline. This antibiotic has a unique characteristic—it binds well with calcium—so much so that it causes yellowing of teeth in children. Tetracycline may strip the calcium coating from nanobacteria as well as killing the organisms. Nanobacterial infection is being treated experimentally at the present time with nutrients, EDTA, and antibiotics of the tetracycline family.

Smashing kidney stones with ultrasound may help temporarily, but those who hold to the nanobacterial hypothesis suggest this may release billions of nanobacterial particles into the body, triggering regrowth of calcified deposits.

Removal of calcium deposits from nanobacteria, called "unroofing," appears to transform them from a semi-dormant form to a suddenly active state. They cluster together and produce protective films called biofilms. EDTA, commonly used to treat heart disease, "unroofs" nanobacteria. This may be undesirable unless other steps are taken to prevent the consequences of activation of the organism. One writer observed that "unroofed nanobacteria plant themselves as 'seeds' from which new growths develop."[13]

The questions that remain to be answered with regard to nanobacteria are many. What is the source of infection? What conditions favor the growth of the organisms? What role can diet and nutritional supplements play in enabling the immune system to eradicate this infection? The role of certain nutrients in benefiting diseases characterized by calcium accumulation indicates they

Tiny, slow-growing infectious particles named nanobacteria were first isolated from kidney stones in 1998.

RELATED TOPICS

JOINT AND MUSCLE PAIN

RHEUMATOID ARTHRITIS

TARTAR ON THE TEETH

The very existence of nanobacteria is still a subject of heated scientific debate. The discussion allows us to observe some rather remarkable similarities between such diverse health conditions as tartar formation, kidney stones, fibromyalgia, and arthritis. These disorders evidence similarities centering around deranged calcium and phosphorus metabolism. Nutrients of significance for these abnormalities include magnesium, vitamins B6, C and D, and essential fatty acids.

probably do play a role in combating nanobacterial infection. Included among these nutrients are amino acids, essential fatty acids, B complex vitamins, and antioxidants. Many of these nutrients are discussed under RELATED TOPICS. Nanobacterial research will prove interesting in the coming years.

SUGGESTIONS

- Avoid sugar.

- Be cautious of avoiding calcium.

- Consider the possibility of overgrowth of nanobacteria.

- Do not consume high-oxylate foods.

- Supplement with B complex (especially vitamin B6) and magnesium.

Pink Urine

SIGN

The urine turns pink after eating beets

SIGNIFICANCE

This sign may indicate an iron deficiency or lack of hydrochloric acid which makes it difficult to absorb iron. If beets have not been consumed, pink urine may indicate blood.

DISCUSSION

Pink urine after eating beets is considered by some to suggest a possible iron deficiency. Iron deficiency is also indicated by a craving for ice (phagophagia), cracks at the corner of the mouth and nose, paleness under the eyelid, spoon-shaped fingernails, and a pale or painful red tongue. Iron is difficult to absorb and deficiency is common, especially in menstruating women. The pink urine will usually clear within a week of iron supplementation.[14]

If the red color of the urine goes away when baking soda is added to the urine and returns when vinegar is added, the red color is from beets. If the red does not go away, the color could be blood which should be checked by a physician since it could be a tumor or bleeding.[15]

RELATED TOPIC

FLATTENED OR
SPOON-SHAPED
NAILS

SUGGESTIONS

■ Consider possible deficiency of stomach acid, which inhibits iron absorption.

■ Test for iron deficiency.

Stool Bulk and Transit Time

SIGN

The stool is small and moves through the digestive tract very slowly

SIGNIFICANCE

A small stool and infrequent elimination indicate inadequate fiber intake. A number of common health problems are associated with small stool and slow transit time, including hiatus hernia, diverticulosis, constipation, appendicitis, varicose veins, and obesity.

DISCUSSION

The stool of individuals on a high-fiber diet is significantly larger (500 grams) than the stool of an individual on a low-fiber diet (100 grams). In other words, the stool on a high-fiber diet can easily be as much as five times the weight of the stool on a low-residue diet. Small, stiff pebble-like stools indicate a low fiber intake. Bulky, soft stools reflect a more adequate consumption of fiber.

Transit time refers to the lapse of time between the consumption of a food and the time it is eliminated in the stool. This can be roughly measured by consuming corn on the cob and noting how long it takes the corn kernels to pass through the body. Some have used beets to measure transit time, but the red color tends to bleed through and gives an inaccurate measurement.[16] Cochineal and charcoal powder tablets have also been used to measure transit time.

Fibers are divided into soluble and insoluble to indicate whether they tend to absorb water or not. Insoluble fibers are generally preferred for the purpose of bulking up the stool. Soluble fibers are more effective in establishing a stable blood sugar. Pectin, another form of fiber, is a valuable detoxifier of the digestive tract. My suggestion to clients is to consume the wide varieties of fiber found in nature to obtain all the benefits that the different types of fiber offer.

RELATED TOPIC

CONSTIPATION

Cochineal is a red dye made from a Mexican red scale insect that feeds on cacti.

SUGGESTIONS

- Add acidophilus to the diet, particularly if antibiotics have been used.
- Correct low stomach acid if this is an issue.
- Eat high-fiber foods or supplement with a variety of fibers.
- Obtain all essential nutrients.

Yellow Urine

SIGN

The urine becomes a vivid yellow or yellow-green color.

SIGNIFICANCE

A yellow or green color to the urine usually indicates nothing more than the presence of vitamin B2 or riboflavin. This is a good sign.

DISCUSSION

Most people who sell nutritional products can tell a story about the customer who purchases a package of vitamins and calls in alarm the next day. The cause of distress is a dramatic fluorescent yellow color in the urine. The customer will accusingly say, "I never had this problem until I took your vitamins."

This yellow color of urine is caused by vitamin B2 or riboflavin. Urine that is unfailingly white is probably issuing a warning that the diet is deficient in the B complex vitamins. Dr. Abram Hoffer, a physician who struggled with delivery of adequate quantities of nutrients to his patients, wrote, "This (yellow color of the urine) is a good test whether or not the vitamins are being absorbed in the gastrointestinal tract."[17] In other words, if you take a supplement that contains riboflavin and the urine does not turn yellow the product may not be digesting. More than one nurse has told me about "bedpan clink." They are referring to supplements that pass through the body and show up in the bedpan without ever being broken down. One company that specializes in developing supplements that are easily digested shared that a competitive product sat in an agitated container of hydrochloric acid for a week without ever dissolving.

The yellowness of the urine will fluctuate with the amount of water consumed and with the quantities of vitamin B2 in the diet. A yellow color of the urine after taking a vitamin supplement is no cause for alarm. Failure of the

Yellow color of the urine is usually caused by the fluorescent yellow color of riboflavin or vitamin B2.

A yellow color of the urine is a good test, indicating whether B complex vitamins are being absorbed in the digestive tract.

urine to turn yellow after taking a B complex supplement would be more of a concern.[18] Maintenance of a consistent yellow color to the urine with a good source of the B complex vitamins rather than isolated riboflavin increases the likelihood that the entire family of these nutrients will be adequately supplied. Excessively dark and yellow urine may indicate not only the presence of vitamin B2, but also chronic dehydration.

Riboflavin or vitamin B2 has been shown to help prevent migraine. In one study this vitamin helped 59% of sufferers while a placebo helped only 15%. The dosage given was 400 mg of riboflavin a day. Some of the patients experienced a little diarrhea and frequent urination with the high dose of the vitamin. The benefit of riboflavin for migraine compares favorably with medications designed to prevent the problem, and the side effects are far less serious.

Riboflavin may prevent migraine by increasing energy production in the brain. This vitamin does not dissolve easily in fat, the primary building block of brain tissue. Researchers suspect the high doses of riboflavin facilitate the delivery of the vitamin to the mitochondria or energy factories in the brain. This is not a normal nutritional use of vitamin B2, but rather a megavitamin approach. Do not neglect to read the caution regarding use of such large quantities of vitamin B2 at the end of this discussion.[19]

Further evidence of the importance of riboflavin for the brain is the use of the vitamin to treat Parkinson's disease in Brazil. Researchers found that 31 Parkinson's patients they tested were deficient in riboflavin. Supplementation of 19 of these for six months with 30 milligrams of vitamin B2 three times a day improved functional motor capacity from 44% of normal to 71% of normal. Patients were also instructed to discontinue eating red meat, which releases hemin, a potential neurotoxin, during the process of digestion.[20]

Many years ago one of our family friends suffered with emphysema and Parkinson's disease. He suffered a heart attack and while in the hospital his physician instructed him to supplement with three brewers yeast–based B complex tablets per meal. This provided 45 mg of vitamin B2 per meal. Over a period of five years his emphysema and Parkinson's symptoms almost completely disappeared. He never had another heart attack. The only time he ever suffered a relapse of the Parkinson's is after traveling to Mexico to undergo an anti-cancer nutritional program even though he did not have cancer. The clinic took him off his vitamins and his Parkinson's returned within a couple of weeks. He once told me he would never take a treatment for a disease he did not have again! It took this man a year to reestablish the health he had experi-

Maintenance of a consistent yellow color to the urine with a good source of the B complex vitamins rather than isolated riboflavin increases the likelihood that the entire family of these nutrients will be adequately supplied.

Supplementation of Parkinson's patients with 30 milligrams of vitamin B2 three times a day for six months improved functional motor capacity from 44% of normal to 71% of normal.

enced prior to discontinuing the supplements. The riboflavin in this man's supplement program, along with other nutrients, may have been responsible for his remarkable Parkinson's improvement.

Supplement with megadose quantities of riboflavin only under the supervision of a nutritionally knowledgeable medical professional. High doses of vitamin B2 do have potential toxic effects. Riboflavin reacts readily with light. The toxic byproducts of this reaction can damage cells in the eyes, skin, liver, connective tissues, and mitochondria. Megadose intake of vitamin B2 is not a desirable nutritional objective unless the need is indicated by laboratory testing and supervised by a physician, since more of the vitamin is available to interact with light. Unfortunately, some supplements have literally hundreds of milligrams of vitamin B2. A toxicologist once shared with me, "The mantra of the toxicologist is that the dose makes the poison."[21]

Other nutrients in addition to riboflavin are involved in energy production in the brain. The mitochondria where energy is produced require vitamins B3, B6, and magnesium. Vitamin C reduces risk of migraine in some people and plays a role in energy production.[22] Omega-3 oils are an important building block of healthy brain tissue.

SUGGESTION

- Supplement with a source of the B complex vitamins on a regular basis.

Food for Thought

Do you know your transit time? How would you change your diet to modify the time food takes to move through your body? What foods do you think would speed or slow transit time?

In what ways do you feel poor elimination could cause a loss of quality of life? David Reuben in *The Save Your Life Diet* associates lack of fiber with the following diseases: heart attacks, cancer of the colon and rectum, diverticulosis, appendicitis, constipation, varicose veins, hemorrhoids, phlebitis, and obesity. Have you experienced any of these conditions?

Have you ever observed the yellow urine phenomena? How does the color of the urine vary when you drink an abundance of fluids or become dehydrated?

Appetite and Digestion: *Our Energy Supply*

Hist017 tells us Louis XIV of France was a memorable glutton. He consumed two meals a day at 2:00 P.M. and 10:00 P.M. His appetizer was 100 oysters and four large plates of soup. A typical meal was a French specialty called Pot-a-oie which consisted of a large goose stuffed with pheasants, quail, woodcock, pigeons, ortolans, turtle doves, and aromatic spices. Most men consumed only the inside, but Louis ate the goose as well. Having warmed up to the meal, Louis would then consume a partridge, a pheasant, plates of vegetables, salads, two or three thick slices of ham and several servings of mutton. Dessert consisted of eggs and various cakes.

It is no surprise that Louis developed severe digestive problems and lost his teeth. An autopsy was performed after his death that revealed a stomach three times the size of that of a normal man—with a huge tapeworm seated regally in the middle.[1]

Kings have the opportunity to practice unrestrained eating and they often suffer the consequences. It would have been possible to illustrate unrestrained eating by citing many kings throughout history, but this story has one little twist—there was a readily visible cause for this huge appetite. Many people experience uncontrollable appetite today and in this chapter we shall discuss some of the reasons why this may take place.

At the other end of the spectrum is the loss or aberration of appetite. Here too we must look beyond mere psychology to explain why some lose the desire for food, or develop cravings for very strange foods. The digestive tract is the doorway to good nutrition. No one can long remain healthy if there is no desire for food or cravings for foods that do not nourish adequately. We call these changes in appetite food addictions, anorexia, and pica.

Kings have the opportunity to practice unrestrained eating and they often suffer the consequences.

Food is so abundant in the United States that the average citizen has the opportunity to practice the unrestrained eating which once was the luxury of the very wealthy and powerful.

The process of nutrition begins with the desire for and selection of a food which is then chewed. Chewed food passes to the stomach and small intestine where hydrochloric acid and pancreatic enzymes are released to break down or digest the meal. The body is now ready to absorb the nutrients through the lining of the intestines. Food particles then circulate through the bloodstream to the cell wall where a process called assimilation takes place—the movement of nutrients into the cell. The final step in this nutritive process is elimination of waste products. Failure anywhere along this continuum sets the stage for a gradual deterioration of health. This chapter focuses on abnormalities in desire for food and impediments to the proper utilization of the nutrients in the foods we eat.

Anorexia

SIGN

Loss of the desire for food

SIGNIFICANCE

Anorexia is life-threatening—life cannot continue without eating.

DISCUSSION

One of my clients suffered with anorexia. She feared eating more than two cookies a day would cause her to gain weight even though she looked like a toothpick. I spent considerable effort persuading this woman that two cookies would not provide her the nutrition her body needed. She agreed to add a couple of calories to her diet in the way of a nutritional supplement. I persuaded her to begin using a "chain of life" package of nutrients with a generous quantity of B complex vitamins and zinc. Changes in her attitude were obvious within a few months—she became less obsessive about dieting, and completely recovered over a period of about a year. Anorexia is no laughing matter. One out of five anorexics die and only 30 to 40% ever fully recover. The problem is increasing among young women.

The word anorexia means "without a longing to eat," which aptly describes this often life-threatening disorder. Dr. Alexander Schauss is a specialist on the subject of eating disorders. He retold a remarkable story that appeared in *The Lancet* in 1984. Tina, a 13-year-old, had no menstrual cycle, was miserable, withdrawn, and tearful. She weighed only 69.5 pounds and was diagnosed anorexic. Tina was placed on zinc supplementation. Within two weeks there

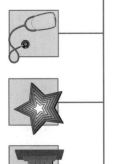

One out of five anorexics die and only 30 to 40% ever fully recover.

Chapter 12 – Appetite and Digestion

was an obvious improvement. She was able to smile. A year later she weighed 97 pounds.[2]

Dr. Schauss suggested that zinc deficiency is a common cause of anorexia.[3] Zinc is essential for proper function of the tastebuds. Imagine how you would enjoy eating if everything tasted like sawdust.

The anorexic is a prime candidate for widespread nutritional problems. Inadequate protein intake alters the thinking process. Lack of B complex vitamins decreases not only energy, but the desire for food. Early indications of thiamine or vitamin B1 deficiency include loss of appetite, abdominal discomfort, and constipation.[4]

Several times over the years mothers have complained to me that their children simply have no appetite. Some of these children respond nicely to vitamin B complex. Those who consume large quantities of sugar, including most of these children who lose their appetite, are at considerable risk for developing deficiency of vitamin B1. It is probable that anyone who has lost his appetite has developed or is in the process of developing a number of serious nutritional deficiencies.

SUGGESTIONS

- Avoid sugar and junk fats.

- Supplement with essential fatty acids, zinc, and B complex vitamins.

- Supplement with other essential nutrients, including amino acids.

Binging

SIGN

The inability to stop eating, resulting in consuming far more calories than are necessary.

SIGNIFICANCE

Binging contributes to obesity, which is associated with a multitude of health problems. Binging also leads to digestive disorders and intolerance to foods.

Early indications of thiamine or vitamin B1 deficiency include loss of appetite, abdominal discomfort, and constipation.

DISCUSSION

I once dated a young woman who was bulimic. She felt compelled to purge herself after eating. It was obvious to me that this woman's diet contained far too much sugar and junk fats. It is a tragedy that millions of young people have developed habits of binging, with many following their binges with purging.

Consumption of sugar, salt, or hydrogenated fats increases appetite and may contribute to binging.

Every form of overeating from the mild to the extreme has become part of the American landscape. Bulimia (literally "ox hunger") is an extreme form of binging, characterized by eating large quantities of food followed by purging. This condition has become epidemic among young people, affecting as many as one out of four college-age women. Dr. Alexander Schauss suggested that zinc deficiency may cause bulimia.[3] Other nutritional problems undoubtedly contribute to binging.

A number of years ago the theory that sugar decreased appetite encouraged advertisers to promote sugar as a low-calorie food and an aid to weight loss. In hindsight, the whole episode seems to have been foolish.

Small amounts of sugar actually did reduce appetite. Larger amounts, however, caused the rabbits to eat twice as much as normal.

Researcher Dr. Paula Geiselman of UCLA took on the challenge of disproving this theory and demonstrating that in actuality sugar increases appetite. She fed rabbits different quantities of sugar. Small amounts of sugar actually did reduce appetite. Larger amounts, however, caused the rabbits to eat twice as much as normal. They ate faster and they ate longer when large amounts of sugar were added to the diet. Unfortunately, humans rarely eat small quantities of sugar.

Consumption of a food decreases as it becomes more nutritious. Food processors have every motivation to decrease the nutritional value of their products in order to reach their sales targets.

Dr. Geiselman observed the same increases in appetite when animals were fed salt. The giant food processors of the world have known for many years that they are able to increase consumption of their products by adding large quantities of salt and sugar.[5] Biochemist Paul Stitt, an expert on how foods affect appetite, referred to the ability of refined foods to increase appetite as the "Can't Eat Just One Syndrome." This phrase is borrowed from a popular potato chip commercial. Stitt noted that the "Conspiracy of the Sales Curve" dictates that consumption of a food decreases as it becomes more nutritious. As a result, food processors have every motivation to decrease the nutritional value of their products in order to reach their sales targets.[6] Stitt purchased a bakery and improved the nutritional quality of the bread. He almost went bankrupt due to the decline in sales of his bread until he increased his marketing area. The better the quality of the bread, the less of it needed to be consumed to satisfy appetite.

Most of us become addicted to sugar at an early age because it activates the opiate receptors in the brain. In the mid-1980s Dr. Elliott Blass demonstrated that an 11.5% sugar solution had the ability to block pain perception in mice when their front foot was placed on a hot plate. The time necessary to perceive the pain increased from 10 seconds to 20 seconds.

Dr. Blass then demonstrated that this pain-blocking effect was related to the beta-endorphin receptor. He gave the animals Naltrexone, a drug that blocks the pain-killing effect of opioid drugs by occupying the opiate (beta-endorphin) receptor site. The mice reacted to the hot plate in eight seconds. This study demonstrated that sugar has addictive properties similar to opiate drugs like heroin. Once consumption of sugar begins, it becomes very difficult to stop because sugar consumption makes us feel good.[7] Sugar is commonly added to processed foods because it makes the consumption of those foods pleasurable, as well as increasing overall intake of the food.

Sugar and salt are not the only substances capable of triggering binging or causing us to eat excessively. Partially hydrogenated oils have a similar effect. Dr. Johanna Budwig, a physician experienced in the use of nutrition to treat degenerative diseases, made the observation that: "Testing on animals and humans has shown that when these preserved fats, poor in electrons, are ingested, animals and humans eat six times their normal amount of food."[8] Those ignoring the quality of the fats they consume are virtually foreordained to overeat. Quality fats decrease appetite, but junk fats make us eat more.

One of the keys to breaking virtually any kind of addiction is taking steps to assure that the brain has availability of all the amino acids it needs. Amino acids are the raw materials the brain uses to synthesize powerful chemicals that enable us to experience pleasure, satisfaction, and relaxation. It is almost impossible for a protein-starved brain to break an addiction to carbohydrates and sweets. Julia Ross, a pioneer in the use of amino acids to treat a variety of addictions, wrote "My clients consistently report that within twenty-four hours after taking amino acids, their moods lift and their food cravings disappear. Like them, you will no longer need to diet because you will have stopped eating—naturally. These benefits soon become permanent."[9] The protein-starved individual is far more likely to become a sugar or drug addict than someone consuming adequate protein.

Amino acids may help break addictions to salt, sugar, and partially hydrogenated oils, but these food additives should also be avoided. Read labels

Sugar has addictive properties similar to opiate drugs like heroin.

Amino acids are the raw materials the brain uses to synthesize powerful chemicals that enable us to experience pleasure, satisfaction, and relaxation.

It is almost impossible for a protein-starved brain to break an addiction to carbohydrates and sweets.

"A food addiction differs only in degree of severity from a drug addiction. In all other respects, the two phenomena are remarkably similar."
Dr. Theron Randolph

Binging may also be triggered by nutrient starvation, which leads to "hidden" hungers.

carefully. You will find that most processed foods and those which are most difficult to stop eating are high in one or more of these substances.

Binging may take place even when eating only healthy foods, although this is much less common. In this situation, suspect that an allergic response or sensitivity to a food may be involved. Test yourself to see if eating a particular food seems to trigger the appetite.

Allergists know that food addiction may lead to binging. Dr. Theron Randolph has been referred to as the most exceptional and outstanding physician in the entire field of allergy. He wrote, "A food addiction differs only in degree of severity from a drug addiction. In all other respects, the two phenomena are remarkably similar."[10] Dr. Marshall Mandell, another physician who has conducted pioneering work in the allergy field, believed that daily compulsive food cravings and unrestrained eating habits of the obese are based on "a physiologic need to stop the withdrawal symptoms caused by food addiction."[11]

Binging may also be triggered by nutrient starvation which leads to "hidden" hungers. The body has a tendency to desire to eat until nutritional needs have been met, even if this requires excess consumption of calories. Supplement the diet with all essential nutrients, what Dr. Roger Williams called "the chain of life," to decrease this kind of food craving.

Poor digestion of foods results in "hidden hungers" as well. One of my relatives was hungry continually until she began to supplement with a stomach acid support. Her constant hunger then disappeared. She lost weight and her dress size reduced considerably. Ingestion of food should not be equated with digestion. Unless food is adequately digested, absorbed, circulated, and assimilated the cells will starve. You may find yourself overfed, but undernourished. Allergic responses to foods may interfere with the normal process of utilization of nutrients from our foods.

SUGGESTIONS

- Avoid sugar, salt, and partially hydrogenated oils.

- Do not overconsume processed foods or foods you strongly crave.

- Eliminate from the diet foods to which you are allergic.

- Supplement with amino acids or consume quality protein in the diet.

Bloating, Burping, and Bad Breath

SIGN

A common cluster of symptoms consists of bad breath, bloating, belching, and burping. Sometimes intolerance to fruit acids will exist. Pruritis ani or itching around the rectum may also be associated with bad breath.

SIGNIFICANCE

All these signs are often associated with low stomach acid.[12]

DISCUSSION

Stomach acid kills harmful bacteria and assures complete and proper breakdown of foods. Lack of stomach acid allows bacteria to proliferate in the stomach. Food ferments rather than digests, which may result in bad breath, bloating, or burping.

Many years ago I made the observation in a seminar that iced beverages with meals tend to inhibit hydrochloric acid production. A physician in the group presented me with a copy of a volume he had written on emergency care, which recommended cold temperatures for control of stomach acid in serious ulcer situations.[13]

After years of careful observation I have been surprised how often those who routinely use antacids have a strong and lifetime habit of consuming iced beverages with meals. These iced beverages often interfere with digestion, creating the need for antacids. Most people assume that the use of antacids is a reasonable solution to a problem of indigestion. In actuality, many digestive difficulties disappear when iced beverages are consumed apart from meals.

Several people have told me over the years they "picked up" an intestinal infection in Mexico by adding ice cubes made from unpurified water to their purified drinking water or soda pop. Apparently the microbes survive the freezing and more easily create an infection after the cold temperature of the beverage inhibits stomach acid secretion.

I met with one young man who had suffered with serious digestive problems from the time he was 12 years of age. He had a lifetime habit of drinking large quantities of iced beverages with meals. Thinking his digestive problems were tied to excess stomach acid he began taking antacids, which only made his

Stomach acid kills harmful bacteria and assures complete and proper breakdown of foods.

Lack of stomach acid allows bacteria to proliferate in the stomach.

Production of hydrochloric acid (HCL) is dependent upon many nutrients. A lack of any of these nutrients decreases the ability to produce stomach acid.

Stomach acid assures proper digestion of food, improving nutritional status and also prevents bacteria and other pathogens from entering the body via the digestive tract.

digestive problems worse. His digestive complaints cleared up when he discontinued the iced beverages and antacids.

Avoiding iced beverages with meals is only one way of encouraging normal stomach function. Warm soups, with protein content, consumed prior to meals facilitate production of stomach acid. Digestive bitters, available in grocery stores, may also be helpful and are a time-tested treatment for indigestion.

Production of hydrochloric acid (HCL) is dependent upon many nutrients. A lack of any of these nutrients decreases the ability to produce stomach acid. Appropriate supplementation will often resolve the issue of low stomach acid. (See the footnote for a list of 12 nutrients required for adequate HCL production).[14]

Dr. Hugh Tuckey, a physician and lifelong researcher on the subject of hydrochloric acid, observed an association between bad breath and low stomach acid. He wrote, "In some of the halitosis cases, people who have a bad breath will find it will disappear very quickly when the HCL is normalized in the stomach. This is because normal emptying time of the stomach is improved so that there is no putrefaction taking place in the stomach."

He then cited an example, "One of my professors, who is now dead, God rest his soul, was a vegetarian. (Of course, I knew nothing about HCL therapy at the time.) He had been a vegetarian for possibly 30 or 40 years. When he spoke to you, you had to turn your back to him. His breath was the most fetid, bloomin' thing, it could knock you down at 30 paces. He died of cancer."[15]

Low stomach acid increases the risk of stomach cancer. Bacteria proliferate in the stomach and convert nitrates to nitrosamines—potent carcinogens—when stomach acid is low. Adequate HCL prevents the formation of nitrosamines in the stomach by killing the bacteria which might otherwise produce them.[16]

Tests are available for HCL production. One of these is the Heidelberg capsule. This involves swallowing a miniature transmitter which provides information on the pH of the digestive tract.[17] Low stomach acid can also be indicated by stool analysis.

Stomach acid typically declines as we age. Dr. Jonathan Wright suggested that the widespread use of antacids by the elderly in the United States is often harmful. A great many of these people desperately need stomach acid support. If excess stomach acid were really the problem it is made out to be, we would be treating the younger population with antacids rather than the geriatric population—young people produce more stomach acid than senior citizens.

Stomach acid assures proper digestion of food, improving nutritional status and also prevents bacteria and other pathogens from entering the body via the digestive tract.[18] Antacids trigger the emptying of the stomach but do not improve nutrient utilization. Neutralizing stomach acid promotes the invasion of the digestive tract by harmful microbes which would normally be destroyed by the stomach's hydrochloric acid.

SUGGESTIONS

- Avoid iced beverages or excessive beverage consumption with meals.

- Consume a warm soup with added protein at the beginning of a meal.

- Do not consume rancid or excess fat.

- Supplement with stomach acid if it is low.

Chinese Restaurant Syndrome

SIGN

Becoming ill after eating foods that contain monosodium glutamate

SIGNIFICANCE

Sensitivity to MSG may indicate marginal or inadequate intake of vitamin B6 and magnesium.

DISCUSSION

Chinese restaurant syndrome is characterized by symptoms such as "warmth, stiffness, weakness in the limbs, tingling, pressure, headache, lightheadedness, heartburn or gastric discomfort." Dr. Karl Folkers, a leading nutritional biochemist, suggested that this response takes place because glutamate intensifies a borderline deficiency of vitamin B6. In a study conducted by Folkers, a good many individuals no longer reacted to MSG when given daily supplements of vitamin B6 for twelve weeks prior to consuming MSG.

Bacteria proliferate in the stomach and convert nitrates to nitrosamines— potent carcinogens —when stomach acid is low.

The widespread use of antacids by the elderly in the United States is often harmful.

Glutamate intensifies a border-line deficiency of vitamin B6.

Many individuals no longer reacted to MSG when given daily supplements of vitamin B6 for twelve weeks prior to consuming MSG.

RELATED TOPIC
QEW TEST

Ingestion of refined and concentrated glutamate in the form of MSG has the potential to overwhelm the protective mechanisms of the brain cells.

Becoming ill after consuming monosodium glutamate may reflect marginal B complex intake.[19]

MSG makes food taste better than it actually is, which is why it is a popular additive to many processed foods. Glutamate is an important neurotransmitter commonly found in foods. It is slowly released from foods because it is linked to protein. High amounts of glutamate in a rapidly-absorbed form such as MSG will overexcite nerve cells, even to the point of death in extreme cases. John Olney, a research scientist, named this process "excitotoxicity."

Ingestion of refined and concentrated glutamate in the form of MSG has the potential to overwhelm the protective mechanisms of the brain cells. Nutrients such as vitamins B6, E, and magnesium protect brain cells from these "excitotoxins."[20]

MSG is a common additive to the food supply, but often hidden in foods creating challenges for those who react to it or wish to avoid it. Those who wish to avoid MSG should read a book by Dr. George R. Schwartz entitled *In Bad Taste: The MSG Syndrome*. Schwartz noted that MSG is added to a wide range of processed foods.[21] Most people tolerate small amounts of MSG in the diet as long as intake of protective nutrients, including vitamin B6, is adequate.

SUGGESTIONS

■ Do not allow blood sugar to become unstable by excess sugar consumption.

■ Minimize exposure to MSG.

■ Supplement with a source of vitamins B complex, E, and magnesium.

Craving for Salt

SIGN

The tendency to add excess salt to food or to crave very salty foods

SIGNIFICANCE

Salt craving may indicate zinc deficiency or weak adrenal glands.

DISCUSSION

Zinc depletion may result in cravings for salt. When zinc is low, food loses its taste and there is a tendency to add excess salt in order to improve the flavor and taste. Dr. Carl Pfeiffer observed that *the mother who is zinc deficient will add excess salt to the food served the entire family.*[22, 23] I think of this often when I taste food at a restaurant that has so much salt that the taste is repulsive to my tastebuds.

Zinc plays a very special role in the perception of taste and smell. The unusual cravings associated with pregnancy may be caused or contributed to by zinc deficiency. Changes in taste are common after delivery of an infant. Pregnancy tends to challenge not only zinc reserves, but also vitamin B6 adequacy.[24]

The strange tastes of those who are mentally ill are often as unusual as those of a pregnant woman. Dr. Carl Pfeiffer, speaking of the mentally ill, noted that vitamin B6 should always accompany zinc supplementation. "Otherwise, zinc alone can increase hallucinatory experiences and/or depression. Patients with loss of taste are usually severely depressed, and for a good reason: the food they eat tastes like so much sawdust."[25]

Zinc is not abundant in the food supply as it is frequently low in the soil. Those with zinc deficiency should supplement with this mineral rather than try to obtain an adequate intake from foods alone. Zinc is rapidly depleted when we are under emotional or physical stress.

Those with weak adrenals often have low blood pressure and may also develop cravings for salt because they feel better when they consume it. One of the functions of the adrenal gland is to retain adequate salt for the body's day-to-day functioning. Consuming salt reduces the work the adrenal must perform to accomplish this goal. Those with weak adrenals should not be put on a low-salt diet. Dr. Jonathan Wright emphasized, "Yes, that's salt, sodium chloride (sea salt is best), an important item in staying healthy for anyone with low blood pressure and weak adrenal glands." Dr. Wright also suggested augmenting salt with a little licorice extract for those with weak adrenals and low blood pressure.[26]

Dr. John Tintera, who spent a lifetime researching weak adrenals, emphasized a diet that would build the strength of the adrenals and treat low blood sugar resulting from the poorly functioning glands. He permitted all meats including fish, all dairy products, eggs, nuts including salted ones (excellent between meals), all vegetables and fruits except for those to be avoided, peanut

When zinc is low, food loses its taste and there is a tendency to add excess salt in order to improve the flavor and taste.

Vitamin B complex, expecially B6, should always accompany zinc supplementation of the mentally ill.

Those with weak adrenals often have low blood pressure and may also develop cravings for salt because they feel better when they consume it.

butter, soybean products, and low-carbohydrate breads. To be avoided were all sugars and honey, strong coffee and tea, dates, raisins and other dried fruits, all hot and cold cereals except for occasional oatmeal, all alcoholic beverages, potatoes, corn, spaghetti, rice, breads, cakes, pies, pastries, and candy. Dr. Tintera wrote, "We cannot overemphasize the importance of a proper diet. The diet essentially consists of strict elimination of rapidly-absorbed carbohydrates in order to obviate the sudden rise in blood sugar with its subsequent fall."[27] Dr. Tintera emphasized the importance of a substantial breakfast.

SUGGESTIONS

- Avoid rapidly absorbed carbohydrates.

- Don't avoid salt if blood pressure is low and the adrenals are weak.

- Eat breakfast.

- Supplement with an adrenal glandular.

- Supplement with zinc, vitamins C and B complex, omega-3 oils, phospholipids and phytosterols.

Gallstones

SIGN

Formation of stones in the gallbladder

SIGNIFICANCE

Gallstones are the most costly and common digestive disease in the United States. About one million cases are diagnosed annually and billions are spent for treatment. Gallstones may result from allergic response to foods or deficiencies of fiber and hydrochloric acid.

DISCUSSION

Gallstones are often caused by poor tolerance to foods. A remarkable study by Dr. James C. Breneman found that 93% of those with stones in his study were intolerant to egg, 64% to pork, and 52% to onion.[28] Consuming these foods increased the likelihood of developing stones, while avoiding them reduced the chances of losing one's gallbladder. Food allergies in this situation apparently prevented normal emptying of the gallbladder, resulting in the development of stones.

Low stomach acid secretion may also contribute to development of gallstones. Several studies indicate that approximately half of those with gallstones have low stomach acid secretion, which can delay or hinder emptying of the gall bladder allowing stones to form.[29]

Vitamin C may be an important preventative for gallstones. Guinea pigs, like humans, do not produce their own vitamin C and develop gallstones when they are not provided an adequate quantity of this vitamin. Sixteen patients with gallstones were given 500 mg of vitamin C four times a day. The concentrations of phospholipids in the bile increased significantly. It took cholesterol crystals 7 days to form in the bile of those supplemented with vitamin C and only 2 days for crystals to form in the bile of the control group not supplemented with vitamin C.[30]

Common steps that can be taken to prevent gallstones include regular exercise, consumption of fiber-containing foods or supplementing with fiber, and avoiding excess coffee. These measures tend to normalize emptying of the gallbladder.

If the gallbladder is removed, and this happens to tens of thousands of people each year, intolerance to fats may develop. This may usually be overcome by supplementing with pancreatic enzymes or bile acids.

SUGGESTIONS

- Avoid foods to which you are allergic.

- Address any deficiency of stomach acid.

- Avoid excess coffee.

- Exercise regularly and eat a high-fiber diet.

- Supplement with vitamin C and lipotropics.

Pica

SIGN

A craving for or eating of things that would not normally be considered food

It took cholesterol crystals 7 days to form in the bile of those supplemented with vitamin C and only 2 days for crystals to form in the bile of the control group not supplemented with vitamin C.

Lipotropics are nutrients that help the body handle fats properly.

SIGNIFICANCE

Pica may indicate nutrient deficiencies, especially of certain trace minerals.

DISCUSSION

Pica is the Latin word for magpie, a bird that picks up non-food objects in its beak. This is a disorder in which there is a craving for specific foods or for substances that would not normally be eaten. Both I and one of my siblings suffered with pica as youngsters. My parents had difficulty keeping dirt out of my mouth, while my sibling craved chicken feed. Looking back on this strange eating behavior with an understanding of nutrition, I realize that the food the chickens were fed was probably quite a bit more nutritious than the white bread covered with margarine and sugar we delighted in as children.

Pregnant women are notorious for their cravings for strange foods. One study found 14.4% of the pregnant women examined suffered from some form of pica. These women craved everything from dirt to soap, ashes to chalk, and paint to burnt matches.[31]

Pica has been associated with a deficiency of a number of trace minerals, including iron, zinc, calcium, and magnesium. Iron appears to be the most common deficiency in children.[32]

Zinc is not only frequently low in the diet, but may be involved with the development of pica. Zinc is essential for the ability to taste and smell.

RELATED TOPICS

ANOREXIA

CRAVING FOR SALT

FLATTENED OR SPOON-SHAPED NAILS

PINK URINE

ZINC TASTE TEST

SUGGESTIONS

■ Supplement or obtain in the diet essential trace minerals, including iron, zinc, calcium, and magnesium.

Stomach Acid Self-Test

Low

SIGN

Consuming a tablespoon of apple cider vinegar or lemon juice makes heartburn go away.

SIGNIFICANCE

Hydrochloric acid is necessary for the breakdown and digestion of protein in the diet. It also kills harmful bacteria in foods.

Discussion

If heartburn goes away when consuming apple cider vinegar or lemon juice, stomach acid is probably low. If heartburn becomes worse there is a possibility of excess stomach acid, according to Dr. James Balch.[33] Neither lemon juice nor hydrochloric acid are sufficiently strong acids to replace the hydrochloric acid normally produced by the stomach. Deficiencies should be treated with betaine hydrochloric acid and pepsin.

Hydrochloric acid supplements should be designed to release in the stomach rather than the mouth or small intestine. Early researchers on stomach acid had patients drink hydrochloric acid through a glass straw. Unfortunately, this increased the risk of damage to the teeth. A properly designed stomach acid support will be specially coated so it does not damage the teeth and will also release slowly in the stomach so it does not damage the stomach lining.

Related Topics

Bloating, Burping, and Bad Breath

Brittle Nails

Forehead Furrows or Wrinkles

Osteoporosis

Suggestions

- Confirmatory tests are available for stomach acid secretion.
- Supplement with stomach acid if needed.

Zinc Taste Test

Sign

A simple test for adequate zinc reserves requires holding 1 to 2 teaspoons of a zinc sulfate solution in the mouth for 10 to 30 seconds.

Significance

A strong taste usually indicates adequate zinc status. Lack of taste is associated with zinc deficiency.

Discussion

A breakthrough taste test for zinc deficiency was introduced in the British medical journal *Lancet* in 1984. This is a simple taste test of a liquid zinc solution which is 0.1% zinc sulfate in a base of distilled water. The test involves not eating, drinking, or smoking for an hour before the test. About 1 teaspoon of test solution (10 milliliters) is placed in the mouth and swished around for 10 seconds. The solution can then be swallowed.

After 30 seconds, the subject is asked how the solution tastes. Responses fall into four categories:

1. Tasteless or like water.

2. A gradually developing taste described as dry, mineral-like, bubbly, furry, or even sweet.

3. A definite, but not unpleasant taste, which gets stronger over time.

4. An immediately unpleasant taste, which is strong and sometimes metallic. The taste can linger.

[zinc deficiency]

The first two suggest the benefit of zinc supplementation, according to Alex Schauss, Ph.D. He observed that most anorexics fall into category one and most bulimics fall into category two. Among those who could not taste the solution were sufferers from hyperactivity, hearing problems, alcoholism, infertility, ulcers, chronic fatigue, and postpartum depression. None of these people showed any obvious signs of zinc deficiency.[34]

This is an interesting test to perform on young boys, who often fail the test. Zinc is particularly important for male sex hormone production. Some believe that zinc deficiency contributes to the fact that boys, who require more zinc than girls, seem to lag about two years behind girls in development. Zinc is important for growth in both boys and girls and severe deficiency can result in decreased stature. Zinc deficiency is also associated with incomplete sexual maturation.[35] Zinc is as vital for cell growth as it is for overall growth.

SUGGESTION

- Supplement with zinc if needed.

Food for Thought

Why is binging undesirable? What foods or beverages tend to make you or others binge?

Why is a healthy appetite so essential for good nutrition? A study was once conducted which demonstrated that infants would choose a balanced and nutritious diet until sugar was introduced. How do sugar and salt alter food choices?

Some pathologists believe that most people starve to death because illness causes loss of appetite. How does this speak to the need for support of proper digestion and the consumption of foods and supplements that are capable of being digested and absorbed, particularly in those who are ill?

How do you feel after consuming a Chinese meal to which MSG has been added? How does this illustrate the way in which potentially harmful ingredients may be unknowingly ingested when eating out?

The Brain and Nerves: *Our Onboard Computer System*

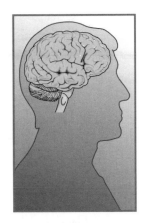

Disorders of the brain and nerves are among the most pervasive of all health conditions in the United States. This is indicated by the prescriptions to treat depression among adults and attention deficit among children.

Disorders of the brain and nerves are among the most pervasive of all health conditions in the United States. This is indicated by the prescriptions to treat depression among adults and attention deficit among children. One cannot help but conclude that something is seriously awry with our "onboard computer systems."

Brain and nerve tissues require a tremendous amount of quality nutrition to function properly. The brain is an energy hog. It consumes 25% of the glucose used by the entire body even though it consists of only about 2% of the body's weight. The brain also consumes about 20% of the body's oxygen. Almost a liter of blood flows through the brain each minute to supply necessary oxygen and fuel and to carry away waste products.[1] Proper vitamin and mineral intake is essential for the ongoing energy production of brain cells. B complex vitamins are particularly important for this energy generation.

The brain is an energy hog. It consumes 25% of the glucose used by the entire body even though it consists of only about 2% of the body's weight.

Not only are the brain's energy demands extraordinary, but the raw materials necessary for construction of healthy brain cells simply are not present in the poor-quality diets many people choose to eat. Over 60% of brain cell structure is fat. Dr. Michael Schmidt, a professor of biochemistry and clinical nutrition, wrote that "the brain requires specific fats of specific size, length, shape, and function in order to conduct its daily business."[2]

A great many of the fats in the standard American diet have been sufficiently altered that they form unsatisfactory building materials for healthy, well-functioning brain cells. These dietary fats are often rancid or oxidized because they have been subjected to high temperatures or allowed to spoil due to careless handling.

The raw materials necessary for construction of healthy brain cells simply are not present in the poor-quality diets many people choose to eat.

Our dietary and bodily fats are often contaminated with a number of toxins including PCBs, pesticides, herbicides, solvents, and mercury compounds. Some of these toxins have the ability to damage the energy-producing machinery or interfere with the structural development of brain and nerve cells.

Finally, the American diet is heavily weighted in favor of the omega-6 family of fats. These promote inflammation and blood clotting, neither of which is a desirable environment for maintaining healthy, functioning brain cells. Poor-quality fats both impair blood flow to and block energy production within brain cells. Our choice of dietary fat is one of our most important nutritional decisions when considering the proper functioning of the brain.

The primary building blocks of brain cells are phospholipids, found in whole grains and legumes, and DHA, a fat supplied by cold-water fish. These fats are the major structural components of brain and nerve tissues. DHA has been shown to improve eyesight and IQ in infants. Deficiency of either of these quality building materials forces the body to build brain and nerve cells from inferior materials that may not be sufficient to withstand the psychological and physical stress many of us encounter on a day-to-day basis.

Imagine our brains as equivalent to the houses built by the three little pigs. The big bad wolf blew down the house built from wood and the house built from straw. These houses were built from inferior building materials. The third little pig built his home from bricks, and it proved to be impervious to the wolf's huffing and puffing. The test of the quality of construction of a home is not its ability to remain standing on a sunny day, but its ability to withstand a ferocious storm. The same is true of brain and nerve cells—they will be more resistant to emotional trauma, depression, or illness if built from healthy materials.

Fats are prone to oxidation or spoilage whether they are outside the body or inside. I encourage clients to make sure they include not only quality fats in the diet, but also rich sources of antioxidants in both food choices and dietary supplements to prevent brain fats from oxidizing.

Attention Deficit Hyperactivity Disorder (ADHD)

SIGN

Difficulty paying attention or controlling behavior

Our choice of dietary fat is one of our most important nutritional decisions when considering the proper functioning of the brain.

The primary building blocks of brain cells are phospholipids, found in whole grains and legumes, and DHA, a fat supplied by cold-water fish.

Significance

The National Institute of Mental Health estimates that as many as one in 20 children may suffer from ADHD. Children diagnosed with this condition are often placed on potent medications with many undesirable side effects.

Discussion

Likely contributors to ADHD include common pollutants and poor diets that poison or fail to properly nourish brain and nerve cells. Elizabeth Guillette and Maria Mercedes Meza conducted a study in 1994 which indicated that pesticides have powerful effects on brain function. They compared the development of children, who are more susceptible to the harmful effects of pesticides than adults, in two neighboring communities in Sonora, Mexico.

The first community is in the foothills where pesticide use is rare. Here the researchers found bugs and butterflies in abundance. Development of the children in this area was normal.

The second community is in a valley with very heavy pesticide use. The researchers saw few bugs and butterflies and learned that farmers grow two crops a year, applying pesticides up to 45 times per crop. The children were different in this valley area. In the pesticide-ridden valley, girls developed breasts at the age of 7, while in the foothills girls developed breasts at about 12 years of age. This precocious puberty was most likely due to the estrogenic effects of the pesticides in use in the valley.

The valley children had severe deficits in hand and eye coordination. Their ability to catch a ball or drop raisins in a bottle cap, tests used by pediatricians to measure development, showed that four and five-year-olds could not accomplish what three-year-old children should have been able to accomplish. Perceptual ability, memory and nerve and muscle coordination were far superior in the foothill children.

Generalized physical endurance in these children was measured by jumping in place. The longest a valley child jumped was 110 seconds compared to 336 seconds for a foothill child. The average jumping for valley children was 52.2 seconds versus 86.9 seconds for foothill children.

The most striking difference in the two groups of children was the ability to draw people. One point was given for head, body, arms, legs, and facial features. Valley children averaged 1.6 body parts and foothill children averaged 4.4 body

Likely contributors to ADHD include common pollutants and poor diets that poison or fail to properly nourish brain and nerve cells.

parts. The differences in these drawings were stunning. In essence, foothill children could draw figures that looked like people, valley children could not.[3]

The mechanism by which many pesticides kill insects is through powerful activation of the nerves, making them fire repeatedly like a machine gun. These electric impulses trigger convulsions, paralysis, and death. It is entirely possible and rational that smaller quantities of these compounds might trigger hyperactivity or attention deficit in children.

Another substance to which children are exposed that may increase the risk of ADHD is fluoride. Phyllis Mullenix, a prominent toxicologist, published a study on the neurotoxicity of sodium fluoride in 1994. She found that fluoride could trigger behavioral changes in rats at blood concentration levels found in children with a high level of exposure. She discovered that fluoride has the ability to damage an area of the brain called the hippocampus which plays an important role in memory and emotions.[4]

Heavy metals including mercury and lead have the potential to wreak havoc with brain function as well. Dr. Robert Tuthill, a professor of epidemiology at the University of Massachusetts, found that hair lead levels of children closely paralleled teacher evaluations of classroom attention deficit behavior. Teachers rated only 13.5% of students with less than 1 ppm hair lead as suffering from attention deficit, but when hair lead was over 6 ppm 62.5% of the children were classified in this way. There was an even stronger association between hair lead levels and physician-diagnosed ADHD.[5]

Lead is much more toxic to children than to adults because they are not able to excrete it as efficiently, they are smaller in size, and they have developing nervous systems. We may never know the full extent of problems created by the widespread use of leaded gasoline for many years and the use of lead in paint prior to 1980. Many older buildings are surrounded by soil that is heavily contaminated with lead.

The contribution sugar makes to ADHD should not be overlooked. Brain and nerve cells become much more susceptible to damage from toxic exposures of every kind when blood sugar is low. A high intake of refined sugar triggers episodes of high followed by low blood sugar. Low blood sugar can increase risk to brain cells when exposed to toxic substances one hundred fold![6]

Sugar decreases ability of the brain to cope with what are called excitotoxins. Some chemicals, particularly MSG, have the ability to excite brain cells in a manner similar to the pesticides already mentioned. High sugar intake

---

The mechanism by which many pesticides kill insects is through powerful activation of the nerves, making them fire repeatedly like a machine gun.

RELATED TOPICS

ALZHEIMER'S DISEASE

CHINESE RESTAURANT SYNDROME

FLUOROSIS

MERCURY AMALGAMS

Fluoride has the ability to damage an area of the brain called the hippocampus which plays an important role in memory and emotions.

Chapter 13 – The Brain and Nerves

disables the protective mechanisms against these excitotoxins in brain cells. This is discussed in more detail under CHINESE RESTAURANT SYNDROME. Children should not be given adult size servings of sweets—their body size is smaller.

SUGGESTIONS

- Do not overindulge children in sweets.

- Reduce exposure to toxic substances, including pesticides, heavy metals, and food additives.

- Supplement with essential brain-building and sustaining nutrients, including phospholipids, omega-3 oils, vitamins, minerals, and antioxidants.

Alzheimer's Disease

SIGN

Memory loss and confusion

SIGNIFICANCE

Those with Alzheimer's are a tremendous burden to caretakers and a tremendous cost, both in terms of dollars and lost productivity.

DISCUSSION

One of the best horror films of which I am aware resulted from the work of Fritz Lorscheider and his associates of the Faculty of Medicine at the University of Calgary in Alberta, Canada, in 2001. In this video neurons of snails that are virtually identical to those of human beings are exposed to low levels of mercury. The neurons literally begin to disintegrate before the eyes of the viewer.[7] (See the footnote for location of the video.)

This research shows that low levels of mercury exposure can cause the kind of damage to brain neurons (neurofibrillar tangles) we see in Alzheimer's disease. Other metals, including aluminum, did not cause this kind of damage to nerve cells in this study.

Mercury is found in amalgams in the teeth, some fish, polluted air, and in the preservative thimerosol that is often added to vaccines. I spoke with a friend

This research shows that low levels of mercury exposure can cause the kind of damage to brain neurons (neurofibrillar tangles) we see in Alzheimer's disease.

Individuals consuming municipal water with high levels of aluminum for over ten years increase their risk of Alzheimer's 2¹/₂ times.

RELATED TOPICS

AUTISM

MERCURY AMALGAMS

SMALL WAIST AND ALZHEIMER'S

Moderate to severe deficiencies of vitamin D are found in 80% of those with Alzheimer's.

who suffers from rather severe respiratory problems recently. She was advised to take the flu shot as a protective measure. She chose not to do this, but had an allergy workup done. The allergy testing indicated she was quite sensitive to thimerisol. She works in a hospital. After learning of her sensitivity to thimerisol, she checked the flu vaccine with which she would have been immunized and learned that it contained thimerisol as a preservative. She would not have tolerated this vaccine well. Unfortunately, patients are rarely tested for sensitivities to vaccines or medications before they are administered. Patients are also uninformed as to whether immunizations contain mercury.

Aluminum is toxic to nerves and brain cells. Individuals consuming municipal water with high levels of aluminum for over ten years increase their risk of Alzheimer's 2¹/₂ times, while those consuming water with low levels of aluminum have a 70% increased risk of the disease. Aluminum (frequently aluminum sulfate) is commonly added to municipal water supplies as a coagulant to settle out particulates. Aluminum is also commonly found in baking powder and antacids.

Electromagnetic radiation may also be a risk for Alzheimer's. Occupations with a high degree of exposure to electromagnetic fields have *four times* more risk for developing Alzheimer's disease than those who are unexposed to powerful electromagnetic fields. This study was conducted prior to the widespread popularity of computers and cell phones.[8]

A number of antioxidants reduce risk of Alzheimer's or improve the condition. Among the most helpful antioxidants are vitamin E, ginkgo biloba, alpha lipoic acid, N-acetyl-cysteine, and vitamin D. Moderate to severe deficiencies of vitamin D are found in 80% of those with Alzheimer's.[8]

The most important and most abundant antioxidant in the human body is glutathione. N-acetyl-cysteine, vitamin C, and alpha-lipoic acid all enhance activity or production of this important antioxidant. Glutathione is what we call a tripeptide because it is made up of three amino acids: glutamate, cysteine, and glycine. Direct supplementation with this tripeptide is ineffective and a waste of money because it is simply broken down into amino acids. Glutathione is quite effective when given by injection. Of the three amino acids that make up glutathione, the most likely to be missing in the diet is L-cysteine, which explains the value of foods or supplements that contain this amino acid.[9] Foods that boost glutathione production include asparagus, garlic, broccoli, spinach, eggs, milk, and avocado.

Dr. Michael Gold, Assistant Professor of Neurology and Psychiatry at the University of South Florida, found that many patients with Alzheimer's are deficient in thiamine or vitamin B1. This was not true of other forms of dementia. Lack of this nutrient may be one of the weak links, making brain cells more susceptible to death in this brain disease.[10] A generous supply of all the B complex vitamins is probably wise. These nutrients supply brain cells with energy which they use to protect themselves.

A brain cell without energy is like a soldier without a shield. The cell becomes susceptible to every dart, arrow, or spear tossed at it. The energy of the brain cell is derived from glucose, which is why low blood sugar has a devastating effect upon brain function and long-term brain health. A number of nutrients, including the B complex vitamins and magnesium, are essential for the production of energy from blood sugar, while lead, mercury, aluminum, and pesticides do much of their damage by interfering with cellular energy generation.[11]

Many patients with Alzheimer's are deficient in thiamine or vitamin B1.

A brain cell without energy is like a soldier without a shield.

SUGGESTIONS

- Avoid exposure to mercury, lead, aluminum, and pesticides.

- Don't allow brain cells to become depleted of antioxidants.

- Never allow low blood sugar situations to develop.

- Supplement with quality oils, B complex vitamins, and other essential nutrients.

Autism

SIGN

Staring into space, uncontrollable tantrums, or lack of ability to relate to people

SIGNIFICANCE

A substantial body of evidence points to mercury exposure as a cause or major contributor to autism. Mercury is one of the most toxic natural substances on earth.[12] According to Dr. Rashid Buttar, an expert on autism, this disease has increased from about 1 in 10,000 in the 1970s to about 1 in 175 in the early 21st century.[13]

RELATED TOPICS

ALZHEIMER'S
DISEASE

MERCURY
AMALGAMS

MIGRAINE

NEUROPATHY

A recent study found autistic children have reduced capacity to cope with mercury, which could be bolstered with methyl donors (vitamins B6, B12, folic acid, and betaine) and glutathione enhancement.[56]

The number of immunizations given to children increased dramatically in the 1990s, which may account for the apparent increase in the number of cases of autism.

DISCUSSION

At a recent clinical nutrition meeting two physicians spoke on autism. Their talks were most unusual in that both had sons suffering from autism. Both treated their sons for mercury toxicity. Both saw remarkable improvements in behavior after treatment. Both found that their sons needed nutritional help in order to be able to excrete mercury, which the physicians concluded probably resulted from exposure to thimerisol in childhood immunizations. The pivotal nutrient in both these situations was glutathione. The physicians observed that many children with autism do not have the ability to excrete mercury due to deficiency of this internally synthesized detoxifier.

Inability to excrete mercury creates a problem for diagnosis. Common tests may not show the presence of mercury because those who are most at risk have the poorest ability to excrete the metal, allowing its existence to remain easily hidden.

Much of a child's exposure to mercury is a result of the use of mercury in the form of thimerosol to preserve vaccines. Thimerosol is almost 50% mercury. The number of immunizations given to children increased dramatically in the 1990s, which may account for the apparent increase in the number of cases of autism.[14]

Mercury has been removed from many children's vaccines, which should decrease exposure of this susceptible population in the future. An excellent discussion of immunizations called "The Vaccine Controversy" will be found in a book by Russell Blaylock, M.D., entitled *Health Secrets That Could Save Your Life.*[15]

Dr. Bernard Rimland, who has spent much of his medical career studying autism, finds that nutrients such as vitamin C, vitamin B6, and DMG are helpful for autism.[16] DMG is a form of glycine, an amino acid that relaxes and calms the brain and nerve cells. Vitamin C improves the body's ability to cope with mercury and other toxins. Vitamin B6 aids the body in its use of magnesium, a mineral that not only calms and relaxes, but also provides a bulwark of defense for brain cells.

Any of the foods or supplements that boost glutathione production should benefit autism. Autistic children will sometimes demonstrate an aggravation of symptoms when exposed to gluten, milk, or other foods to which they are allergic.

SUGGESTIONS

- Avoid mercury in fish, dental fillings, and vaccines.

- Consume foods rich in sulfur-containing amino acids such as asparagus, avocado, cruciferous vegetables, garlic, and eggs.

- Investigate the possibility of a mercury detox program.

- Supplement with all essential nutrients, including "methyl donors."

- Supplement with fish oils.

Depression

SIGN

A person is often considered to be suffering major depression if the mood is low for two weeks. The sufferer loses interest in and does not derive pleasure from usual activities—feeling helpless and hopeless.

SIGNIFICANCE

You are one hundred times more likely to suffer major depression if born after 1945 than the person who was born before 1914—increased pollution and deterioration of the diet are probably factors responsible for this change. Serious depression may result in inability to function and can lead to suicide.[17]

DISCUSSION

Phyllis, a client of many years, was quivering although I had never seen her exhibit anything like this before. I commented on her shaking and she explained that she had been under a great deal of stress. I told her that I had never seen stress of the kind she described do this to someone. She explained that her doctor had given her an antidepressant medication. I immediately had a clue to the cause of her uncontrollable behavior. It is a common side effect of antidepressant medications called akathisia. I showed her the following paragraph from Dr. Peter Breggin's work:

"Akathisia is characterized by inner tension or anxiety that drives or compels afflicted individuals to move their bodies. Typically the sufferer cannot sit still and frantically moves about. Where severe, akathisia feels like internal

The client's name has been changed.

torture, and those who suffer from it can wear out the soles of their shoes, the rug beneath their chair, or their clothing."[18]

This woman shared the information on this side effect with her physician and he immediately lowered her dose of the drug.

Depression is often treated as a deficiency of serotonin—a chemical that stabilizes mood, focuses the mind, and helps us sleep. Prior to 1989 depression was commonly treated rather successfully with the amino acid L-tryptophan, which is the nutrient precursor to serotonin production. In that year the Showa Denko company of Japan introduced contaminated tryptophan on the market. The FDA responded by stopping the sale of all L-tryptophan.

Coincidentally, the year before, Prozac was introduced and within two years became one of the best-selling drugs of all time. This medication belongs to a class of drugs called serotonin reuptake inhibitors (SSRIs). These drugs do not increase serotonin production, but prevent the body from removing serotonin from nerve synapses. In other words, these medications block the body's balancing mechanism for maintaining a stable and consistent level of serotonin in the brain. The destruction of the body's self-regulation of this brain chemical may contribute to some of the serious side effects of these medications, including akathisia, tics, and increased risk of suicide or violence.

Tryptophan, the amino acid precursor to serotonin, is not abundant in foods. In addition, conversion of tryptophan to serotonin is dependent upon adequate intake of vitamin B6 or pyridoxine, which is often deficient in the diet. High intake of sugar, blood sugar imbalances such as hypoglycemia and diabetes, or alcohol consumption can interfere with serotonin production. One of the best means of assuring adequate serotonin production is to avoid sugar and other refined carbohydrates and to obtain adequate B complex to enable the body to synthesize its own serotonin.

Tranquilizers cause a major toxic reaction called tardive dyskinesia which is very similar to akathisia. Dr. Abram Hoffer suggested that these medications bind to manganese and carry it out of the body. He wrote, "If drug companies would put 1 mg of manganese into every tranquilizer tablet, tardive dyskinesia would disappear."[19] Research needs to be conducted to determine if this potentially irreversible and tortuous condition can be prevented by a small amount of manganese. It might provide a clue to prevention of akathisia when patients use antidepressants as well.

Prior to 1989 depression was commonly treated rather successfully with the amino acid L-tryptophan, which is the nutrient precursor to serotonin production.

Conversion of tryptophan to serotonin is dependent upon adequate intake of vitamin B6 or pyridoxine, which is often deficient in the diet.

One possible cause for depression is immune activation. The macrophage (literally "big eater") is a major player in the game of immune defense. This white blood cell releases a number of chemical messengers when activated. These chemical messengers are able to cause numerous nerve and endocrine abnormalities that are consistently found with major depression.

Volunteers given one of these chemical messengers (INF-α) developed a major depression over a period of five days that disappeared after two weeks. All patients had a short euphoric phase similar to mania on the second day after being given the chemical messenger. The volunteers also developed moderate to severe fatigue, loss of appetite, physical activity dependent upon thinking slowed down, confusion and inability to concentrate were observed, and sleep was prolonged.[20]

The kind of immune activation and subsequent depression described above could easily result from allergic response to common foods such as those containing gluten. Dr. James Braley, an expert on food allergies and gluten sensitivity, reported that "depression is the most common symptom of gluten intolerance."[21] Ronald Smith, author of a number of papers on immune activation suggested that milk is also a common cause of depression.[20]

Depression is positively associated with rheumatoid arthritis, which is also characterized by activated macrophages. Both of these problems are two to three times more common in women than men. Estradiol, a powerful estrogen found in great quantity in younger women, increased concentrations of one of the chemical messengers (IL-1) associated with depression fourfold. Hormone imbalance, particularly excess estrogen, apparently contributes to depression by increasing immune activation in a number of ways.[20]

One of the hormones significantly elevated in depression is cortisol. This hormone is elevated not only by immune activation, but also by high sugar intake and caffeine consumption. This suggests that sugar and caffeine may contribute to depression. Both of these substances have been shown to increase cortisol levels dramatically.[22] Renowned biochemist, researcher, and physician John Yudkin conducted research showing that sugar could increase cortisol levels 300 to 400%.[23]

The brain is largely composed of phospholipids and DHA, a fat found in cold water fish. Fish oil also contains a fat called EPA which calms macrophages and decreases their release of chemical messengers from 40 to 60% in as little as six weeks in some studies.[20] Dr. Andrew Stoll, Director of the Psychopharmacology Research Laboratory at McLean Hospital in Boston, has

Volunteers given one of these chemical messengers (INF-α) developed a major depression over a period of five days that disappeared after two weeks.

Depression is the most common symptom of gluten intolerance.

Sugar and caffeine may contribute to depression.

written an entire book emphasizing the importance of fish oils for treating depression and promoting mental health.[17]

A number of other nutrients may help fight depression. Psychiatrist Abram Hoffer has treated depression with surprising success using the trace mineral selenium. Lithium and thiamine (vitamin B1) have also been successfully applied to the treatment of depression.[24] The brain is a complex organ with many nutrient requirements. Complete and adequate nutrition is ideal in treating any mental disorder.

SUGGESTIONS

- Avoid refined sugar and caffeine.

- Avoid gluten, milk, or other foods to which one has an allergic response.

- Supplement with all essential nutrients including amino acids.

- Priority nutrients include vitamin B complex, fish oils, phospholipids, and fat-soluble antioxidants.

Dream Recall

SIGN

Inability to remember dreams in the morning

SIGNIFICANCE

Lack of dream recall may indicate vitamin B6 (pyridoxine) deficiency.

DISCUSSION

Dr. Jeffrey Bland, a pioneering nutrition researcher, observed that inability to remember dreams may be associated with inadequate intake of vitamin B6. This nutrient plays many roles in mood and memory. Intake of vitamin B6 may need to be rather high for dream recall.[25] Pyridoxine deficiency is often accompanied by deficiencies of zinc. Deficiencies of vitamins B6 and B3 may lead to altered perception and hallucinations.[26] Vitamin B6 improves vitamin B3 nutriture due to the fact that it is part of the enzyme that converts the amino acid tryptophan to niacin (vitamin B3).

SUGGESTION

■ Supplement with vitamin B complex.

Migraine Headache

SIGN

A very bad headache that sometimes results in nausea or vomiting—often affecting only one side of the head and making one sensitive to light or noise

SIGNIFICANCE

Migraines result from altered blood flow to or through the brain. They are frequently associated with allergic responses to foods and deficiencies of omega-3 oils and magnesium. A severe migraine attack has the ability to totally incapacitate an individual.

DISCUSSION

Studies of migraine often find low magnesium levels in the body of those who suffer from this condition. An easily assimilated magnesium supplement often produces substantial benefit.[27] Magnesium improves blood flow through the brain.

Fish oils also improve circulation as well as reducing inflammation in the brain. Regular use of fish oil may decrease the severity of migraine or eliminate it.[28] If fish oils are going to improve migraine, adequate quantities must be used for a period of two or three months.

A generous intake of vitamin B2 (up to 400 mg a day) has shown itself to be remarkably effective for some migraine sufferers.[29] This is not a nutritional benefit of vitamin B2, but rather a pharmaceutical or drug-like effect. This approach should be used with medical supervision.

Migraines are often caused by food intolerances. One study found chocolate a common trigger for migraine.[30] Other common triggers include alcohol, gluten, caffeine, and high-fat diets.[31] Gluten intolerance should be considered in chronic headache conditions, including migraine. Gluten intolerance often results in alterations of the blood flow in the brain, and avoidance has benefited many migraine and headache sufferers.[32, 33]

Studies of migraine often find low magnesium levels in the body of those who suffer from this condition.

Regular use of fish oil may decrease the severity of migraine or eliminate it.

I have repeatedly encountered individuals with a passion for "eating a healthy diet" who suffer all manner of health difficulties, including migraine. These people often go to extra effort to consume whole wheat or whole grain breads rather than white breads, not realizing that whole grain products actually have greater gluten content than refined grains. Their migraine problems often disappear or are greatly decreased in severity when gluten is avoided.

Establishing a more normal sleep pattern reduces incidence of migraine among children. The researchers found the children benefited from getting to bed before 11:00 P.M. and getting up before 8:00 A.M. This is not bad advice for adults.[34]

Surprisingly, the smell of a green apple has been shown to alleviate migraine.[35] Feverfew, an herb, sometimes effectively prevents migraine.[36]

Migraines that occur only at premenstrual times may be contributed to by excess estrogen or estrogen dominance.

RELATED TOPICS

AUTISM

CHINESE
RESTAURANT
SYNDROME

NUMBNESS OF THE
HANDS OR FEET

SUGGESTIONS

- Avoid or reduce consumption of chocolate, sugar, and alcohol.

- Consider the possibility of intolerance to gluten or other foods.

- Increase magnesium intake from foods and supplements.

- Supplement with B complex vitamins and fish oils.

Multiple Sclerosis (MS)

SIGN

The body attacks its own myelin-producing cells in the central nervous system. Common symptoms include blurred vision, loss of muscle strength, numbness and tingling in the extremities, and loss of control of the bowels.

SIGNIFICANCE

Multiple sclerosis may develop as a result of immune dysfunction due to vitamin D deficiency. Gluten intolerance, estrogen excess, and heavy metal exposure, including lead or mercury, may also be factors in causing MS.

DISCUSSION

One of the amazing stories I have been privileged to hear over the years is that of a middle-aged woman who was diagnosed with MS as a young woman. Her father was an eye doctor who attempted everything medically and nutritionally possible to reverse his daughter's MS. Despite this she lost the vision in one eye. Nothing seemed to be working for her. At this point she was sold a partially predigested protein product. She had used many other supplements, including a number of protein products in the past, but this one made a significant difference and her disease has been in remission for decades. This particular product was manufactured for ease of digestion and probably overcame her inability to digest protein. Subsequently this young woman found that salmon oil also benefited her condition tremendously.

In the 1940s Dr. Hinton Jonez treated MS with a good deal of success using histamine, which the body manufactures from the amino acid histidine. Histamine is produced in response to allergy. Jonez felt those with MS suffered from serious allergies and became depleted of histamine, a substance produced by the body to defend itself. I have already discussed the ability of gluten to cause damage to the nervous system under the topic of NUMBNESS OF THE HANDS OR FEET. Dr. Jonez was addressing this kind of neurologic damage resulting from allergic response to foods. He did allergy workups on his patients, removed the allergens from the diet, and supported the patient with injectable histamine. The Tahoma Clinic that unburied Dr. Jonez's work reported improvement in 72% of patients with the use of histamine.[37]

Multiple sclerosis provides a model for autoimmune disease. It has similarities to juvenile diabetes and rheumatoid arthritis. One of the most remarkable characteristics of MS is that occurrence is inversely related to vitamin D intake. This is true whether the vitamin D is obtained by consuming fish oils or exposure to the sun. Incidence of MS in equatorial regions is nearly zero. It is also much less common on the Norwegian coast where fish oils rich in vitamin D are consumed. MS rates are low in high altitudes in Switzerland where more direct sunlight is available and high in low altitudes where less sunlight is available.[38] Vitamin D deficiency has been identified not only in MS but also in juvenile diabetes (IDDM) and rheumatoid arthritis.

There is a mouse model for multiple sclerosis called EAE. Vitamin D3, the biologically active form of vitamin D, has been shown to prevent EAE. Deficiency of vitamin D increases susceptibility to EAE. Vitamin D targets the cells (Th1, including T-helper cells) that cause EAE. This vitamin decreases

Those with MS often suffer with digestive problems. Poor protein digestion may result in deficiency of the amino acid histidine, which the body uses to manufacture histamine.

One of the most remarkable characteristics of MS is that occurrence is inversely related to vitamin D intake.

Vitamin D has been shown to alter developing immune cells so they are less likely to engage in autoimmune activity.

Dr. Rhonda Voskuhl, who heads up the UCLA research project on MS, has determined that both estriol and testosterone produce improvement in MS.

both the reproduction and activity of cells responsible for autoimmune activity in mice.[39] Vitamin D has been shown to alter developing immune cells so they are less likely to engage in autoimmune activity.

Many autoimmune diseases are found more frequently in women than in men. This suggests that hormones play a role in these problems. Dr. Rhonda Voskuhl, who heads up the UCLA research project on MS, has determined that both estriol and testosterone produce improvement in MS.[40] Estriol is the weakest of the estrogens and was shown to reduce risk of breast cancer by Henry Lemon in 1966. Lemon found that estriol could block some of the more harmful effects of estrone and estradiol, the stronger estrogens in a woman's body.[41] The stronger estrogens appear to increase risk of autoimmune disease, while hormones that counteract strong estrogens produce improvement in many autoimmune conditions. Reducing estrogen dominance may decrease the risk of multiple sclerosis.

Dr. Roy Swank, a prominent neurologist and physician, spent years treating those with MS with a low-fat diet. He felt that high intake of saturated fat and partially hydrogenated oils caused a breakdown in brain and nerve structure and function. He was able to prevent progress or relapses for years in MS patients who were willing to reduce total fats, especially the saturated ones that make white and red blood cells clump together.[42] The low-fat diet Dr. Swank used would tend to reduce estrogen levels.

Nutrients that build healthy brain and nerve cells include omega-3 oils, lecithin, and antioxidants. These should replace the junk fats in the diet, which cause a deterioration in the vitality and health of brain and nerve cells.

SUGGESTIONS

- Avoid junk fats in the diet.

- Consider the possibility of gluten intolerance or other allergies.

- Correct hormone abnormalities, especially estrogen dominance.

- Investigate the possibility of heavy metal poisoning.

- Obtain adequate vitamin D from sunlight or cod liver oil.

- Obtain nutrients essential for building and supporting healthy brain and nerve cells, including B complex vitamins, antioxidants, and quality fats.

Schizophrenia

SIGN

Hallucinations, fears, disorientation, confusion, and incoherence

SIGNIFICANCE

Schizophrenia can make an individual incapable of functioning normally.

DISCUSSION

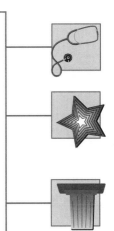

Some immune cells that line the gut produce a chemical messenger called interleukin-2 (IL-2). Injecting this substance into patients has resulted in all the symptoms of schizophrenia. No other chemical messenger has this toxic effect on brain and nerve cells. Schizophrenia is common in those who are intolerant to gluten. This may be a common trigger for activation of the white blood cells that line the digestive tract to produce IL-2. Those with rheumatoid arthritis and depression have a totally different kind of immune activation (IL-1) and have far less incidence of schizophrenia than the general population.[43]

That schizophrenia is associated with food intake is supported by the use of fasting to treat it. Professor Yuri Nikolaev has treated thousands of schizophrenics at the Moscow Psychiatric Institute with fasting. Seventy percent of patients recover on fasts that can last up to 30 days.[44] Fasting eliminates food allergens, allows the digestive tract to heal, and cleanses the digestive tract of harmful bacteria. It is unknown which of these is the primary cause for improvement observed in schizophrenics as a result of fasting.

Schizophrenics are often deficient in a number of nutrients, including vitamin C, zinc, magnesium, and vitamins B6 and B3. The omega-6 fatty acid DGLA (dihomogamma linolenic acid) may be deficient as well.[45]

One of the symptoms of pellagra or extreme vitamin B3 deficiency is mental illness. Use of high doses of vitamin B3 and vitamin C to treat schizophrenia was pioneered by Dr. Abram Hoffer, a prominent Canadian psychiatrist. One of the objects of this treatment was to reduce accumulation of adrenochrome, a byproduct of oxidation of adrenalin. Adrenochrome is a hallucinogen. [46] Adrenochrome is also toxic to heart muscle and may cause fibrillation and death. Niacin reduces accumulation of this toxic compound,

Some immune cells that line the gut produce a chemical messenger called interleukin-2 (IL-2). Injecting this substance into patients has resulted in all the symptoms of schizophrenia.

One of the symptoms of pellagra or extreme vitamin B3 deficiency is mental illness.

which may explain not only why it benefits schizophrenia, but also one of the reasons it is so beneficial for the heart.[47]

I worked in a psychiatric hospital for a year. Many of the patients appeared to be perpetually pumped with adrenalin. Hoffer's hypothesis makes a good deal of sense to me. I have seen vitamins C and B complex work wonders with schizophrenics.

Dr. Hoffer discovered that prolonged deficiency of niacin can result in a permanent dependency on the vitamin. In the 1930s it was learned that dogs maintained on a pellagra-producing diet for an extended period thereafter required large doses of niacin to remain pellagra-free. Early researchers on pellagra found that 60 times more niacin was required to treat pellagra than was necessary to prevent it.

Dr. Hoffer was researching the benefit of niacin for senility in 1960. The director of the facility in which he was working asked if he could test the niacin on himself. This man had been a prisoner of war of the Japanese for 44 months. Since the war he had suffered with crippling arthritis, irrational fears, difficulty sleeping at night, a tendency to sleep during the day, depression, and intolerance to cold. All these symptoms disappeared after he began taking one gram of niacin three times a day and symptoms returned only once when he went on a two-week camping trip and forgot to take his vitamins. [47] Dr. Hoffer came to refer to this requirement for a larger-than-normal amount of a nutrient "acquired dependence."

Dr. Hoffer stumbled upon the fact that many schizophrenics are vitamin B3 dependent. [48] "Acquired dependence" for a larger amount of a nutrient than normally present in the diet should be considered as a possibility by anyone who has experienced severe malnutrition. Supplementation by these people can sometimes produce electrifying improvements in health.

Hoffer and others have observed that many schizophrenics excrete a hallucinogenic substance called kryptopyrrole in the urine. This substance binds with zinc and vitamin B6, creating a deficiency of these nutrients. Vitamin B6 is involved in the conversion of the amino acid tryptophan to niacin (NAD), creating a biochemical block to the use of the vitamin. Schizophrenics often benefit from the addition of zinc and vitamin B6 to the diet as well as niacin.

Dr. Donald Rudin has observed that the amount of vitamin B3 necessary to create a flush in psychoses associated with niacin deficiency is reduced by as much as tenfold when omega-3 oils are present.[49] This suggests the interde-

Early researchers on pellagra found that 60 times more niacin was required to treat pellagra than was necessary to prevent it.

Dr. Hoffer came to refer to this requirement for a larger-than-normal amount of a nutrient "acquired dependence."

Dr. Donald Rudin has observed that the amount of vitamin B3 necessary to create a flush in psychoses associated with niacin deficiency is reduced by as much as tenfold when omega-3 oils are present.

pendency of these two nutrients. This is not unusual as nutrients usually do work together in the same way an orchestra does. Doctors Harte and Chow reviewed over 200 scientific studies years ago and concluded that "the shortage of a single essential vitamin, mineral element, amino acid, or fatty acid will create a shock wave that spreads to affect the utilization and/or function of every other essential nutrient."[50] Asking the body *or brain* to function without an essential nutrient may be likened to asking a musician to play an orchestral piece with a violin that has a broken string.

SUGGESTIONS

- Consider the possibility of acquired dependence for a larger-than-normal amount of some nutrients.

- Consume only high-quality oils.

- Eliminate gluten and other allergens from the diet.

- Supplement with vitamin C, zinc, and vitamin B complex.

Sense of Humor

SIGN

Inability to laugh at humorous stories or incidents

SIGNIFICANCE

Loss of a sense of humor accompanies deficiency of vitamin B3 or the B complex.

DISCUSSION

Noted nutritionist Dr. Tom Spies observed that when his patients were short tempered and "swimmy-headed" and could not laugh at a funny story they were often deficient in vitamin B3. "After hundreds of trials he learned that one of the early signs of niacin depletion is the loss of a sense of humor."

Dr. Abram Hoffer, who has probably studied the relationship of niacin to behavior as much as anyone, felt that a total lack of the vitamin resulted in the deficiency disease pellagra, but low levels of intake produced "humorless, overemotional, down-in-the-dumps individuals who are rarely recognized for what they are: 'minipellagrins.' "[51] The B complex vitamins are central to the use of carbohydrate for the energy production necessary to fuel brain cells. Deficiencies of these vitamins are known to influence mood. It may well be true that the most pleasing personalities among those we know are contributed to in a significant way by superior nutrition.

Excessive intake of sugar, illness, nutrient deficiencies, and consumption of foods to which one is allergic may also contribute to a poor disposition. Dr. Francis Pottenger found that cats, the females in particular, not only lost their good temperament, but became aggressive and dangerous when malnourished. He named three of these animals Tiger, Cobra, and Rattlesnake. [52]

RELATED TOPICS

ARTHRITIS (OSTEOARTHRITIS)

CASAL'S NECKLACE

SUGGESTIONS

- Avoid refined carbohydrates, especially sugar.

- Avoid brain-damaging heavy metals, pesticides, and other toxic chemicals.

- Eat a healthy diet.

- Supplement with vitamin B complex and quality oils.

Sudden Infant Death Syndrome (SIDS)

SIGN

A child dies suddenly, often while sleeping

SIGNIFICANCE

This sign may indicate vitamin C deficiency or heavy metal poisoning.

DISCUSSION

When an infant has scurvy or severe vitamin C deficiency, there is a tendency to lie on the back and to make little effort to move the arm or leg that hurts. This is because tissues deprived of vitamin C are painful, and this pain is one of the earliest signs of scurvy. An infant with scurvy may also cry a great deal or engage in high-pitched screaming, especially when limbs are touched or moved. Bruising can occur.[53]

A remarkable account of infant scurvy is found in a book entitled *Every Second Child* by Dr. Archie Kalokerinos, a physician who worked among the

Australian aborigines. Every other child under his care died after being immunized. This physician eventually discovered that the infant formulas being given the children were deficient in vitamin C. The immunizations depleted what little vitamin C was in the bodies of the children, resulting in death from scurvy. The death rate dropped to zero for an entire year after vitamin C was added to the diets of the children.

Dr. Kalokerinos found that these infants suffered from many ear infections and runny noses. Since young children cannot tell parents something is wrong, the astute parent should look for signs that vitamin C intake may be inadequate.[54]

There are other theories regarding the causation of SIDS. Dr. T. James Sprott, a New Zealand chemist and forensic scientist, suggested that SIDS is caused by release of toxic gases from flame-retardant clothing and mattresses. Flame-retardant materials contain phosphorus, arsenic, and antimony. Toxic gases are released when flame-retardant materials become wet and fungi feed on these minerals. The toxic gases phosphine, stibine, and arsine interrupt nerve impulses from the brain to the heart and lungs, resulting in death. High levels of antimony in particular have been identified in many babies have died of SIDS.

Flame-retardant materials become wet as a result of perspiration, urine, or drooling. Toxic gases are heavy and hang close to the mattress. Simply having an infant sleep on its back greatly reduces the risk of death. Dr. Sprott developed the BabeSafe® mattress cover to protect infants in New Zealand. He feels that vaccinations may contribute to SIDS by elevating body temperature and depleting vitamin C, but feels exposure to toxic gases is the primary cause of death.

Dr. Sprott has developed an entire protocol for protecting infants from toxic gases. There have been no SIDS deaths reported among families in New Zealand following his suggestions for protecting infants.[55]

SUGGESTIONS

■ Be especially cautious when body temperature is elevated as this increases the risk of release of toxic gases. This can be caused by too many blankets.

■ Do not immunize infants when they are ill.

■ Make sure nutritional intake is adequate, including sufficient vitamin C intake.

■ Have infants sleep on the back.

The immunizations depleted what little vitamin C was in the bodies of the children, resulting in death from scurvy.

■ Take steps to make sure mattresses are wrapped and toxic materials are not present in mattresses or bedding materials.

Food for Thought

Have you ever noted a relationship between headache and diet?

Gluten is found in wheat, rye, barley, triticale, spelt, and oats. How do you feel after eating these foods? Do you know anyone who suffers with gluten intolerance? What symptoms do they experience?

Have you ever observed an apparent relationship between what people eat and their mood or temperament? Has your mood ever changed after eating particular foods?

What measures could be taken to improve the health of young children?

Internal Organs and Conditions:

The Ghost in the Machine

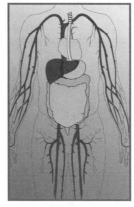

The Greek storytellers attribute the beginning of the war between Greece and Troy to a beauty contest between three goddesses. Paris, the judge, chose the goddess of beauty who rewarded him with Helen, the wife of the king of Sparta. Paris kidnapped Helen and took her to his home in Troy. The Greek city-states combined to attack Troy. The walls of Troy withstood all the fury of the massed Greek armies for nine years until Odysseus devised a clever plan. He had a large hollow horse built. Soldiers were placed inside and the Greek fleet sailed away. The deceived Trojans believed they were victorious. They brought the horse within the walls of the city and engaged in a drunken orgy to celebrate their victory. The soldiers emerged from the horse in the middle of the night and opened the gates of the city which allowed the Greek armies who had returned under the cover of darkness to sack and destroy the city of Troy.

This chapter discusses Trojan horses—conditions that may escape notice and yet undermine health in powerful ways. It provides insights into adrenal weakness, insulin resistance, joint and muscle pain, and allergy detection that may just protect your immune fortifications and prevent "the fall of the city."

Allergy has been discussed a good deal already, yet I have only touched on the many ways in which intolerance to foods may be manifested and act as a Trojan horse undermining our health. A number of other allergy indicators could have been discussed, including red or warm earlobes, swollen and puffy lips, cracks at the corner of the mouth similar to vitamin B2 deficiency, pimples around the mouth and chin, hoarseness, a raised pitch of the voice, stiff hands in the morning, becoming cold after eating certain foods, swelling in different parts of the body, and excessive perspiration. This chapter provides a simple

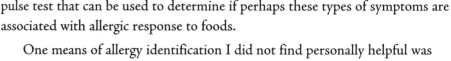

pulse test that can be used to determine if perhaps these types of symptoms are associated with allergic response to foods.

One means of allergy identification I did not find personally helpful was the blood-type diet. It identifies safe and unsafe foods based on blood type.[1] In my situation this allergy detection scheme identified as safe, foods that my own experience and other forms of allergy testing indicated were unsafe. The blood-type diet also suggested removing foods that other allergy testing did not indicate were problems. I felt this ran the risk of unnecessarily removing from my diet potentially valuable sources of good nutrition. I do not recommend relying on blood type alone as a guide for those with allergic problems. The gold standard for allergy detection should be some type of measurement of what a food actually does to the human body as indicated by blood testing of actual foods, by symptoms, or other evidence of immune reactivity.

This chapter also discusses a simple little test for weakness of the adrenal glands, which enable us to cope with stress. Americans put their adrenals through a considerable amount of stress on a day-to-day basis with jolts of caffeine-containing beverages, a huge intake of sugar, and stress-filled lives. Building strong adrenals is a central issue in enabling the body to cope with allergy and in the prevention of autoimmune disease.

I have also included a discussion of three blood measurements in this chapter. Physicians often miss the association between these factors and insulin resistance. This leaves a patient taking unnecessary medications while progressing on a path that may lead to diabetes.

Dizziness Upon Rising

Sign

Dizziness when rising suddenly from a reclining position

Significance

This sign may indicate weak or exhausted adrenal glands.

Discussion

The pancake-shaped adrenal glands that sit on top of the kidneys are the body's primary means of responding to stress or changes in the environment. Stress may be physical or emotional—temperature changes, arguments, illness, divorce, a horror movie, a roller coaster ride, eating a sugar-sweetened food, or

The gold standard for allergy detection should be some type of measurement of what a food actually does to the human body as indicated by blood testing of actual foods, by symptoms, or other evidence of immune reactivity.

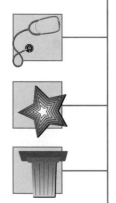

drinking a caffeinated beverage. Poor diet contributes to adrenal exhaustion as readily as emotional stress. All these lifestyle habits stimulate the adrenal glands. Unfortunately, overstimulated glands become exhausted.[2]

Dizziness or lightheadedness when rising suddenly from a reclining position is called postural hypotension and this is an excellent indicator of low adrenal function. Edward Schwartz, Ph.D., provided the details for a simple little test of the ability of the adrenal glands to regulate blood pressure.

Schwartz recommended having an individual relax completely. Take blood pressure in the sitting position and then in the standing position. It is normal for the systolic or higher blood pressure reading to rise 4 to 10 mm of mercury upon standing. If the blood pressure drops or fails to rise, low adrenal function is suspected. When an individual faints or becomes dizzy upon rising suddenly, the adrenals most likely have not initiated an increase in blood pressure.[3]

Vitamin C is concentrated in the adrenal glands. Inadequate intake of this nutrient results in adrenal weakness. Other nutrients that support adrenal function include the B complex vitamins (especially vitamin B5), amino acids (especially tyrosine), and trace minerals.[4]

The adrenal glands produce many types of hormones. One of these, aldosterone, is involved in salt retention. Salt intake decreases the need for aldosterone production and takes quite a burden off the adrenals. Blood pressure is generally low when the adrenals are weak, which reduces or eliminates problems associated with consumption of salt.[5]

ACTH is a hormone the body produces to stimulate adrenal function. One of the medical tests for adrenal health is to administer ACTH to a patient and see if cortisol production goes up. Cortisol is the body's major stress-coping hormone. If cortisol does not increase when ACTH is released, it indicates that the adrenals do not have much in the way of reserve capacity to cope with stress situations.[6] ACTH levels tend to be excessively high when the adrenals are weak. Elevated ACTH tends to produce hyperpigmentation or darkening of the skin and mucous membranes—making this a clue to adrenal weakness.[7]

Dr. Jonathan Wright made an interesting observation regarding adrenal weakness compared to other glandular problems. He observed, "Although underfunction of the thyroid and other endocrine glands generally is recognized and treated in conventional medicine prior to the stage of total glandular failure, underfunction of the adrenal glands generally is not considered or diagnosed until its 'endstage' of total adrenal failure, termed 'Addison's disease.'"

Dizziness or lightheadedness when rising suddenly from a reclining position is called postural hypotension and this is an excellent indicator of low adrenal function.

"Underfunction of the adrenal glands generally is not considered or diagnosed until its 'endstage' of total adrenal failure, termed 'Addison's disease.'"

Jonathan Wright, M.D.

Many of the manifestations of weak adrenals appear to be psychological in origin and patients are often referred to psychologists.

Dr. John Tintera associated weak adrenals with a number of health problems, including fatigue, nervousness, depression, weakness, craving for salt and sweets, alcoholism, mental confusion, poor memory, and allergies.

Low-carbohydrate diets are not recommended for those with weak adrenal function because they force the adrenals to work harder manufacturing carbohydrate from protein.

Many of the manifestations of weak adrenals appear to be psychological in origin and patients are often referred to psychologists.[8] Dr. Edward Schwartz noted that weak adrenals can be indicated by the psychological symptoms of depression, insomnia, and mental instability as well as more typical symptoms such as low blood pressure, loss of appetite, weight loss, impaired digestion, diarrhea, dizziness, allergic responses, arthritic conditions, low blood sugar, and nausea.

The adrenals make it possible to convert protein to carbohydrate. Low-carbohydrate diets are not recommended for those with weak adrenal function because they force the adrenals to work harder manufacturing carbohydrate from protein. Complex carbohydrate consumption is far preferable to refined sugars for the individual with weak adrenals since refined carbohydrates and sugars tend to overexert and exhaust the glands.[9]

Adrenal hormones such as cortisone have been administered medically for a number of conditions. Unfortunately, physicians have not used the amounts of these hormones normally found in the human body. Excesses of cortisone have a variety of undesirable side effects. Cortisone has therefore obtained a reputation for being a dangerous medication.

If cortisone is needed, it can be used safely, according to at least one expert, Dr. William Jefferies, author of *Safe Uses of Cortisone*. He explained that if correct physiologic doses of this hormone are used with patients the hormone is quite safe. He wrote, "Employment of safe dosages on a proper schedule has demonstrated a promising potential in patients with gonadal dysfunction with or without infertility, rheumatoid arthritis, allergic rhinitis, asthma, recently recognized autoimmune disorders such as hyperthyroidism with diffuse goiter, chronic thyroiditis, and diabetes mellitus, and common clinical problems such as functional hypoglycemia, hirsuitism, acne, and chronic cystic mastitis." Jefferies suggested that adrenal weakness may cause unexplained chronic fatigue.[10]

The adrenal glands are the source of the body's most powerful anti-inflammatory hormones. It is no accident that adrenal hormones benefit a wide range of inflammatory and autoimmune disorders. Properly caring for our adrenal glands provides many benefits.

A complete discussion of the condition of low adrenal function will be found in a book by Dr. John W. Tintera entitled *Hypoadrenocorticism*. Tintera associated weak adrenals with a number of health problems, including fatigue, nervousness, depression, weakness, craving for salt and sweets, alcoholism, mental confusion, poor memory, and allergies. [11] Modern man lives in a stress-filled world, eating a diet that provides little adrenal support. It is not surprising that weak adrenal function is a common phenomenon.

Weak adrenals are often accompanied by symptoms associated with high insulin and low blood sugar. The adrenals are the buffer that prevents blood sugar levels from dropping excessively low when refined carbohydrates are consumed. Dr. Abram Hoffer observed that low blood sugar was often accompanied by dizziness, migraine and other headaches, muscle cramps and restless legs, swelling, anxiety, and depression. He believed many neuroses and psychological symptoms could be traced to poor diet and low blood sugar.[12]

The most natural solution for weakness of the adrenals is not to administer adrenal hormones, but rather to strengthen the glands so they are capable of functioning normally. The adrenal glands are strengthened by consuming adequate protein with meals and avoiding refined carbohydrates, caffeine, and emotional trauma. Supplements that support adrenal function include B complex vitamins, trace minerals, vitamin C complex, adrenal glandulars, phospholipids, and phytosterols. This same nutritional approach is beneficial for low blood sugar. Quality is important with any supplementation, but particularly so with regard to use of glandulars and essential fats.

SUGGESTIONS

- Avoid sugar and caffeine.
- Consume fresh raw foods and quality fats.
- Consume adequate protein and complex carbohydrate.
- Supplement with vitamins B complex and C.

High Blood Pressure and Blood Fats

SIGN

Elevated blood measurements of cholesterol, triglycerides, and blood pressure

SIGNIFICANCE

These elevated measurements are often associated with insulin resistance or "Syndrome X." Weight gain often accompanies insulin

The adrenals are the buffer that prevents blood sugar levels from dropping excessively low when refined carbohydrates are consumed.

resistance. If uncorrected, insulin resistance will often lead to the development of diabetes.

DISCUSSION

Dr. Jonathan Wright, one of America's leading nutritional physicians, pointed to the fact that physicians often fail to diagnose the insulin resistance problem and treat elevated cholesterol and blood pressure as separate entities. The elevated cholesterol is treated with medication (usually statin drugs) to lower cholesterol. The high blood pressure is treated with anti-hypertensive medications.

Not only do these medications fail to address the underlying problem, but they can have side effects of their own. Statin drugs interfere with the body's synthesis of CoQ10, a nutrient that protects the energy factories within the cells. Lack of CoQ10 can lead to heart damage. Anti-hypertensive medicines can wash important nutrients out of the body, including B complex vitamins, potassium, and magnesium, which should be replaced as deficiencies of these nutrients may increase the risk of heart problems.

Health agencies have been establishing health guidelines that suggest ever lower cholesterol and blood pressure levels. Placing these people on medications without establishing glucose tolerance is missing the mark. Physicians should be encouraged to test insulin resistance before suggesting medications. Dr. Wright suggested the glucose-tolerance-insulin-resistance test (GT-IRT).[13]

RELATED TOPIC

BEER BELLY
SYNDROME

SUGGESTIONS

- Avoid sugars—stevia is an excellent natural sweetener.

- Exercise regularly. Five or more times a week is ideal.

- Obtain all essential nutrients.

- Supplement with fish oils.

Joint and Muscle Pain

SIGN

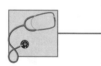

Constant nonspecific muscle and skeletal pain, or pain and discomfort when the sternum is pressed with thumb or forefinger (the latter is a sign of vitamin D deficiency).

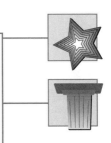

SIGNIFICANCE

Constant pain may indicate deficiency of vitamin D.

DISCUSSION

It has been known for some time that if brushing a child's hair elicits pain, vitamin D deficiency is indicated. Recent studies, however, indicate that lack of this vitamin may create much more pervasive and debilitating pain.[14]

Physician Gregory Plotnikoff examined 150 patients suffering with severe chronic pain in 2002. Ninety-three percent (140) were deficient in vitamin D. Less than 10% of these people were taking a vitamin supplement. Nine out of ten had been treated by a doctor for at least a year. None had been tested for deficiency of vitamin D.

Five of the patients in this study had no detectable vitamin D in their bodies. Their symptoms included low back pain, weakness, fatigue, insomnia, depression, headache, and chest pain. These patients had been prescribed non-steroidal anti-inflammatory drugs and antidepressants. Dr. Plotnikoff concluded that all patients with vitamin D deficiency are at risk of misdiagnosis.[15]

Those with vitamin D deficiency may be diagnosed with fibromyalgia. It is interesting that Dr. R. Paul St. Amand, author of *What Your Doctor May Not Tell You About Fibromyalgia*, noted that disordered phosphate metabolism is an underlying factor in fibromyalgia.[16] Overlooked in his discussion is the fact that inadequate vitamin D sets up a chain of events that alters calcium phosphate levels, making it impossible to properly mineralize bone. The rubbery matrix of bone then absorbs water, putting pressure on sensory pain fibers.[17]

Vitamin D deficiency contributes to poor bone development in youth and risk of bone fractures among the elderly. Young women were found to have the lowest levels of vitamin D. Almost half of those found vitamin D deficient (46%) were obtaining the recommended daily intake of the vitamin, suggesting that the recommendation is too low.[15]

The great majority of our vitamin D would come from sunlight if we were spending sufficient time outdoors. A dark skin or sunscreen (SPF 8) can block most of the vitamin D formation in the skin. Little vitamin D is formed in the skin during the winter months in the northern latitudes, even if considerable time is spent outdoors. Deficiency of this vitamin is undesirable as vitamin D inhibits cell growth, protecting from tumors, helps prevent autoimmune diseases, reduces blood pressure, and protects against heart disease.

All patients with vitamin D deficiency are at risk of misdiagnosis.

Almost half of those found vitamin D deficient (46%) were obtaining the recommended daily intake of the vitamin, suggesting that the recommendation is too low.

Deficiency of this vitamin is undesirable as vitamin D inhibits cell growth, protecting from tumors, helps prevent autoimmune diseases, reduces blood pressure, and protects against heart disease.

Dr. Amand's discussion of the disordered calcium and phosphate metabolism associated with fibromyalgia is very reminiscent of discussions of nanobacteria. Disordered calcium and phosphate metabolism is apparently contributed to by excess intake of sugar and phosphates, vitamin D excess or deficiency, and deficiencies of magnesium and vitamin B6.

Dr. Amand observed that those with fibromyalgia tend to have fingernails that break or peel. He wrote, "With each attack of what we now call fibromyalgia, new, excessive crystals are laid down at the nail root. As the nails grow out in layers similar to concentric rings of a tree, they chip when the defect reaches the tip. This is why the nails all seem to break at once."[16]

Dr. Amand concluded that accumulation of inorganic phosphate was a trigger for fibromyalgia symptoms. He wrote, "The increased and repetitive intake of carbohydrates causes equally frequent release of insulin. This hormone causes an increase in renal reabsorption of inorganic phosphate and promotes its uptake in a variety of cells throughout the body."[18] If inorganic phosphate proves to be a trigger for growth of nanobacteria it would explain why sugar makes fibromyalgia symptoms worse. Consumption of sodas loaded with phosphate might also prove to be a problem.

Dr. Amand made one other interesting observation. He felt fibromyalgia is a harbinger of osteoarthritis: "If fibromyalgia is allowed to progress unchecked, it is my experience that it will eventually lead to joint damage."[19] Dr. Amand found that medications that improve gout also improve fibromyalgia. It is of interest that vitamin C appears important in prevention of both gout (see PAIN IN THE BIG TOE) and osteoarthritis (see OSTEOARTHRITIS).

Fibromyalgia and chronic pain may be caused or aggravated by allergic responses, immune dysfunction, and repair deficits resulting from poor nutrition. This is the conclusion of a study conducted by Dr. Russell Jaffe and Dr. Patricia Deuster. Test subjects were evaluated for intolerance to foods and chemicals. Almost half the test subjects (17 out of 40) reacted to MSG. Other frequently reactive items included Candida albicans, caffeine, food coloring, chocolate, shrimp, dairy products, sulfites, xylene, yogurt, aspartames, BHA, cadmium, lead, Tylenol, sodium benzoate, and orange.

Patient compliance in taking the vitamin supplements and avoiding reactive items was a little under 90%. Nevertheless, after six months the treatment group "experienced 50% less pain, 70% less depression, 50% more energy, and 30% less stiffness." The control group had an increase in pain and depression while stiffness and energy remained the same.

One interesting aspect of this study was the observation that men and women with similar symptoms were given different diagnoses. Women were more likely to be diagnosed with fibromyalgia. Men were more likely to be diagnosed with multiple chemical sensitivity or chronic fatigue syndrome. Both men and women were suffering from a widespread dysfunction of nerves, hormones, and the immune system.[20]

Support for the ability of immune activation to cause severe pain is found in research that demonstrates that a chemical messenger (TNF) produced by the white blood cells (macrophages) causes severe muscle pain, loss of appetite, and fatigue "in a dose-response fashion."[21]

Allergic responses weaken the immune system because they elicit an immune response. The end result of strong allergic responses to foods or chemicals is that the immune system becomes distracted from its primary task of protecting the body from invading bacteria and viruses. Instead, the immune system attacks food remnants or chemical residues, creating inflammation and increased susceptibility to viral and bacterial attack.

SUGGESTIONS

- Obtain adequate exposure to sunlight (avoid burning).
- Reduce sugar and refined-carbohydrate consumption.
- Supplement with cod liver oil, particularly in the winter months.
- Supplement with all essential nutrients.
- Test for vitamin D deficiency.
- Test for food allergies.

The Pulse Test

SIGN

The pulse rate increases after eating a meal

SIGNIFICANCE

A pulse over 84 beats a minute after eating often indicates an allergic response.

RELATED TOPICS

ARTHRITIS (OSTEOARTHRITIS)

ARTHRITIS (RHEUMATOID)

KIDNEY STONES

PAIN IN THE BIG TOE

RICKETS

TARTAR ON THE TEETH

Men and women with similar symptoms are often given different diagnoses.

A pulse rate over 84 beats a minute strongly suggests an allergic response or an infection.

RELATED TOPICS

ALLERGIC SALUTE

MIGRAINE HEADACHE

NUMBNESS OF THE HANDS OR FEET

PUFFY, DARK, INFLAMED, OR WRINKLED UNDER THE EYES

DISCUSSION

Dr. Arthur Cocoa developed what has been called the "pulse test." Cocoa found the pulse would often rise when an individual consumed foods to which he or she was allergic. This rise in pulse rate is accompanied by the release of adrenal hormones, which enable the body to deal with allergens.

Dr. Cocoa found that under normal circumstances the pulse was rarely over 84 unless an individual was fighting an infection. He felt a pulse over 84 was strongly suggestive of allergic response. Conduct of the test required avoiding known allergens such as cigarette smoke at the time of the testing.[22]

Dr. Cocoa advised taking the pulse before meals and three times after a meal at one-half-hour intervals. The pulse should also be taken just before going to bed and just after waking up in the morning. Single food tests are the most revealing. Cocoa advised keeping a record of foods consumed.[23]

The pulse is taken by placing the hand in the lap with the palm up. The first two fingers of the right hand are placed about 3/4 of an inch above the wrist. Search for the arteries here.[24] The pulse must be counted for a full 60 seconds. Even minor variations in the pulse are significant and may indicate an allergic response.[25] Cocoa found many health conditions associated with foods using this technique. These problems included allergies, digestive pain, migraine, chest pain, and others.[26]

SUGGESTIONS

- Foods to which one is allergic should be avoided.

- Support adrenal function to improve tolerance.

- Test foods to see if pulse rate is altered.

Food for Thought

Postural hypotension is a common indicator of weak adrenal. Do you recall becoming dizzy more easily after a stressful life event?

Have you ever noticed changes in pulse rate after being exposed to some substance or food?

Do you experience more muscle or joint pain in the winter months than during the summer months? Have your muscles ever appeared to be more relaxed and comfortable after sunbathing?

Male and Female: *Provision for Posterity*

Iwas sitting in a hotel lobby in San Antonio when an older, distinguished-looking man entered the area where I was seated. Under his arm was a round pillow with a hole in the middle. Out of curiosity I asked about the pillow. He explained that he had gone through treatment for prostate cancer with radiation and was suffering radiation burns.

This led to a discussion of the increasing incidence of cancer. He suddenly became quite serious and said, "I am a veterinarian. I have practiced for many years and when I first began I never saw cancer in animals. Now people bring in their cats, dogs and even their birds and they all have cancer. Something has changed…something in the environment is very different."

I then proceeded to share with him what I had learned about the widespread worldwide pollution with hormone mimics. Many of our environmental exposures today are estrogenic in character, including many electromagnetic fields, plastics, pesticides, herbicides, pharmaceutical drugs, and surfactants in soaps. This estrogenic pollution is wreaking havoc in both animal and human populations. It is my belief that this kind of pollution is a major contributor to hormone-related cancers.

Increased exposure to hormone mimics is only the tip of the iceberg when considering the widespread environmental changes to which modern man has become habituated. Technology tends to move people away from sunlight. This chapter describes how inadequate exposure to light and deficiency of vitamin D increases the likelihood of developing breast and prostate cancer.

Lack of essential nutrients contributes to several conditions associated with one or the other of the sexes. Iodine appears to be essential for preventing lumps in the breasts of women. Zinc and essential fatty acids are important in

Estrogenic pollution is wreaking havoc in both animal and human populations.

Inadequate exposure to light and vitamin D deficiency increases the likelihood of developing breast and prostate cancer.

prevention of swelling of the prostate gland. Vitamin A may prevent heavy menstrual bleeding. Vitamin C and flavonoids may be particularly important in coping with hot flashes. The amino acid arginine may be significant for addressing the problem of impotence.

Breast Cancer

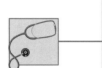

SIGN

A lump or growing mass in the breast

SIGNIFICANCE

Breast cancer is one of the most common cancers in women, and it often appears to be associated with excess estrogen exposure. Inadequate exposure to sunlight also increases risk of breast cancer.

DISCUSSION

Breast cancer is linked to increased exposure to estrogenic hormones and xenoestrogens, environmental pollutants that have an estrogen-like effect on the body. Hormone replacement therapy and exposure to organochlorine pesticides like DDT are known to increase the risk of breast cancer.[1] Women with breast cancer have elevated levels of these hormones and pesticides in their fat.[2] When Israel banned three organoclorine pesticides in 1978, breast cancer rates dropped by about 8% in the next few years when they should have risen as they did everywhere else in the technologically advanced world.

Natural estrogen-like substances (phytoestrogens) in plant foods may protect the breast to a certain degree by blocking the ability of more harmful synthetic estrogen-like substances such as DDT from activating the estrogen receptors in the breast tissues and causing abnormal cell growth.[3]

Hormone mimics that should be considered as risk factors for the development of breast cancer include not only exposure to pesticides and herbicides, but also exposure to strong electromagnetic fields, estrogenic surfactants in soaps, and estrogenic substances in plastics. The ability of fat cells in the body to produce estrogen should not be overlooked as a contributor to excessive bodily estrogen accumulation.

Cruciferous vegetables reduce the risk of breast cancer by directing the metabolism of estrogen in a pathway that is not harmful. This is referred to as sending estrogen down a pathway where it becomes "good" estrogen rather

Cruciferous vegetables reduce the risk of breast cancer by directing the metabolism of estrogen in a pathway that is not harmful.

Chapter 15 – Male and Female

than "bad" estrogen. The Southern Research Institute found that a cruciferous blend slowed breast cancer cell growth in culture by 37%.[4]

Flavonoids, the water-soluble coloring pigments in fruits and vegetables, dramatically slow the growth of breast cancer cells in culture. The Southern Research Institute found that one flavonoid blend slowed breast cancer cell growth in culture by an amazing 92%.[5] Carotenoids, the fat-soluble coloring pigments in fruits and vegetables also appear to help prevent breast cancer. The red pigment found in tomatoes, pink grapefruit, and watermelon called lycopene is one of the most potent of all antioxidants and has been shown to reduce both size and number of breast tumors in rats.[6]

The hormone issues associated with breast cancer are discussed in far greater detail in Dr. John Lee's excellent book entitled *What Your Doctor May Not Tell You About Breast Cancer: How Hormone Balance Can Help Save Your Life.*

RELATED TOPIC

BREAST LUMPS

SUGGESTIONS

- Avoid excessive exposure to estrogens, including xenoestrogens

- Consider use of progesterone if the ovaries are surgically removed.

- Consider alternatives to hysterectomy such as myomectomy to preserve progesterone production.

- Eat fish rich in omega-3 oils or supplement with fish oils.

- Eat richly-colored fresh fruits and vegetables or supplement with phytonutrients, including carotenoids, flavonoids, and cruciferous compounds.

- Supplement with quality oils from grains, legumes, and nuts.

- Use a good-quality multiple vitamin.

Breast Lumps

SIGN

Benign lumps in the breast of a woman

SIGNIFICANCE

These are often associated with excessive caffeine (methylxanthine) intake. Lack of iodine may contribute to the problem as well. Lumps

in the breast can make cancer detection more difficult. Iodine deficiency, if involved, may result in immune compromise.

DISCUSSION

The work of John Minton, M.D., demonstrated that avoidance of methylxanthines improved fibrocystic breasts. This involves avoiding sources of caffeine, including coffee, tea, chocolate, and sodas. Minton discovered that avoiding caffeine resulted in complete resolution of breast disease in 82.5% of participants in one study and significant improvement in 15%. Complete avoidance of methylxanthines resulted in 97.5% clinical benefit![7] A study of 48 pairs of twins found that the twins with fibrocystic breast disease consumed significantly more coffee.[8] Risk of fibrocystic breast disease increased in direct proportion to caffeine intake. Women who consumed 31 to 250 mg of caffeine a day had a 1.5-fold increase in risk of the condition. Women who consumed over 500 mg a day had a 2.3-fold increased risk of breast disease.[9]

Reducing fat intake lowers risk of fibrocystic breast disease. In one study of ten premenopausal women, all improved by reducing fat intake to 20% of total calories. The reduced fat intake reduced estradiol (a very powerful estrogen) by an average of 28%, estrone by 36%, and prolactin by 29%.[10] Many Americans have excessively high female hormone levels due to excessive weight gain or a diet containing excess fat. Reducing fat intake also appears to benefit prostate problems, which may also be associated with excess estrogen.

Dr. John Myers, an early nutrition pioneer, pointed to iodine as a central factor in the causation of fibrocystic breast disease. Myers found that he could spray an iodine solution on the mucous lining of a woman's vagina and observe a softening of her breast tissue within five minutes. Iodine is involved in keeping cholesterol fluid and eliminating excess cholesterol. The ovary of the woman is second only to the thyroid in its concentration of iodine.[11]

An iodine-dependent hormone called diiodotyrosine keeps the fats and cholesterol in the breast soft and in a fluid state. Myers found that administration of this hormone, and/or the administration of the trace elements iodine, zinc, manganese, copper, cobalt, and silver could soften the breasts within a short period of time. The amino acid tyrosine is also essential for the manufacture of diiodotyrosine.[11]

Iodine treatment has been used successfully to treat fibrocystic breasts.[12, 13] A good deal of research supports Myers contention that iodine is important for

Complete avoidance of methylxanthines may benefit fibrous breasts.

Reducing fat intake lowers risk of fibrocystic breast disease.

Iodine deficiency may be a contributing factor to fibrocystic breast disease.

Chapter 15 – Male and Female

this breast disorder. Induction of a fibrocystic breast disorder in rats was accomplished by giving them an iodine-blocking agent (sodium perchlorate). This makes one wonder if the widespread use of fluoride in toothpaste and drinking water might not contribute to breast disease. Fluoride is known to interfere with thyroid function and was once used to treat overactive thyroid. One also wonders if caffeine does not interfere with thyroid function or iodine metabolism in some way since it appears to be so intimately involved with fibrocystic breast disease.[14]

Not everyone tolerates iodine well. Myers was fond of Lugol's Iodine for treating fibrocystic breasts. One study found that 70% of those who used this solution had clinical improvement, although the rate of side effects was high. Molecular iodine appeared to be the most beneficial with the fewest side effects.[15] Kelp or sea vegetation is an excellent natural source of iodine and other trace minerals.

Dr. John Lee, a pioneer who improved our understanding of how hormone therapy works, reported that women with fibrocystic or lumpy breasts often have estrogen dominance. He found that progesterone supplementation for a few months would often alleviate the condition.[16] Progesterone is known to improve thyroid function.

Vitamin E is commonly recommended for fibrocystic breast disease. Several studies have indicated that it appears to result in improvement. Vitamin E supports progesterone function in the body. Iodine appears to work more effectively than vitamin E supplementation and may be more effective than progesterone.[17, 18]

SUGGESTIONS

- Avoid caffeine-containing foods and beverages.

- Avoid excessive fluoride intake.

- Supplement with a source of iodine if tolerated and give vitamin E a trial.

- Consider progesterone use if needed.

Iodine treatment has been used successfully to treat fibrocystic breasts.

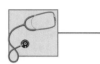

The majority of men in the United States over 50 years of age will develop benign prostatic hypertrophy.

Frequent Urination

SIGN

The need to urinate frequently, decreased urine flow, and the need to awake in the middle of the night to urinate (Scientific terms: benign prostatic hypertrophy, prostate cancer)

SIGNIFICANCE

These signs are often indicators of an enlarged prostate (benign prostatic hypertrophy) or prostate cancer. Elevated estrogen levels or exposure to chemicals with estrogenic effects may be causative factors. Inadequate exposure to sunlight or vitamin D deficiency increases the likelihood of developing prostate cancer.

DISCUSSION

The majority of men in the United States over 50 years of age will develop benign prostatic hypertrophy. The stream of urine begins to slow to a trickle. By the time this symptom begins to appear, the problem is frequently quite advanced, yet it is often the first indication of swelling of the prostate. A physician should be consulted as this symptom can be caused by either prostatic hypertrophy or prostate cancer.

The prevailing opinion among physicians at this time is that testosterone is responsible for prostatic hypertrophy, especially when it is converted to DHT (dihydrotestosterone). Medications have been developed to block the enzyme (5 alpha-reductase) that converts testosterone to DHT. The drug Proscar® functions in this way. Unfortunately, only a little over a third of the men who use Proscar® for a year experience any improvement in symptoms. About one in twenty users suffer side effects such as impotence and loss of sex drive. This medication does not appear to decrease the risk of prostate cancer.

A number of physicians, including Tiberius Reiter and George Debled, have treated prostatic hypertrophy with testosterone. They reported that this treatment actually resolved many cases of hypertrophy and seemed to provide protection against the later development of prostate cancer. This suggests that prostatic swelling strikes older men due to a drop in testosterone. These findings make sense since young men, overflowing with testosterone, rarely have problems with prostatic hypertrophy.

A cloud of uncertainty hangs over the issue of whether testosterone promotes the growth of prostate cancer once it exists. Natural testosterone has been widely used in treatment of prostatic hypertrophy and appears to be effective. Physicians who have worked with natural testosterone report satisfactory results with this approach.[19]

Estrogen, which normally rises in men as they age, may be a culprit. Weight gain tends to increase estrogen levels in both men and women. The epidemic of weight gain in the United States has been paralleled by increases in prostate cancer in men and breast cancer in women.

A wide range of nutrients are known to promote prostate health, including essential fatty acids, zinc, carotenoids, vitamin E, vitamin D, and selenium. Supplementation with essential fatty acids and zinc has a long history of safe and effective use in treating swollen prostate glands. Dr. Jonathan Wright emphasized the importance of using these nutrients as a priority over saw palmetto. He wrote, "The difference is simple: Both zinc and essential fatty acids are essential nutrients, while saw palmetto is not....we can die of either zinc or essential fatty-acid deficiencies; *we wouldn't die if we never swallowed even a microgram of saw palmetto.*"[20] There is a role for herbs like saw palmetto in treating prostatic hypertrophy, but nutrients should have a priority.

The carotenoid lycopene is a prostate superhero. One ten-year study of 48,000 health professionals found that men who consumed ten servings of lycopene-rich foods a week cut their risk of prostate cancer by half![21] Some studies have shown that lycopene may actually help the body fight prostate cancer after it has developed as well as preventing it. Lycopene is found in red foods, including tomato, pink grapefruit, and watermelon.

I encourage supplementation with a wide spectrum of carotenoids as found in foods. Different carotenoids have been shown to provide different kinds of protection to various parts of the body. High intake of a single carotenoid, such as lycopene, may depress levels of another member of the carotenoid family of nutrients, which provides a totally different kind of protection in a different part of the body.

Fish consumption reduces the risk of prostate cancer. A study in Sweden found that men who ate four servings of fish a week cut their risk of prostate cancer in half, and they were only one-third as likely to die of prostate cancer as men who did not eat fish. Researchers suspected the benefit came from the oils in the fish.[22]

The epidemic of weight gain in the United States has been paralleled by increases in prostate cancer in men and breast cancer in women.

Men who ate four servings of fish a week cut their risk of prostate cancer in half, and they were only one-third as likely to die of prostate cancer!

A number of sulfur-containing vegetables, including garlic, onion and broccoli, reduce the risk of prostate cancer.[23, 24] These foods tend to increase glutathione, the body's major antioxidant and thereby support what is called Phase II detoxification. The body has a twofold process of ridding itself of toxic substances such as pesticides. Firstly, they are made more soluble. This is called phase I detox. Unfortunately, this often makes them more toxic. It is crucial to eliminate these substances as rapidly as possible once they have undergone phase I detox, and this is accomplished with phase II detox. The body often rids itself of these unwanted substances by combining them with sulfur compounds and excreting them.[25] Sulfur-containing foods support this important function by providing the body with the sulfur it requires for detoxification.

The trace mineral selenium works along with sulfur compounds to support phase II detox and also plays an important role as an antioxidant. Intake of 200 mcg/day of selenium was shown in one study to reduce prostate cancer risk by 63%.[26]

Cruciferous vegetables play a very special role in prevention of prostate cancer and other prostate problems. One study found that consuming as few as three servings of cruciferous vegetables per week reduced prostate cancer risk by 41%. Cruciferous vegetables not only support phase II detox, but they also decrease a bad form of estrogen (16 alpha-hydroxy-estrogen) and increase a good form of estrogen (2-hydroxyestrogen). Most men with prostate cancer have increased levels of the bad estrogen.[27]

Studies suggest that men with the lowest levels of testosterone are at the greatest risk for developing prostate cancer and prostatic hypertrophy. Maintaining a healthy weight keeps testosterone elevated and estrogen low in men. Exposure to sunlight also increases testosterone in men in a very natural and safe manner, and this may be an important preventative against reduced testosterone levels as we age.[28] The elderly are known to obtain less exposure to sunlight than younger people.

Sunlight is powerful medicine when it comes to prevention of prostate (and breast) cancer. A study that divided men into four groups based on their exposure to sunlight found that those receiving the least sun exposure were *three times* more likely to develop prostate cancer. Those spending the most time in the sunlight also tended to develop prostate cancer almost *five years later* than those with the least exposure to sunlight (67.7 years vs. 72.1 years). Similar work suggests increased sun exposure or vitamin D supplementation might reduce incidence and death rate from breast cancer by 25% or more.[29]

Considerable research supports the use of plant sterols to improve symptoms of benign prostatic hypertrophy.[30] Plant sterols have an efficacy of their own, but they also appear to function by blunting the effects of cholesterol, which contributes to hypertrophy and speeds the growth of hormone-linked cancers. Phytosterols are quite protective against prostatic hypertrophy and may prove to be one of the best long-term preventatives for prostate problems.[31]

Phytosterols have reduced the rate of growth and spread of prostate cancer significantly in laboratory animals. Tumors were 40 to 43% smaller in animals given plant sterols as compared to animals receiving cholesterol. Cholesterol actually increased the rate of growth of prostate cancer cells while plant sterols reduced growth considerably—up to 70%.[32]

Legumes, including peanuts and soy, are excellent sources of phytosterols with anti-cancer properties.[33] The soybean appears to have a number of anti-cancer compounds present, including protease inhibitors, phytic acid, isoflavones, saponins, genistein, and phytosterols. These compounds appear to be particularly effective in reducing risk of colon, breast, and prostate cancers.[34]

Cells of the body have a double (bilayer) wall or membrane around them which is composed of whatever fats are available from the diet. Proper control and function of hormone chemistry is dependent to a large extent upon an adequate supply of essential lipids—particularly those available from grains and legumes. As long ago as 1959, researcher Paul Meynell wrote, "…the essential lipids control cell metabolism. They also determine the efficiency of those gonadal and adrenocortical hormones that have the most to do with the effective use of all classes of food for bodily nutrition."[35] Sex hormones, including testosterone, enable the body to build bone and muscle. Meynell's research led him to the conclusion that lipids played a key role in the normal function of these sex hormones.

Much more recently Dr. Jeffrey Bland wrote, "…over the past several years it has become increasingly clear that alterations in membrane lipid composition and membrane fluidity influence important cellular functions…The nature of the fatty acids within the phospholipid bilayer determines the physiochemical properties of membranes that, in turn, influence cellular functions, including hormone responsiveness."[36] Dr. Bland is saying that hormones cannot function normally if quality lipids are missing from the double-layered cell wall. Deficiency of quality fats and excessive consumption of junk fats may contribute to prostate cancer or speed its growth by interfering with normal sex hormone function.

Considerable research supports the use of plant sterols to improve symptoms of benign prostatic hypertrophy.

Cholesterol actually increased the rate of growth of prostate cancer cells while plant sterols reduced growth considerably—up to 70%.

SUGGESTIONS

- Consume carotenoids in foods and supplements (especially lycopene).

- Consume quality oils, including phytosterols and fish oils while avoiding excess cholesterol.

- Engage in reasonable sunbathing or assure adequate vitamin D intake from cod liver oil or other sources.

- Eat cruciferous and allium vegetables or supplement with these compounds.

- Use a basic multiple that includes zinc.

Heavy Menstrual Bleeding

SIGN

Abnormally heavy bleeding during the menstrual cycle (Scientific term: menorrhagia)

SIGNIFICANCE

Heavy menstrual bleeding contributes to iron deficiency. Vitamin A may remedy the condition.

DISCUSSION

Physicians often prescribe birth control pills for this condition, although vitamin A has been shown to substantially improve excessive menstrual bleeding for the majority of women. Lithgow and Politzer, the original researchers, used 50,000 units of vitamin A daily for 15 days.[37] Dr. Jonathan Wright reported similar benefits although he extended the intake for 30 days followed by a reduced intake thereafter.[38] Exercise caution with high intake of vitamin A if pregnancy is a possibility as this vitamin is believed to cause birth defects at fairly low levels of intake.

SUGGESTIONS

- Supplement with vitamin A if safe.

- Watch iron levels which may drop, creating anemia and increasing the severity of the condition. Supplement with iron if necessary.

Hot Flashes

SIGN

Sensations of flushing or feeling warm, sometimes accompanied by sweating in menopausal women

SIGNIFICANCE

Hot flashes result from fluctuating hormone levels during menopause.

DISCUSSION

Menopausal symptoms result from swings in hormone levels. In order to understand why American women have such a difficult time with menopause while such problems are rare among women in many other countries one needs to understand one basic fact: *estrogen levels in women in the United States are often far higher than those of women in many other parts of the world.* The relative change of hormone levels at menopause is therefore greater for American women. The greater the fluctuation in hormone levels, the greater the menopausal symptoms will tend to be.

The high estrogen levels of American women are caused by excessive body fat, poor nutrition, and lack of exercise. This situation is aggravated by exposure to hormone mimics (called xenoestrogens) released into the environment in the form of pesticides, herbicides, plastics, surfactants, and other chemicals. Ovulation that is accompanied by the release of progesterone protects a woman from many of the worst effects of elevated estrogen levels during the child-bearing years, but ovulation ceases at menopause. Progesterone production ceases almost totally at menopause while estrogen levels fall much less dramatically. An American woman at menopause may have an estrogen level higher than women of childbearing age in other parts of the world, while she has no counterbalancing progesterone. This scenario explains why progesterone supplementation will often alleviate menopausal symptoms—even though it is not a natural solution to the difficulties of menopause in the sense that this has never been practiced historically.

One of the characteristics of societies without a menopause problem is a lower estrogen level to begin with and a diet high in phytoestrogens or plant estrogens, which has a net effect of further lowering estrogen. Supplementation

The greater the fluctuation in hormone levels, the greater the menopausal symptoms will tend to be.

with plant estrogens such as soy and flavonoids will often alleviate menopausal symptoms. These weak estrogenic substances block some of the action of stronger estrogens produced within the body.

Flavonoids, water-soluble coloring pigments found in fruits and vegetables, offer a very special benefit for hot flashes. Not only are flavonoids weakly estrogenic, but they also work to improve functioning of the circulatory system—a key benefit where hot flashes are involved. In 1964 Charles Smith wrote that 1200 mg of flavonoids with an equal amount of vitamin C could alleviate hot flashes with remarkable effectiveness.[39] Flavonoids vary greatly in biological activity—some are much more effective than others.

Phospholipids and phytosterols, B complex vitamins, minerals including calcium and magnesium, and vitamin E all improve hormone balance and offer promise for hot flashes and menopausal symptoms. The liver is an important player in overall hormone balance and each of these nutrients plays a role in improving liver function. I vividly remember a woman who was suffering hot flashes around the clock. She began supplementing with the above nutrients and her hot flashes disappeared within a week. The B complex vitamins, in this instance, were supplied with brewer's yeast.

An important study on the use of brewer's yeast to treat premenstrual syndrome may have implications for menopause as well. Women were given a supplement with brewer's yeast (1,000 mg), magnesium (400 mg), vitamin B6 (1.5 mg), folic acid (.2 mg) vitamin E (12 mg), iron (20 mg), and copper (4 mg). This placebo-controlled, double-blind study found that 81% of the women using the brewer's yeast had reduced symptoms of PMS by the sixth month.

Dr. Alan Gaby considered brewer's yeast the primary reason for the improvement, possibly due to its wide range of nutrients and ability to suppress undesirable, and promote beneficial, intestinal bacteria. He wrote, "Women with PMS have been reported to have abnormal intestinal flora, which might be favorably affected by taking brewer's yeast." Since abnormal intestinal bacteria can cause reabsorption of estrogen the body is attempting to excrete, restoring normal intestinal flora might relieve various conditions that are related to hormone imbalance.[40] Fiber and acidophilus supplementation, as well as brewer's yeast, could be expected to encourage normal bowel function and promote better hormone balance.

Michael Holick, discoverer of the active form of vitamin D, pinpointed low serotonin as a trigger for PMS. Serotonin is a chemical messenger produced

Flavonoids, water-soluble coloring pigments found in fruits and vegetables, offer a very special benefit for hot flashes.

Phospholipids and phytosterols, B complex vitamins, minerals, and vitamin E all improve hormone balance and offer promise for hot flashes and menopausal symptoms.

from the amino acid tryptophan with the help of vitamin B6. Serotonin levels naturally drop prior to a woman's period. Some women have such low base levels of serotonin that this drop leaves insufficient amounts of this chemical messenger to maintain psychological health. Holick found bright light increased serotonin levels and reduced PMS symptoms by 76%.[41]

Dietary and lifestyle changes may also make menopause easier to survive. High intake of sugar and fat promotes weight gain and causes estrogen levels to spiral upwards. Exercise keeps weight down and lower weight is usually reflected in lower estrogen levels.

Millions of American women have been prematurely thrown into menopause, with the accompanying symptoms, by hysterectomies. Dr. Stanley West argued in his book *The Hysterectomy Hoax* that most hysterectomies are unnecessary. Myomectomy (surgical removal of uterine fibroids) is one available alternative.[42]

The ultimate solution for an easy transition through menopause is lower estrogen levels. A way of living that leads in this direction combines a diet high in vegetables rich in phytochemicals and fiber while low in fat and sugars with a reasonable amount of exercise. Reducing excessive estrogen levels offers many benefits, including improving sluggish circulation, decreasing risk of stroke and clotting, reducing mood swings by normalizing copper and zinc levels, decreasing risk of migraine, fibroids, endometriosis, and autoimmune diseases.[43]

Bright light increased serotonin levels and reduced PMS symptoms by 76%.

SUGGESTIONS

- Avoid excess sugar and fat intake.

- Consume a variety of seeds, beans, grains, and vegetables, which are rich in phytonutrients and fiber.

- Supplement with vitamins B complex and C with flavonoids to support hormone regulation.

- Supplement with vitamin E complex, calcium, magnesium and other minerals, essential fatty acids, and phytosterols.

Impotence

SIGN

Inability to achieve an erection

Impotence before sixty years of age is a risk indicator for development of heart disease later on.

SIGNIFICANCE

Impotence before sixty years of age is a risk indicator for development of heart disease later on. Impotence is often caused by diabetes. The older a man becomes, the greater the likelihood he will become impotent, although impotence usually results from disease rather than a natural consequence of aging.

DISCUSSION

A man's erection begins with secretion of acetylcholine, followed by release of a chemical messenger called nitric oxide. Lecithin is an excellent raw material for acetylcholine manufacture. The primary role acetylcholine plays in a man's performance is as a trigger for production of nitric oxide.

Viagra is one of the best-selling drugs of all time. It works by potentiating the activity of nitric oxide, which makes it possible for smooth muscles in the circulatory system and in the penis to relax. This chemical is made from an amino acid called L-arginine. Obtaining adequate intake of this amino acid not only offers possibility for ending impotence, but it also improves heart function and provides a wealth of other benefits.[44]

Benefits of arginine and nitric oxide

- ▸ Reduces blood pressure
- ▸ Keeps coronary arteries open
- ▸ Reduces risk of blood clots by acting as a blood thinner
- ▸ Helps the immune system kill bacteria and viruses
- ▸ Acts as a messenger molecule between nerve cells
- ▸ Makes breathing easier
- ▸ Functions as an antioxidant
- ▸ Reduces the risk of diabetes
- ▸ Stimulates production of human growth hormone

N.B.

Arginine supplementation may be undesirable in some circumstances. It may not be well tolerated by the migraine sufferer, where depression exists, and in autoimmune diseases.[44]

Arginine is known to be essential for herpes simplex viral replication. Restriction of arginine-containing foods such as nuts, chocolate, and gelatin, and supplementation with lysine, which is thought to compete with arginine, is sometimes quite effective in preventing viral outbreaks. Arginine, while it is

Chapter 15 — Male and Female

not just the herpes virus.

considered a nonessential amino acid, is sufficiently beneficial in most circumstances that one would not wish to significantly depress tissue levels.[45] Remember, however, that arginine may improve not only human reproduction, but also that of viruses and avoid too much of a good thing.

Garlic contains some arginine, but it also has the ability to increase nitric oxide activity apart from its arginine content. Garlic may be an option for obtaining additional nitric oxide activity in situations where arginine supplementation is not an option, as in severe viral infection.[46]

SUGGESTIONS

■ Supplement with arginine and lecithin.

■ Supplement with garlic.

Garlic may be an option for obtaining additional nitric oxide activity in situations where arginine supplementation is not an option, as in severe viral infection.

Food for Thought

Intake of large amounts of caffeine has been noted to alter perception. How does caffeine affect your perception of the world? Withdrawal from caffeine often results in a headache for several days. Have you ever experienced this?

What steps could be taken to reduce exposure to estrogenic substances found in pesticides, herbicides, plastics, and surfactants in soaps and cosmetics?

How does our society handle male and female health issues differently?

What part do economics and politics play in how health conditions and nutrition are addressed in the United States? What differences do you see between the way men and women relate to nutrition and health problems?

Conclusion: *The Journey Continues*

Many older people are familiar with the "Code Talkers" of World War II. The military called upon the Navajo Indians who have a complex tonal language to deliver secret messages on the battlefield. If it were not for the active and vital communications of these brave Navajo, the United States might have lost many battles during World War II. These Navajo speakers successfully transmitted military codes in their own language, which was so unintelligible to the Japanese that even their best linguists could not crack the code.

Our body has a universal "code talker" system with its own complex signs and symptoms. Any attempt to crack the body's complex biochemical code can be a daunting task. Still, I hope that I have presented a fair and balanced view of important nutritional insights and have brought a measure of preliminary understanding to the average person regarding how to apply these insights to one's life and experience.

We are fortunate to live at a time when nutritional testing for a wide range of abnormalities is available. This capability will only increase in the coming years. It is possible to examine how the body tolerates foods, how foods are digested, the strength or weakness of metabolic pathways, and how nutrients actually work in the body. We can also test toxic exposures in a number of ways. These are great advances in science and medicine.

Despite the great advances that have been made, health of the general population is deteriorating rapidly. One reason for this is that people often refuse to take an interest in their health until after they have lost it. Our disease-oriented medical system encourages this approach. One of the purposes

Despite the great advances that have been made, health of the general population is deteriorating rapidly.

of this book has been to create an interest and awareness of the need to improve health *prior* to the development of problems.

My choice of body signs is simply a tool to open the eyes to biomarkers—physical indicators that may result from neglect of proper nutrition. Millions of people see no connection between basic dietary or lifestyle habits and the development of conditions like obesity or chronic pain. Hopefully this book will result in a clearer understanding that there may indeed be a connection. I hope the reader walks away with several key nutritional principles.

Nutrients Work Together

Throughout this book I have emphasized that nutrients are linked together in a "chain" that makes life processes possible. Lack of an essential nutrient breaks the chain, impacting the use of other nutrients.

Our medical system has taught people to look for a single pill for a single symptom. Nutrients do not function in this manner. Throughout this book I have emphasized that nutrients are linked together in a "chain" that makes life processes possible. Lack of an essential nutrient breaks the chain, impacting the use of other nutrients. I have talked about the association of signs with specific nutrients, but in reality the goal of sound nutrition should be to obtain a daily intake of all essential nutrients.

Deficiencies of isolated nutrients are rarely found. The poor diets that fail to meet nutritional requirements often result in multiple nutritional gaps.

Deficiencies of isolated nutrients are rarely found. The poor diets that fail to meet nutritional requirements often result in multiple nutritional gaps. The best means of plugging these gaps is through use of a wide spectrum of nutrients from sources that are as natural as possible. The most important nutrients for any given individual will rarely be those receiving the most "glamorous" attention in the media. The most critical nutrients are those that are essential and are inadequately supplied in the diet.

Incomplete nutrition makes us susceptible to infection by bacteria and viruses. It also sets the stage for the development of degenerative diseases. No one would think of building a wall with holes in it, yet human beings routinely provide the body with an inadequate and incomplete supply of nutrients.

Nutritional Priorities

In place of a complete supply of essential nutrients people often purchase and utilize a wide spectrum of herbs, isolated nutrients, or the latest miracle substance being advertised by media "hype-meisters." Herbs have their place, as I have indicated in the pages of this book, but nutrients must have a priority. Cells *die* without essential nutrients, while such is not the case with herbs. Isolated nutrients will never produce the benefits of the complete spectrum of

Conclusion – The Journey Continues

essential nutrients. Miracle substances, even the most researched, will rarely produce the long-term health improvement associated with regular use of a well-rounded intake of essential nutrients. One of the messages of this book is, DON'T MAJOR IN MINORS: Don't focus on the use of one vitamin or herb to the neglect of all other essential nutrients.

Another area where priorities are misplaced is medications. Many people eagerly seek out medications, but are reticent to add essential nutrients to the diet. Medications do not build healthy cells. I recently met a woman who reduced her intake of medications from 17 to 3 after implementing a well-rounded supplement program and improving her diet. Many of her symptoms had been caused by tissue starvation for essential nutrients.

Structural Nutrients

Many leading researchers have come to the conclusion that the underlying nutrient problem today is an inadequate supply of quality oils, including omega-3 fats, phospholipids, and phytosterols. These quality fats have been largely stripped from foods because they spoil rapidly. In their place have been substituted oxidized or rancid fats, which rapidly deplete the body's antioxidant reserves and interfere with normal cellular and glandular functioning. Restoring these essential oils is central to reestablishing proper nutrient utilization. One study found that addition of phospholipids and phytosterols to the diet of laboratory animals improved overall nutrient utilization by 50%. Equally important are the omega-3 fish oils that govern the functioning of tissue hormones at the cellular level.

Quality oils are the primary building blocks of much of the body. All the cells of the body have lipid membranes. Very high-quality oils are the primary building blocks of brain and nerve cells. These oils have profound effects upon endocrine function and prostaglandin chemistry. These roles alone determine that the quality oils play a role in thinking and emotions, nutrient utilization or the lack of it, and the nature of inflammatory processes in the body. As I have indicated in the pages of this book, no nutritional approach that neglects the quality of the fats in the diet has established the proper nutritional priorities.

Not All Problems Are Nutritional

Finally, not all health problems have their origin in inadequate nutritional intake. A sizeable portion of this book has been dedicated to toxicological issues. Nutrition is an essential component of enabling the body to cope with toxic exposures, as discussed in these pages. The most profound means of coping with toxins is to avoid them.

There is a story of a man who sat on the edge of a river. A giant scorpion came up to him and asked to be taken across the river. The man refused, saying, "You will poison me with your stinger."

The scorpion assured the man that he would not sting him. The man finally relented and consented to carry the scorpion across the river. In the middle of the river the scorpion stung the man. The man said, "You promised you would not sting me!"

The scorpion replied, "What can I say? I am a scorpion!"

The modern industrialized world is filled with potentially dangerous substances capable of creating harm even when they do not appear to. In these pages I have discussed fluoride, mercury, pesticides, and estrogenic pollutants. Hopefully society will one day reach the point where the youngest and most vulnerable, as well as the rest of us, are protected from the most dangerous pollutants. Learn to identify toxic substances and take steps to assure that your family and friends avoid them.

Proactive or Reactive

There are two approaches to health-related issues. One is to treat our health as a precious commodity and do everything possible to preserve it or improve it. The alternative is to wait until health problems develop and then attempt to repair the problem. The health care model in America reminds one of a poem I learned as a child:

> *Humpty Dumpty sat on a wall:*
> *Humpty Dumpty had a great fall.*
> *All the King's horses and all the King's men*
> *Couldn't put Humpty Dumpty in his place again.*

It is tragic to see generations of people throwing away the most meaningful asset in life and not having the slightest idea why good health spreads its wings and flies from them. It only takes a few simple and easy steps to build vital health, yet most of us settle for mediocre or worse "disease care." Do we wish to plug the small hole now or clean the town after the dam bursts? Medical practices today have proven themselves to be the cleanup crew after the flood, yet we as individuals have the power to plug that small hole, catching the problem before the water engulfs our health, finances, and happiness.

A wise physician once encouraged a successful businessman to build a company selling nutritional products. He was heard saying, "Make these supplements available and you will be doing something sixteen times more important than we doctors do, because 'an ounce of prevention is worth a pound of cure!' " The primary goal of this book parallels this physician's remark. By recognizing problems at an early stage and preventing them through improved nutrition, we are taking decisive measures to safeguard ourselves not only from pain, suffering and palliative medicine, but also from extraordinary expenses.

We can choose to be old at 40 or old at 80. We can choose to live in the regret of "If I had only…" or the satisfaction of knowing "My priorities were correct." We all realize that we have to make wise choices, but willpower and discipline do not come easily for most of us.

This book is the beginning of a journey, not a destination. You can visit my website for further guidance, encouragement, and motivation for your journey. The afterword provides the information necessary to take this step.

I sincerely desire that this guidebook be a beacon of light that excites and inspires you to take action to fortify your physical well-being for an extended and satisfying life. Let each day ahead bring a clearer mind and a stronger body. May the potential you were born with be fully materialized. Most of all, may you enjoy the best of health each and every day.

Afterword

A Continuing Resource: www.imageawareness.com

ACCESS THE IMAGE AWARENESS WEB SITE FOR A WEALTH OF INFORMATION INCLUDING:

- ▶ Availability of other books and audiotapes
- ▶ Laboratories
- ▶ Newsletters on various topics
- ▶ Seminar scheduling
- ▶ Types of nutritional assessments

YOU CAN CONTRIBUTE TO THIS PROJECT

You are welcome to make contributions to a future edition of this volume. Either mail or email any information on body signs or biomarkers which you think worthwhile including. Be sure and include sources. Additional insights on the material presented in this volume are also welcome.

CONTACT INFORMATION

Email: mail@imageawareness.com

Image Awareness Corporation
1271 High Street
Auburn, CA 95603
(530) 823-7092

The Concept of Body Signs
Chapter 1

1. Balch, James, and Balch, Phyllis, *Prescription for Nutritional Healing*, Garden City, NY: Avery Publishing Group, 1997, 229.

2. Scudder, Samuel, Look at your fish. In Marlys Mayfield, *Thinking for Yourself: Developing Critical Thinking Skills Through Reading and Writing*, 2nd Ed., Wadsworth: Belmont, CA, 1994. Web: http://people.morrisville.edu/~snyderw/courses/natr252/agassiz.html.

3. Selye, Hans, They all looked sick to me, *Human Nature*, February 1978; 58.

4. Selye, Hans, *The Stress of Life*, New York: McGraw-Hill, 1956, 14, 31, 176.

5. Selye, plates 1–7, 174.

6. Barthes, Roland; Carter, Angela; Brodbeck, Didier; and Baltrusaitis, Jurgis, A rose is a nose is a rose, *FMR*, January/February 1987; 25–62. Craig, Diana, *The Life and Works of Arcimboldo*, Bristol, Great Britain: Parragon Book Service, Ltd., 1996.

7. Cheraskin, E.; Ringsdorf, W. M., Jr.; and Brecher, Arline, *Psychodietetics*, New York: Bantam Books, 1976, 152–153.

8. Williams, Roger, *Nutrition Against Disease*, New York: Pitman Publishing Corporation, 1971, 21.

9. Bland, Jeffrey, *Genetic Nutritioneering*, Los Angeles: Keats Publishing Co., 1999.

10. Sheldon, William H., *The Varieties of Human Physique*, New York: Harper, 1940; and *The Varieties of Human Temperament: A Psychology of Constitutional Differences*, New York: Harper, 1941.

11. Peshek, Robert, *Student's Manual for Balancing Body Chemistry with Nutrition*, Riverside, CA: Color Coded Systems, 1977, 68.

12. Abravanel, Elliot, and King, Elizabeth, *Dr. Abravanel's Body Type Diet and Lifetime Nutrition Plan*, New York: Bantam, 1983, 21–34.

13. Price, Westin, *Nutrition and Physical Degeneration*, Santa Monica, CA: The Price Pottenger Nutrition Foundation, Inc., 1975, *xvii*.

14. Price, 3, 13, 27.

15. Price, 38–39.

16. Pottenger, Jr., Francis M., *Pottenger's Cats: A Study in Nutrition*, edited by Elaine Pottenger with Robert T. Pottenger, Jr., La Mesa, CA: Price-Pottenger Nutrition Foundation, 1983.

17. Pottenger, Francis M. Jr., The effect of heat-processed foods and metabolized vitamin D milk on the dentofacial structures of experimental animals, *American Journal of Orthodontics and Oral Surgery*, 1946; 32(8): 467–485.

Body Shape
Chapter 2

1. Eades, Michael, and Eades, Mary, *Protein Power*, New York: Bantam Books, 1996, 137–8.

2. Stranges, Saverio, et al, Body fat distribution, relative weight, and liver enzyme levels: A population-based study, *Journal of Hepatology*, March 2004; 39(3): 754–763. Potbelly: It's strongly linked to liver damage, *USA Weekend*, Aug. 13–15, 2004; 10.

3. Reaven, Gerald, *Syndrome X*, New York: Simon & Schuster, 2000, 17–22.

4. Pizzorno, Joseph E., Jr., and Murray, Michael T., *Textbook of Natural Medicine*, Vol. 2, New York: Churchill Livingstone, 1999, 1429.

5. Obesity-breakfast, *Nutrition Week*, March 1, 1996; 7. Ortega, R. M., et al, Associations between obesity, breakfast-time food habits and intake of energy and nutrients in a group of elderly Madrid residents, *Journal of the American College of Nutrition*, February, 1996; 15(1): 65–72.

6. Stitt, Paul A., *Fighting the Food Giants*, Manitowoc, WI: Natural Press, 1981, 156. Subsequently renamed *Beating the Food Giants*.

7. Geiselman, Paula, and Novin, D., Sugar infusion can enhance feeding, *Science* 1982; 218: 490–491. Geiselman, Paula, Feeding patterns following normal ingestion and intragastric infusion of glucose, fructose, and galactose in the rabbit, *Nutrition and Behavior* 1985; 2: 175–188.

8. Budwig, Johanna, *Flax Oil as a True Aid Against Arthritis, Heart Infarction, Cancer, and Other Diseases*, Vancouver, Canada: Apple Publishing Company, 1994, 33.

9. Blaylock, Russell L., *Excitotoxins: The Taste that Kills*, Santa Fe, New Mexico, Health Press, 1995, xx.

10. You can win for losing: Truth about dieting, *Consumer Reports*, June 2002; 26–31.

11. Mandell, Marshall, and Scanlon, Lynne, *Dr. Mandell's 5-Day Allergy Relief System*, New York: Thomas Crowell, 1979, 108–109.

12. Lock, C., A toxic side of weight loss, *Science News*, July 17, 2004; 35.

13. Raloff, J., Inflammatory fat: Unraveling the injurious biology of obesity, *Science News*, Feb. 28, 2004; 165(9): 139.

14. Hitt, Emma, Alzheimer's may be linked to body shape, *Reuters*, Atlanta, October 25, 2001. Moceri, Victoria, Larson, Eric, et al, Blood pressure, BMI, waist-to-hip ratio and Alzheimer's disease, 129th Annual Meeting of APHA (American Public Health Association), October 24, 2001.

15. Luchsinger, J. A., Mayeux, R., et al, Hyperinsulinemia and risk of Alzheimer's disease, *Neurology*, October 2004; 63(1 of 2): 1187–1192.

16. Zandi, Peter, Ph. D., et al, Reduced risk of Alzheimer's disease in users of antioxidant vitamin supplements, *Archives of Neurology*, January 2004; 61: 82.

17. Maugh, Thomas, A new marker for diabetes, *Science*, Feb. 5, 1982; 215: 651.

18. Schulze, M. B., Manson, J. E., et al., Sweetened beverages, weight gain, and incidence of type 2 diabetes in young and middle-aged women, *Journal of the American Medical Association*, August 25, 2004; 292(8): 927–934.

19. Apovian, C. M., Sweetened soft drinks, obesity, and type 2 diabetes, *Journal of the American Medical Association*, August 25, 2004; 292(8): 978–979.

20. Soft drinks implicated in type 2 diabetes, *The Clinical Advisor*, October 2004; 13.

21. Lazarus, S. A.; Bowen, K.; and Gard, M. L., Tomato juice and platelet aggregation in type 2 diabetes, *Journal of the American Medical Association*, August 18, 2004; 292(7); 805–6.

22. Raloff, Janet, D., What's enough? Many people need much more, *Science News*, October 16, 2004; 166: 248.

Hair
Chapter 3

1. Marlowe, Mike, Ph.D., et al, Hair trace element content of violence-prone male children, *Journal of Advancement in Medicine*, Spring 1994; 7(1): 5.

2. Tuthill, Robert W., Hair lead levels related to children's classroom attention-deficit behavior, *Archives of Environmental Health*, May/June, 1996; 51(3): 214–220.

3. Sohler, Arthur; Kruesi, Marcus; and Pfeiffer, Carl, Blood lead levels in psychiatric outpatients reduced by zinc and vitamin C, *Journal of Orthomolecular Psychiatry*, 1977; 6(8): 272–76.

4. Lesko, Samuel M., M.D., et al, A case-controlled study of baldness in relation to myocardial infarction in men, *Journal of the American Medical Association*, February 24, 1993; 269(8): 998–1003.

5. Schnohr, P.; Lange, P.; Nyboe, J.; Appleyard, M.; Jensen, G., Gray hair, baldness, and wrinkles in relation to myocardial infarction: The Copenhagen City Heart Study, *American Heart Journal*, Nov. 1995; 130(5): 1003–1010.

6. Roberts, Janet L., Examining the etiology of telogen effluvium in pre- and postmenopausal women: A chart review study, Conference Presentation #157, European Hair Research Society meeting, Tokyo, 2001.

7. Prendiville, Julie S., and Manfredi, Liliana N., Skin signs of nutritional disorders, *Seminars in Dermatology*, March 1992; 11(1): 88–97.

8. Wise, Robert P., et al, Hair loss after routine immunizations, *Journal of the American Medical Association*, Oct. 8, 1997; 278(14): 1176–1178.

9. Blaylock, Russell, *Health and Nutrition Secrets*, Albuquerque, NM: Health Press, 2002, 157.

10. Rudin, Donald, and Felix, Clara, *Omega-3 Oils*, Garden City, NY: Avery Publishing Group, 1996, 9.

11. Schmidt, Michael, *Smart Fats*, Berkeley, CA: Frog, Ltd., 1997, 59–71.

12. Wright, Jonathan, *Dr. Wright's Guide to Healing with Nutrition*, Emmaus, PA: Rodale Press, 1984, 8.

13. Chase, Deborah, *The Medically Based No-Nonsense Beauty Book*, New York: Pocket Books, 1975, 165.

14. John Yudkin, Sugar and Disease, *Nature*, Aug. 25, 1972 and Sept. 22, 1972; 239.

15. Chase, Deborah, see note 13, 165.

16. Kaaks, Rudolf; Lukanova, Annekatrin; and Kurzer, Mindy S., Obesity, endogenous hormones, and endometrial cancer risk, *Cancer Epidemiology Biomarkers & Prevention*, December 2002; 11: 1531–1543.

17. Scrimshaw, N. S., and Behar, M., Malnutrition in young children, *Science*, 1961; 133: 2039.

18. Hoffer, Abram, and Walker, Morton, *Putting It All Together: the New Orthomolecular Nutrition*, New Canaan, CT: Keats Publishing Co., 1996, 74–75.

19. Libby, Alfred F., and Stone, Irwin, The hypoascorbemia-kwashiorkor approach to drug addiction therapy: A pilot study, *Journal of Orthomolecular Psychiatry*, 1977; 6(4): 300–308. Scher, Jordan, Rice, Harry, et al, Massive vitamin C as an adjunct in methadone maintenance and detoxification, *Orthomolecular Psychiatry*, 1976; 5(3): 191-198.

20. Butler, Ross; Davies, Michael; Gehling, Neil; and Grant, Allan, The effect of preloads of amino acid on short-term satiety, *American Journal of Clinical Nutrition*, October 1981; 2045–47.

21. Colgan, Michael, *Optimum Sports Nutrition*, New York: Advanced Research Press, 1993, 159–165.

22. Rosen, Clifford, Premature graying of hair is a risk factor for osteopenia, *Journal of Clinical Endocrinology and Metabolism*, 1994; 79(3): 854–857.

 Eyes and Forehead
Chapter 4

1. Dufty, William, and Nyoiti, Sakurazawa, *You Are All Sanpaku*, New Hyde Park, NY: University Books, 1965, 70.

2. Dufty, 10–12.

3. Hirschhorn, Norbert; Feldman, Robert G.; and Greaves, Ian, Lincoln's blue pills: Did our 16th president suffer from mercury poisoning? *Perspectives in Biology and Medicine*, Summer 2001; 44(3): 315–332.

4. *Newsweek*, April 1981.

5. *Proverbs* 23: 29–30 (NKJV).

6. Cunningham, John J., Ph.D., et al, Vitamin C: An aldose reductase inhibitor that normalizes erythrocyte sorbitol in insulin-dependent diabetes mellitus, *Journal of the American College of Nutrition*, 1994; 13(4): 344–350.

7. Vinson, J. A.; Courey, B. S.; and Maro, N. P., Comparison of two forms of vitamin C on galactose cataracts, *Nutrition Research*, 1992; 12: 915–922.

8. Jacques, P. F., and Chylack, L. T., Jr., Epidemiologic evidence of a role for the antioxidant vitamins and carotenoids in cataract prevention, *American Journal of Clinical Nutrition*, Jan 1991; 53(1 Suppl): 352S–5S.

9. Wright, Jonathan, *Dr. Wright's Guide to Healing with Nutrition*, Emmaus, PA: Rodale Press, 1984, 9.

10. Lewis, Myron, *RDA*, Westport, CT: Lewis Laboratories, LTD, 1.

11. Oxholm, P.; Asmussen, K.; Wiik, A.; Horrobin, D. F., Essential fatty acid status in cell membranes and plasma of patients with primary Sjogren's syndrome. Correlations to clinical and immunologic variables using a new model for classification and assessment of disease manifestations, *Prostaglandins, Leukotrienes, and Essential Fatty Acids*, Oct 1998; 59(4): 239–45.

12. Khraishi, Majed M., et al, Inclusion body myositis in association with vitamin B12 deficiency and Sjogren's syndrome, *Journal of Rheumatology*, 1992; 19(2): 306–309.

13. Lee, John, That's a good question, *The John R. Lee, M.D., Medical Letter*, October 1998; 7.

14. Tsubota, Kazuo, M.D., and Nakamori, Katsu, Ph.D., Eyes and video display terminals, *New England Journal of Medicine*, February 25, 1993; 328(8): 584.

15. Augustin, Albert, J., Oxidative reactions in the tear fluid of patients suffering from dry eyes, *Graefe's Archive for Clinical and Experimental Ophthalmology*, 1995; 233: 694–698.

16. Wright, Jonathan, see note 9, 9.

17. Floaters, *University of California, Berkeley, Wellness Letter*, April 1988; 4(7): 7.

18. Trujillo, Nelson P., and Warthin, Thomas A., The frowning sign: Multiple forehead furrows in peptic ulcer, *Journal of the American Medical Association*, August 5, 1983; 218.

19. Blaser, Martin J., The bacteria behind ulcers, *Scientific American*, February 1996; 104–7.

20. Giannella, Ralph; Broitman, Selwyn; and Zamcheck, Norman, Influence of gastric acidity on bacterial and parasitic enteric infections, *Annals of Internal Medicine*, 1973; 78: 272.

21. Ruddell, W. S. J., Gastric-juice nitrite, *Lancet*, November 13, 1976; 7994.

22. Fahey, Jed W., Haristoy, Xavier, et al, Sulforaphane inhibits extracellular, intracellular, and antibiotic-resistant strains of *Helicobacter pylori* and prevents benzo[a]pyrene-induced stomach tumors, *Proceedings of the National Academy of Sciences*, May 28, 2002; 99(11): 7610–7615.

23. Sivam, G. P., et al, *Helicobacter pylori*—In vitro susceptibility to garlic (Allium sativum) extract, *Nutrition and Cancer* 1997; 27: 118–121.

24. Al-Habbal, M. J.; Al-Habbal, Z.; Huwex, F. U., A double-blind controlled clinical trial of mastic and placebo in the treatment of duodenal ulcer. *Clinical and Experimental Pharmacology and Physiology* 1984; 11: 541–4.

25. Tovey, F. I., et al, Diet: Its role in the genesis of peptic ulceration, *Digestive Diseases*, 1989; 7: 309–323.

26. Ringsdorf, Cheraskin, and Ramsay, R., Sucrose, neutrophilic phagocytosis, and resistance to disease, *Dental Survey*, December, 1976; 52(12): 46–48.

27. Cisternino, A. M., and Freudenheim, J., Diet and duodenal ulcer, *Digest Liver Dis*, 2000; 32: 468–472.

28. Cohen, M. M., Duncan, A. M., Ascorbic acid nutrition in gastroduodenal disorders, *British Medical Journal*, December 2, 1967; 4: 516–518.

29. Segal, I., et al, Dietary factors associated with duodenal ulcer, *South African Medical Journal*, 1991; 32(4): 456.

30. Matushevskaia, V. N., Shakhovskaia, A. K., et al, Optimization of dietary fat composition in erosive and ulcerative diseases of the gastroduodenal area, *Voprosy Pitaniia*, 1996; 6: 35–37.

31. Batmanghlidj, F., *Your Body's Many Cries for Water*, Falls Church, VA: Global Health Solutions, 1992, 35–36.

32. Young, Richard W., personal communication dated February 12, 1996. Details of Richard Young's work are available through his publications: Solar radiation and age-related macular degeneration, *Survey of Ophthalmology* 1988; 32: 252–269; and The family of sunlight-related eye diseases, *Optometry and Vision Science*, 71(2): 125–144.

33. Schalch, Wolfgang, Carotenoids in the retina—A review of their possible role in preventing or limiting damage caused by light and oxygen, *Free Radicals and Aging*, Basel, Switzerland: Birkhauser Verlag, 1992, 280–298.

34. Gao, Xiangqun, and Talalay, Paul, Induction of phase 2 genes by sulforaphane protects retinal pigment epithelial cells against photooxidative damage, *Proceedings of the National Academy of Sciences*, July 13, 2004; 101(28): 10446–10451.

35. Cho, E., et al, Prospective study of dietary fat and the risk of age-related macular degeneration, *American Journal of Clinical Nutrition*, February 2001; 73(2): 209–218.

36. Age-Related Eye Disease Study Research Group, A randomized, placebo-controlled, clinical trial of high-dose supplementation with vitamins C and E, beta carotene, and zinc for age-related macular degeneration and vision loss, *Archives of Ophthalmology* 2001; 119: 1417–1436.

37. Wright, Jonathan, Macular degeneration: Another link to digestion, *Nutrition & Healing*, March 2001, 8(3): 8. Age-Related Eye Disease Study Research Group, Risk factors associated with age-related macular degeneration, *Ophthalmology* December 2000; 107(12): 2224–2232.

38. Yudkin, John, *Sweet and Dangerous*, New York: Bantam Books, 1979, 132–135.

39. Cordain, Loren; Eaton, S. Boyd; Miller, Jennie; Lindeberg, Staffan; and Jensen, Clark, An evolutionary analysis of the aetiology and pathogenesis of juvenile-onset myopia, *Acta Ophthalmologica Scandinavica* 2002; 80: 125–135.

40. Latham, Michael; McGandy, Robert; McCann, Mary; and Stare, Frederick, *Scope Manual on Nutrition*, Kalamazoo, MI: The Upjohn Company, 1975, 37–38.

41. Knapp, Arthur, Vitamin D and retinitis pigmentosa, *Journal of the International Academy of Preventative Medicine*, July 1977; 4(1): 58. Wright, Jonathan, Clinical Tip 3: Vitamin D and retinitis pigmentosa, *Nutrition & Healing*, May 1998; 5(5): 9.

42. Rapp, Doris J., Clinical ecology: Recognition and treatment of unsuspected food and environmental allergies, *The International Journal for Biosocial Research*, 1981; 2(1–9): 35.

43. Nield, Linda, M.D., Milk intolerance presenting solely as periorbital edema, *Clinical Pediatrics*, May 1995; 265–267.

44. Wright, Jonathan, Test yourself for hidden food allergies just by checking your pulse and weight, *Nutrition & Healing*, May 2003; 10(5): 6.

45. Price, Sylvia and Wilson, Lorraine, *Pathophysiology: Clinical Concepts of Disease Processes*, New York: McGraw-Hill, 1982, 112.

46. Peacock, Lamar, M.D. et al, Dark circles: Allergic shiners, *Cortlandt Forum*, April 1992; 112: 50.

47. Blepharitis, *Dorland's Illustrated Medical Dictionary*, 26th Ed., Philadelphia: W. B. Saunders, 1985, 175.

48. Andrews, G. C.; Post, C. F.; and Domonkos, A. N., Seborrheic dermatitis: Supplemental treatment with vitamin B12, *New York State Medical Journal*, 1950; 50: 1921–5.

49. Gilman, Alfred; Goodman, Louis; and Gilman, Alfred, *The Pharmacological Basis of Therapeutics*, New York: MacMillan, 1980, 1566.

50. Goodheart, George, Postural hypotension and functional hypoadrenia, In Peshek, Robert, *Balancing Body Chemistry with Nutrition*, Riverside, CA: Color Coded Systems, 1977, 144. Goodheart, George, Postural hypotension and functional hypoadrenia, *The Digest of Chiropractic Economics*, May–June 1965; 7 (6).

51. *Dorland's Illustrated Medical Dictionary*, 26th Ed., Philadelphia: W. B. Saunders Company, 1985, 746.

52. Ershoff, Benjamin, Beneficial effect of liver feeding on swimming capacity of rats in cold water, *Proceedings of the Society for Experimental Biology and Medicine*, 1957; 77: 488–491.

53. Brown, J., *Stein and Day International Medical Encyclopedia*, New York: Stein and Day, 1971, 325.

54. Williams, Roger, *Nutrition Against Disease*, New York: Pitman Publishing Co., 1971, 164–175.

55. Hart, Archibald, *Hidden Link Between Adrenalin and Stress*, Waco, TX: Word Books, 1986, 14.

 Nose and Ears
Chapter 5

1. Krohn, Jacqueline, *The Whole Way to Natural Detoxification*, Vancouver, B.C.: Hartley & Marks Publishers, Inc., 1996, 55.

2. Price, Sylvia and Wilson, Lorraine, *Pathophysiology: Clinical Concepts of Disease Processes*, New York: McGraw-Hill, 1982, 112.

3. Rapp, Doris, Recognition and treatment of allergies, *International Journal for Biosocial Research*, 1981; 2(1–9): 34.

4. Linday, L. A., Dolitsky, J. N., et al, Study tests nutrients' role in reducing ear infections, *Annals of Otology, Rhinology, and Laryngology*, July 2002; 111(7): Part 1, 642–652.

5. Schmidt, Michael A., *Childhood Ear Infections*, Berkeley, CA: North Atlantic Books, 1990, 102–103.

6. Nsouli, T. M., M.D., et al, Role of food allergy in serous otitis media, *Annals of Allergy*, September 1994; 73(3): 215–219.

7. Treating allergies early can reduce later toll, *Family Practice News*, November 15–30, 1990; 20.

8. Sassen, Maryvonne L., M.D., et al, Breast feeding and acute otitis media, *American Journal of Otolaryngology*, September–October, 1994; 15(5): 351–357.

9. Passwater, Richard, *Supernutrition for Healthy Hearts*, New York: Dial Press, 1977, 307–310. Study confirms link between earlobe crease, cardiac risk, *Family Practice News*, March 15, 1992; 38. *American Journal of Medicine*, 1991; 91: 247–254.

10. Pearson, Durk, and Shaw, Sandy, *Life Extension*, New York: Warner Books, 1982, 323–325.

11. Wyre, H. W., The diagonal earlobe crease: A cutaneous manifestation of coronary artery disease, *Cutis*, March 1979; 328–331.

12. Ishii, Toshiharu, M.D., et al, Earlobe crease and atherosclerosis: An autopsy study, *Journal of the American Geriatric Society*, August 1990; 38(8): 371–376.

13 McCully, Kilmer, *The Homocysteine Revolution*, New Canaan, CT: Keats Publishing Co., 1997, 2–10.

14. McCully, 53–67.

15. Smith, Ronald, *Nutrition, Hypertension & Cardiovascular Disease*, Portland, Oregon: The Lyncean Press, 1989, 15.

16. Ford, Robert S., *Stale Food vs. Fresh Food*, Pascagoula, MS: Magnolia Laboratory, 1977.

17. Rath, Matthias, *Eradicating Heart Disease*, San Francisco: Health Now, 1993, 57.

18. Rojas, C., et al, Effect of vitamin C on antioxidants, lipid peroxidation, and GSH system in the normal guinea pig heart, *Journal of Nutritional Science and Vitaminology*, 1994; 40: 411–420.

19. Hertog, Michael G. L., et al, Dietary antioxidant flavonoids and risk of coronary heart disease: The Zutphen Elderly Study, *Lancet*, October 23, 1993; 342: 1007–1011.

20. Mann, Denise, Purple grape juice, wine and beer all cardioprotective, *Medical Tribune*, May 1, 1997; 26.

21. Ishikawa, Toshitsugu, et al, Effect of tea flavonoid supplementation on the susceptibility of low-density lipoprotein to oxidative modification, *American Journal of Clinical Nutrition*, 1997; 66: 261–266.

22. Murray, Michael, *Encyclopedia of Nutritional Supplements*, Rocklin, CA: Prima Publishing, 1996, 323.

23. Esterbauer, H., et al, Vitamin E and atherosclerosis—An overview, In Mino, Makoto, et al, *Vitamin E—Its Usefulness in Health and in Curing Diseases*, Tokyo: Japan Science and Societies Press, 1993, 233–241.

24. Finding that vitamin E lowers heart attack risk stuns doctors, *Sacramento Bee*, March 26, 1996; A6.

25. Rubin, Daniel, Tocotrienols: Their effects on plasma lipids and regulation of cell division, *Focus*, Hayward, CA: Allergy Research Group, September/October 1998, 4.

26. Carughi, Arianna, and Hooper, Fred, Plasma carotenoid concentrations before and after supplementation with a carotenoid mixture, *American Journal of Clinical Nutrition* 1994; 59; 896–9.

27. Fackelmann, K. A. Beta carotene may slow artery disease, *Science News*, 38: 308.

28. Dixon, Zisca R., Burri, Betty, et al., Effects of a carotene-deficient diet on measures of oxidative susceptibility and superoxide dismutase activity in adult women, *Free Radical Biology and Medicine*, 1994; 17(6): 537–544.

29. Wagner, Richard F., Jr., et al., Ear-canal hair and the earlobe crease as predictors for coronary-artery disease, *The New England Journal of Medicine*, Nov. 15, 1984; 1318.

30. Wright, Jonathan V., and Lenard, Lane, *Maximize Your Vitality and Potency*, Petaluma, CA: Smart Publications, 1999, 119–152, 128. See also, Shippen, Eugene, and Fryer, William, *The Testosterone Syndrome*, New York: M. Evans and Company, Inc., 1998.

31. Ohinata, Y., Yamasoba, T., et al, Glutathione limits noise-induced hearing loss, *Hearing Research*, 2000; 146: 28–34.

32. Scheibe, F.; Haupt, H.; Ising, H., Preventive effect of magnesium supplement on noise-induced hearing loss in the guinea pig, *European Archives of Oto-Rhino-Laryngology*, 2000; 257: 10–16.

33. Houston, D. K., et al, Age-related hearing loss, vitamin B12, and folate in elderly women, *American Journal of Clinical Nutrition*, 1999; 69: 564–571.

34. Bahadori, Robert S., M.D., and Bohne, Barbara A., Ph.D., Adverse effects of noise on hearing, *American Family Physician*, April 1993; 1219–1226.

35. Garry, James, Upper airway compromise and musculo-skeletal dysfunction of the head and neck (MSD), *IAACN Scientific Symposium*, Sept. 6–8, 1996, San Diego, CA.

36. Price, Westin, *Nutrition and Physical Degeneration*, Santa Monica, CA: Price Pottenger Nutrition Foundation, 1975, 359.

37. Pottenger, Francis M., *Pottenger's Cats*, La Mesa, CA: Price-Pottenger Nutrition Foundation, 1983, 23–25.

38. Garry, James, Environmental and iatrogenic influences on orofacial development leading to musculoskeletal dysfunctions of the head and neck (TMJ disorders), IAACN Scientific Symposium, Sept. 6–8, 1996, San Diego, CA.

39. Davison, H. M., The role of food sensitivity in nasal allergy, *Annals of Allergy*, September–October 1951; 568–572.

40. Meggs, William Joel, Rhinolaryngoscopic examination of patients with multiple chemical sensitivity syndrome, *Archives of Environmental Health*, January/February 1993; 48(1): 14–18.

41. Levine, Stephen, and Kidd, Parris, *Antioxidant Adaptation*, San Leandro, CA: Allergy Research Group, 1985, Foreword.

42. Westerveld, Gerrit-Jan, M.D., et al, Antioxidant levels in the nasal mucosa of patients with chronic sinusitis and healthy controls, *Archives of Otolaryngology Head and Neck Surgery*, February, 1997; 123: 201–204.

43. Rangi, S. P., Serwonska, M. H., et al, Suppression by ingested eicosapentaenoic acid of the increases in nasal mucosal blood flow and eosinophilia of ryegrass-allergic reactions, *Journal of Allergy Clinical Immunology*, February 1990; 85(2): 484–489.

44. Jones, A. H., Intranasal xylitol, recurrent otitis media, and asthma: Report of three cases, *Clinical Practice Alternative Medicine*, Summer 2001; 2(2): 112–117.

45. Hiroshi, Kadotani, Tomiko, Kadotani, et al, Association between apolipoprotein E 4 and sleep-disordered breathing in adults, *Journal of the American Medical Association*, 2001; 285: 2888–2890.

46. Hung, Joseph, et al, Association of sleep apnea with myocardial infarction in men, *Lancet*, August 4, 1990; 336: 261–264.

47. Lavie, L.; Perelman, A.; Lavie, P., Plasma homocysteine levels in obstructive sleep apnea: Association with cardiovascular morbidity, *Chest*, September 2001; 120(3): 900–908.

48. Wright, Jonathan, V., *Nutrition and Healing*, March 2002; 9(3): 8.

49. Schwartz, Alan R., M.D., et al, Effect of weight loss on upper airway collapsibility in obstructive sleep apnea, *American Review of Respiratory Diseases*, 1991; 144: 494-498.

50. Kittle, William M., M.D.; and Chaudhary, Bashir, M.D., Apnea and hypothyroidism, *Southern Medical Journal*, November 1988; 81(11): 1421–1425.

51. Bardwell, W. A., Ziegler, M. G., et al, Does caffeine confound relationships among adrenergic tone, blood pressure and sleep apnea? *Journal of Sleep Research*, 2000; 9: 269–272.

52. Christensen, Damaris, Allergies may be linked to obstructive sleep apnea, *Medical Tribune*, February 1997; 3.

53. Edling, Christer, et al, Occupational exposure to organic solvents as cause of sleep apnea, *British Journal of Industrial Medicine*, 1993; 50: 276–279.

54. Wilmshurst, P. and Nunan, T. O., Myocardial infarction risk, ear lobe crease, and sleep apnea syndrome, *Lancet*, September 16, 1989; 676.

Mouth
Chapter 6

1. Hodges, R. E.; Hood, J.; Canham, J. E., et al, Clinical manifestations of ascorbic acid deficiency in man, *American Journal of Clinical Nutrition*, April 1971; 24: 432–443.

2. Parsons, W. B., Introduction of niacin as the first successful treatment for cholesterol control: A reminiscence, *Journal of Orthomolecular Medicine*, 2000; 15(3): 121–126.

3. Lopez, R.; Oyarzun, M.; Naranjo, C.; Cumsille, F., et al, Coronary heart disease and periodontitis—A case control study in Chilean adults: *Journal of Clinical Periodontology*, 2002; 29: 468–473.

4. Huggins, Hal, *Why Raise Ugly Kids?* Westport, CT: Arlington House Publishers, 1981, 116.

5. Krook L., et al, Human periodontal disease. Morphology and response to calcium therapy, *Cornell Veterinarian*, 1972; 62: 32–53.

6. Low antioxidant levels associated with periodontal disease, *Journal of the American Dental Association*, January 2003; 134: 20.

7. Pack, A. R., Folate mouthwash: Effects on established gingivitis in periodontal patients, *Journal of Clinical Periodontology*, October, 1984; 11(9): 619–628.

8. Wilkinson, E. G., et al, Bioenergetics in clinical medicine. VI. Adjunctive treatment of periodontal disease with coenzyme Q10, *Research Communications in Chemical Pathology and Pharmacology*, August, 1976; 14(4): 715–719. Hanioka T., et al, Effect of topical application of coenzyme Q10 on adult periodontitis, *Molecular Aspects of Medicine*, 1994; 15(Suppl): s241–s248.

9. Siblerud, Robert L., MS, Relationship between mercury from dental amalgam and oral cavity health, *Annals of Dentistry*, New York Academy of Dentistry, Winter 1990; 901-902. *Townsend Letter for Doctors*, November 1991; 901–902.

10. Braly, James, and Hoggan, Ron, *Dangerous Grains*, New York: Avery publishing group, 2002, 28, 188. [Those with celiac, a severe form of gluten intolerance, are likely to have the following HLA markers: DQ2 (90%), DQ8 (94%) and HLA-B8 (80%).] Walker D. M., et al., Effect of gluten-free diet on recurrent aphthous ulceration, *British Journal Dermatology*, July 1980; 103(1): 111.

11. Wray, D., Gluten-sensitive recurrent aphthous stomatitis, *Digestive Diseases and Sciences* 1981; 26: 737–740.

12. Biagi, F., Campanella, J. et al, A milligram of gluten a day keeps the mucosal recovery away: A case report, *Nutrition Reviews*, September 2004; 62(9): 360–363.

12. Pizzorno, Joseph E., Jr., and Murray, Michael T., *Textbook of Natural Medicine*, Volume 2, London: Churchill Livingstone, 1999, 1086.

13. Wilson, C. W. M., Food sensitivities, taste changes, aphthous ulcers and atopic symptoms in allergic disease, *Annals of Allergy*, May 1980, 302–307. Aphthous stomatitis is linked to mechanical injuries, iron and vitamin deficiencies, and certain HLA types, *Journal of the American Medical Association*, February 12, 1982; 774–775.

14. Werbach, Melvyn R., and Moss, Jeffrey, *Textbook of Nutritional Medicine*, Tarzana, CA: Third Line Press, Inc., 1999, 116–118.

15. Gaby, Alan, Commentary, In *Dr. Jonathan Wright's Nutrition & Healing*, October 1995; 1, 10–11.

16. Stockton, Susan, *Beyond Amalgam: The Hidden Health Hazard Posed by Jawbone Cavitations*, North Port, Florida: Nature's Publishing, 1998, 7–8, 56.

17. Cheilosis, *International Family Health Encyclopedia*, Los Angeles: AFE Press, 1971; 5: 91.

18. Lesser, Michael, *Nutrition and Vitamin Therapy*, New York: Grove Press, 1980, 53.

19. Siblerud, Robert L., see note 9.

20. Marchesani, Robert B., Crimson crescents facilitate CFS diagnosis, *Townsend Letter for Doctors and Patients*, November 2000; 208: 104–5.

21. Meynell, Paul, Health: Chemical balance, *Herald of Health*, 1959.

22. Dilman, Vladimir, M., and Dean, Ward, *The Neuroendocrine Theory of Aging and Degenerative Disease*, Pensacola, FL: The Center for Bio-Gerontology, 1992.

23. Pressman, Alan, and Adams, Alan, *Clinical Assessment of Nutritional Status: A Working Manual*, New York: Management Enterprises, 1982, 31–32.

24. Kauffman, William, Niacinamide: A most neglected vitamin, *Journal of the International Academy of Preventative Medicine*, Winter 1983; 8(1): 7.

25. Meyer, A., Tongue color and vitamin B deficiency, *Lancet*, June 16, 1975, 116.

26. Wright, Jonathan, Your nutritionally oriented physical examination, Part II, *Nutrition & Healing*, May 1998; 5(5): 2.

27. Meinig, George, *Root Canal Cover-up*, Ojai, CA: Bion Publishing, 1996, 85.

28. Yiamouyiannis, John, *Fluoride: The Aging Factor*, Delaware, OH: Taggart Press, 1983, 24.

29. Jackson, Linda, Colgate pays out for teeth ruined by fluoride, *The Sunday Telegraph* (London), November 24, 1996.

30. Crest toothpaste.

31. Mullenix, Phyllis; Denbesten, Pamela; Schunior, Ann; and Kernan, William, Neurotoxicity of sodium fluoride in rats, *Neurotoxicology and Teratology*, 1995; 17(2): 169–177.

32. Hydrogen bonds show their strength, *New Scientist*, January 22, 1981; 211.

33. Ziff, Sam, *The Toxic Time Bomb*, New York: Aurora Press, 1984, 121–123.

34. Taub, Harold, *Keeping Healthy in a Polluted World*, New York: Harper and Row, 1974, 115. Ganther, H. E., Selenium: Relation to decreased toxicity of methylmercury in diets containing tuna, *Science* 1972; 175: 1122.

35. Queen, H. L., *Chronic Mercury Toxicity: New Hope Against an Epidemic Disease*, Colorado Springs, CO: Queen Company Health Communications, 1988, 49.

36. Meinig, George, see note 27, 75.

37. Jerome, Frank, *Tooth Truth: A Patient's Guide to Metal-Free Dentistry*, Chula Vista, CA: New Century Press, 2000, 308.

38. Wright, Jonathan, *Dr. Wright's Guide to Healing with Nutrition*, Emmaus, PA: Rodale Press, 1984, 11.

39. Tintera, John, W., *Hypoadrenocorticism*, Troy, New York: Adrenal Metabolic Research Society of the Hypoglycemia Foundation, 1980, 98.

40. Pottenger, Francis M., Jr., *Pottenger's Cats*, La Mesa, CA: Price-Pottenger Nutrition Foundation, 1983, 18.

41. Williams, David G., Take a bite out of heart disease, *The Price-Pottenger Nutrition Foundation Journal*, Summer 2001, 4–7. Waters, John E., Correctable systematic disorders indicated by presence of salivary calculus. Paper available from Price-Pottenger Nutrition Foundation.

42. Bertrand, F. R., Vitamin E benefits, *Journal of the American Dental Association*, December, 1975; 91: 1136–1137.

43. Amand, R. Paul St., and Marek, Claudia, *What Your Doctor May Not Tell You About Fibromyalgia*, New York: Warner Books, 1999, 40, 306–307.

44. Price, Weston, *Nutrition and Physical Degeneration*, Santa Monica, CA: Price Pottenger Nutrition Foundation, 1975, 12–13.

45. Jerome, Frank, see note 37, 207–209.

46. Williams, Roger, *Nutrition Against Disease*, New York: Pitman Publishing Corporation, 1971, 119.

47. Ott, John, Light photosynthesis, the occulo-endocrine system and dental caries, *Journal of the American Society for Preventive Dentistry*, 1975.

Neck and Shoulders
Chapter 7

1. Bland, Jeffrey, *Nutraerobics*, San Francisco: Harper and Row, 1983, 45.

2. Price, Sylvia A. and Wilson, Lorraine M., *Pathophysiology*, New York: McGraw-Hill, 1982, 663.

3. Wright, Jonathan, Low stomach acid levels could make symptoms worse and treatment more difficult, *Nutrition & Healing*, March 2002; 9(3): 3.

4. Flippo, Teresa S., M.D., and Holder, Walter D., Jr., M.D., Neurologic degeneration associated with nitrous oxide anesthesia in patients with vitamin B12 deficiency, *Archives of Surgery*, December 1993; 128: 1391–1395.

5. Wright, Jonathan, Treatment of bursitis; gout, *Nutrition & Healing*, January 1997; 4(1): 2.

6. Jaffe, Russell, and Donovan, Patrick, *Guided Health: A Constant Professional Reference*, Health Studies Collegium, 1993, 6.33–6.34.

7. Latham, Michael; McGandy, Robert; McCann, Mary; and Stare, Frederick, *Scope Manual on Nutrition*, Kalamazoo, MI: The Upjohn Company, 1975, 42.

8. Rowe, A. H., and Rowe, A., Jr., Perennial nasal allergy due to food sensitization, *Journal of Asthma Research*, December 1965; 3(2): 141–154.

9. http://www.aace.com/pub/tam1998/card.php.

10. Schutte, Karl H., and Myers, John A., *Metabolic Aspects of Health*, Kentfield, CA: Discovery Press, 1979, 285, 289.

11. Edward, J. F., M.D., Iodine: Its use in the treatment and prevention of poliomyelitis and allied diseases, *The Manitoba Medical Review*, 1954; 34(6): 337–339. Reprinted by Lee Foundation for Nutritional Research, Milwaukee, WI 53201.

12. Kunin, Richard, Clinical uses of iodide and iodine, *Nutrition and Healing*, July 1998; 5(7): 7–8.

The Skin
Chapter 8

1. Pearson, Durk, and Shaw, Sandy, *Life Extension*, New York: Warner Books, 1982, 94–95, 209.

2. Levander, Orville A.; Morris, Virginia; and Ferretti, Renato, Filterability of erythrocytes from vitamin E-deficient lead-poisoned rats, *Journal of Nutrition* 1977; 107: 363–372.

3. Altschule, Mark D., *Nutritional Factors in General Medicine*, Springfield, IL: Charles C. Thomas, 1978, 90–93.

4. Prendiville, Julie S. and Manfredi, Liliana N., Skin signs of nutritional disorders, *Seminars in Dermatology*, March 1992; 11(1): 88–97.

5. Altschule, Mark D., see note 3, 72.

6. Gilman, Alfred; Gilman, Alfred Goodman; and Goodman, Louis, ed. *Goodman and Gilman's The Pharmacological Basis of Therapeutics*, Sixth Edition, New York: MacMillan, 1980, 1578.

7. Michaud, Ellen, et al. *Listen to Your Body*, Emmaus, PA.: Rodale Press, 1988, 486.

8. Marinkovitch, Vincent A., *The Immune System as a Cause of Symptoms*, 6th Int'l Symposium for Functional Medicine, Institute for Functional Medicine.

9. Wright, Jonathan, *Nutrition & Healing*, March 2002; 9(3): 1–3.

10. Reading, Chris, *Your Family Tree Connection*, New Canaan, CT: Keats, 1988.

11. Braly, James, and Hoggan, Ron, *Dangerous Grains*, Garden City, NY: Avery Publishing Group, 2002, 197.

12. Prickett, James D.; Robinson, Dwight; and Steinberg, Alfred, Effects of dietary enrichment with eicosapentaenoic acid upon autoimmune nephritis in female NZBxNZW/F1

mice, *Arthritis and Rheumatism*, February 1983; 26(2): 133–139.

13. Mizel, Steven B., and Jaret, Peter, *In Self-Defense*, New York: Harcourt, Brace, Jovanovich Publishers, 1977, 177–78.

14. Lee, John, R. and Hopkins, Virginia, *What Your Doctor May Not Tell You About Menopause*, New York: Time Warner, 1996, 258.

15. Kauffman, William, Niacinamide: A most neglected vitamin, *Journal of the International Academy of Preventative Medicine*, Winter 1983; 8(1): 6–8.

16. Menne, T., and Maibach, H. I., Nickel allergic contact dermatitis: A review, *Journal of the American College of Toxicology*, 1989; 8(7): 1271.

17. Fisher, Alexander A., M.D., The nickel controversy at home and abroad, *Cutis*, September 1993; 52: 134–135.

18. Wright, Jonathan, Itching and irony: More news on the common skin irritant that may help you erase psoriasis for good! *Nutrition & Healing*, October 2002; 9(10): 6. Exposure to nickel may have potential toxic effects over the long term.

19. Zoler, Mitchel L., Zinc cream blocks absorption of latex allergens, *Family Practice News*, December 1, 1997; 34.

20. Tattoos, *FDA Medical Bulletin*, May 1994; 24(1), 8.

21. Atopic women at risk for sunscreen reactions, *Family Practice News*, May 15, 1997; 48.

22. Moss, Andrew, M. B., Tea tree oil poisoning, *Medical Journal of Australia*, February 21, 1994; 160: 236.

23. Lutz, Michael E., M.D., and El-Azhary, Rokea A., M.D., Ph.D., Allergic contact dermatitis due to topical application of corticosteroids: Review and clinical implications, *Mayo Clinic Proceedings*, 1997; 72: 1141–1144.

24. Machackova, Jirina, and Smid, Pavel, Allergic contact cheilitis from toothpastes, *Contact Dermatitis*, 1991; 24: 311–312.

25. Latham, Michael; McGandy, Robert; McCann, Mary; and Stare, Frederick, *Scope Manual on Nutrition*, Kalamazoo, MI: The Upjohn Company, 1975, 37–38.

26. Gilman, Alfred; Goodman, Louis; and Gilman, Alfred, *The Pharmacological Basis of Therapeutics*, New York: MacMillan, Inc., 1980, 1563.

27. Pearson, Durk, see note 1, 120–121.

28. Bendich, Adrianne, E., Vitamin E and human immune functions, In Klurfeld, David M., ed., *Human Nutrition: A Comprehensive Treatise: Nutrition and Immunology* Vol. 8; Boston, MA: Kluwer Academic, 1993, 217-228.

29. Neve, J., Physiologic and nutritional importance of selenium, *Experientia*, 1991; 47: 187.

30. Jain, Sushil K., et al, Reduced vitamin E and increased lipofuscin products in erythrocytes of diabetic rats, *Diabetes*, October 1991; 40: 124

31. Chase, Deborah, *The Medically Based No-Nonsense Beauty Book*, New York: Kangaroo Books, 1975, 156–158.

32. Kadunce, Donald P., M.D., et al, Cigarette smoking: Risk factor for premature facial wrinkling, *Annals of Internal Medicine*, May 15, 1991; 114(10): 840–844.

33. Joffe, Ian, M.D., Cigarette smoking and facial wrinkling, *Annals of Internal Medicine*, October 15, 1991; 115(8): 659.

34. Purba, M. B., Kouris-Blazos, A., et al, Skin wrinkling: Can food make a difference? *Journal of the American College of Nutrition*, February 2001; 20(1): 71–80.

35. Scurvy and junk food diet, *Nutrition Week*, July 21, 2000; 30(28): 7. *Archives of Pediatric and Adolescent Medicine*, July 2000; 154: 732–735.

36. Wright, Jonathan, Menstrual clotting and vitamin K, *Nutrition & Healing*, September 2001; 8(9): 4.

37. Ryle, H.W., Gastric analysis in acne rosacea, *Lancet*, Dec. 11, 1920; 1195.

38. Lesser, Michael, *Nutrition and Vitamin Therapy*, New York: Grove Press, 1980, 53.

39. Wright, Jonathan, Dry skin: Not a skin-lotion deficiency, *Nutrition & Healing*, March 2000; 7(3): 7.

40. Hoffer, Abram, and Walker, Morton, *Putting It All Together: The New Orthomolecular Nutrition*, New Canaan, CT: Keats Publishing Co., 1996, 78–79.

41. Latham, Michael, see note 25, 74.

42. Margolis, Jack, and Margolis, Lawrence, Skin tags—A frequent sign of diabetes mellitus, *New England Journal of Medicine*, May 20, 1976; 294(21): 1184.

43. Margolis, 1184.

44. Bernstein, Richard K., *Dr. Bernstein's Diabetes Solution*, Boston: Little, Brown and Company, 1997.

45. Philpott, William H., and Kalita, Dwight K., *Victory Over Diabetes*, New Canaan, CT: Keats Publishing Co., 1983.

46. Pfeiffer, Carl C., *Mental and Elemental Nutrients*, New Canaan, CT: Keats Publishing Co., 1975, 230–231.

47. Evans, J., Exposures to paint thinners, removers tied to scleroderma, *Skin and Allergy News*, June 2003; 36.

48. Cooper, G. S.; Miller, F. W.; Germolec, D. R., Occupational exposures and autoimmune diseases, *International Immunopharmacology*, 2002; 2: 303–313.

49. *Physician's Desk Reference*, 49th Edition, 1995, 1113–1114.

50. Grace, W. J.; Kennedy, R. J.; Formato, A., Therapy of scleroderma and dermatomyositis, *New York State Journal of Medicine*, January 1, 1963; 140–144.

51. Bushnell, W.J.; Galens, G.J.; Bartholomew, L. E., et al, The treatment of progressive systemic sclerosis: A comparison of para-amino-benzoate and placebo in a double blind study, *Arthritis and Rheumatism*, 1966; 9: 495–496.

52. Wright, Jonathan, Clinical tip 37, *Nutrition & Healing*, March 1999; 6(3): 3.

53. Ayres, S., and Mihan, R., Is vitamin E involved in the autoimmune mechanism? *Cutis*, March 1978; 21: 321–325.

54. Nishimura, N.; Okamoto, H.; Yasui, M., et al, Intermediary metabolism of phenylalanine and tyrosine in diffuse collagen diseases: II. Influences of the low phenylalanine and tyrosine diet upon patients with collagen disease, *Archives of Dermatology*, October 1959; 80: 124–135.

55. Jablonska, S., Avocado/soybean unsaponifiables in the treatment of scleroderma: Comment on the article by Maheu et al, *Arthritis and Rheumatism*, 1998; 41(9): 1705.

56. Horrobin, D. F., Essential fatty acid metabolism in diseases of connective tissue with special reference to scleroderma and to Sjogren's syndrome, *Medical Hypotheses*, 1984; 14: 233–247.

57. Barnes, Broda O., and Galton, Lawrence, *Hypothyroidism: The Unsuspected Illness*, New York: Thomas Y. Crowell Company, 1976, 46, 50.

58. Ross, Julia, *The Diet Cure*, New York: Viking, 1999, 55.

59. Montes, L. F., et al., Folic acid and vitamin B12 in vitiligo: A nutritional approach, *Cutis*, 1992; 50: 39–42.

60. Howitz, J., and Schwartz, M., Vitiligo, achlorhydria, and pernicious anemia, *Lancet*, 1971; 1: 1331.

 Hands and Fingers
Chapter 9

1. Erlick, Nelson, et al., A dermatoglyphic predictive index for maturity-onset diabetes mellitus, *Journal of the American Podiatry Association*, September 1983; 73(9): 467. Fingerprints may reveal diabetic tendencies, *The Fresno Bee*, March 9, 1983; A11.

2. Childers, Norman F., *Arthritis: Childers' Diet To Stop It*, Gainsville, FL: Horticultural Publications, 1986, 3, 7.

3. Theodosakis, Jason, *The Arthritis Cure*, New York: St. Martin's Press, 1997, 15.

4. Urbano, Frank L., Heberden's nodes, *Hospital Physician*, July 2001; 29.

5. Bucci, Luke, *Pain Free*, Fort Worth, Texas: The Summit Group, 1999, 11–16.

6. Kaufman, William, *The Common Form of Joint Dysfunction: Its Incidence and Treatment*, Brattleboro, Vermont: E. L. Hildreth & Company, 1949, 4.

7. Rudin, Donald, The major psychoses and neuroses as omega-3 essential fatty acid deficiency syndrome: Substrate pellagra, *Biological Psychiatry*, 1981; 16(9): 837.

8. Curtis, C. L.; Rees, S. G.; Cramp, J., et al, Effects of n-3 fatty acids on cartilage metabolism, *Proceedings of the Nutrition Society*, 2002; 61: 381–389.

9. Schwartz, E. R., The modulation of osteoarthritic development by vitamins C and E, *International Journal of Vitamin Research Suppl*, 1984; 26: 141–6.

10. Bucci, see note 5, 29–31.

11. Bucci, see note 5, 55–57.

12. Balch, James, and Balch, Phyllis, *Prescription for Nutritional Healing* (Second Edition), Garden City, NY: Avery Publishing Group, 1997, 140.

13. Brown, Thomas McPherson, and Scammell, Henry, *The Road Back: Rheumatoid Arthritis—Its Cause and Its Treatment*, New York: M. Evans and Company, Inc., 1988, 119.

14. Brown, 130–135.

15. Meinig, George E., *Root Canal Cover-up*, Ojai, CA: Bion Publishing, 1996, 166–7.

16. Poehlmann, Katherine, *Rheumatoid Arthritis: The Infection Connection*, Rolling Hills Estates, CA: Satori Press, 2003, 55–90.

17. Mulhall, Douglas, and Hansen, Katja, *The Calcium Bomb*, Cranston, RI: The Writers' Collective, 2005, 32.

18. Poehlmann, see note 16, 80.

19. Kremer, Joel, et al., Effects of manipulation of dietary fatty acids on clinical manifestations of rheumatoid arthritis, *Lancet*, January 26, 1985; 184.

20. Kjeldsen-Kragh, Jens, Dietary treatment of rheumatoid arthritis, *Scandinavian Journal of Rheumatology*, 1996; 63.

21. Mulhall, Douglas, see note 17, 124.

22. Werbach, Melvyn R., *Nutritional Influences on Illness*, 2nd ed., Tarzana, CA: Third Line Press, 1993, 570–584.

23. Levine, Norman, Nail changes—Local disorder or systemic disease? How to tell, *Modern Medicine*, August 15–September 15, 1979; 75.

24. Hochman, L. G., et al., Brittle nails: Response to daily biotin supplementation, *Cutis*, 1993; 51: 303–305.

25. Wright, Jonathan, *Nutrition & Healing*, May 1995; 2(5): 7. Also, Clinical Tip 55, August 1999; 6(8): 7.

26. Bralley, J. Alexander, and Lord, Richard, *Laboratory Evaluations in Molecular Medicine*, Norcross, GA: Institute for Advances in Molecular Medicine, 2001, 25–6.

27. Giller, Robert M., M.D., and Matthews, Kathy, *Natural Prescriptions*, New York: Carol Southern Books, 1994, 143.

28. Contemporary therapy with vitamin B6, vitamin B2, and coenzyme Q10, *Chemical and Engineering News*, April 21, 1986; 27–29.

29. Cheraskin, E.; Ringsdorf, W.M., Jr.; and Brecher, Arline, *Psychodietetics*, New York: Bantam Books, 1976, 22.

30. Williams, Roger, *Nutrition against Disease*, New York: Pitman, 1971, 47.

31. Spring, Maxwell, and Cohen, Berton D., Dupuytren's contracture: Warning of diabetes, *New York State Journal of Medicine*, May 1, 1970; 1037. Leake, Chauncey, New sign for incipient diabetes, *Geriatrics*, Oct. 1968; 23.

32. Nikolowski, W., Vitamin E in dermatology, *Vitamins*, Nutley, NJ: Hoffman La Roche, 1970, 34.

33. Kirk, J. E., and Chieffi, M., Tocopherol administration to patients with Dupuytren's contracture: Effect on plasma tocopherol levels and degree of contracture, *Proceedings of the Society for Experimental Biology and Medicine*, 1952; 80: 565–8.

34. Balch, James and Balch, Phyllis, *Prescription for Nutritional Healing*, Second Edition, Garden City, NY: Avery Publishing Group, 1997, 400.

35. Fawcett, Robert S., and Linford, Sean, Nail abnormalities: Clues to systemic disease, *American Family Physician*, March 15, 2004; 1420.

36. Schutte, Karl, and Myers, John, *Metabolic Aspects of Health*, Kentfield, CA: Discovery Press, 1979, 99.

37. Stone, R. E., and Spies, T. D., Some recent advances in nutrition, *Journal of the American Medical Association*, 1958; 167: 678.

38. Murray, Michael, *Encyclopedia of Nutritional Supplements*, Rocklin, CA: Prima Publishing, 1996, 209–213.

39. Crawford, Roberta, *The Iron Elephant*, Glyndon, MD: Vida Publishing, Inc., 1993.

40. Scheimann, Eugene, *A Doctor's Guide to Better Health Through Palmistry*, New Delhi, India: Vikas Publishing House, 1979, 44.

41 Levine, Norman, see note 23, 70.

42. Michaelsson G., Gerden B., et al, Psoriasis patients with antibodies to gliadin can be improved by a gluten-free diet, *British Journal of Dermatology*, 2000; 142: 44–51.

43. Luigi, Naldi, M.D., Dietary factors and the risk of psoriasis: Results of an Italian case-control study, *British Journal of Dermatology*, 1996; 34: 101–106.

44. Maurice, P. D., et al, The effects of dietary supplementation with fish oil in patients with psoriasis, *British Journal of Dermatology*, November, 1987; 117(5): 599–606.

45. Michaelsson, Gerd, et al, Selenium in whole blood and plasma is decreased in patients with moderate and severe psoriasis, *Acta Dermato-Venereologica*, Stockholm, 1989; 69: 29–34.

46. Perez, A., et al, Safety and efficacy of oral calcitriol (1,25-dihydroxyvitamin D3) for the treatment of psoriasis, *British Journal of Dermatology*, 1996; 134: 1070–1078.

47. McCarty, M. F., Glucosamine for psoriasis? *Medical Hypotheses*, 1997; 48: 437–441.

48. Prystowsky, Janet H., M.D., Ph.D., et al, Update on nutrition and psoriasis, *Journal of Dermatology*, 1993; 32: 582–586.

49. Gupta, A. K., et al, A higher prevalence of onychomycosis in psoriatics compared with non-psoriatics: A multicentre study, *British Journal of Dermatology*, 1997; 136: 786–789.

50. Giller, see note 27, 290.

51. Ellis, John, *The Doctor Who Looked at Hands*, New York: Arco Publishing Co., 1966, 17–22.

52. Ellis, 130–139.

53. Ellis, 148–150.

54. Ellis, John M., and Presley, James, *Vitamin B6: The Doctor's Report*, New York: Harper and Row, 1973, 11.

55. Ellis, see note 51, 18, 281.

56. Gaby, Alan, *The Doctor's Guide to Vitamin B6*, Emmaus, PA: Rodale Press, 1984, 6–16.

57. Wright, Jonathan, Vitamin B6 and 'Trigger Finger', *Nutrition & Healing*, March 1999; 6(3): 7.

58. Levine, Norman, see note 23, 74.

59. Pfeiffer, Carl, *Mental and Elemental Nutrients*, New Canaan, CT: Keats Publishing Co., 1975, 232.

60. Pfeiffer, Carl, Observations on the therapy of the schizophrenias, *Journal of Applied Nutrition*, Winter 1974; 26(4): 36.

61. Scheimann, see note 40, 41. Pfeiffer, see note 59, 235.

62. Levine, see note 23, 74.

63. Raloff, J., Does fetal zinc affect later immunity? *Science News*, June 13, 1987; 375.

64. Balch, see note 12, 400.

Back, Legs, and Feet
Chapter 10

1. Pickett, Donald E., As I see it, *The Counselor*, September–October 1978; 3.

2. Rittweger, J., Just, K., et al, Treatment of chronic lower back pain with lumbar extension and whole-body vibration exercise: A randomized controlled trial, *Spine*, 2002; 27(17): 1829–1834.

3. Vormann, J.; Worlitschek, M.; Goedecke, T.; Silver, B., Supplementation with alkaline minerals reduces symptoms in patients with chronic low back pain, *Journal of Trace Elements In Medicine and Biology*, 2001; 15(2/3): 179–183.

4. Raloff, Janet, Vitamin D: What's enough? Many people need much more, *Science News*, October 16, 2004; 166: 248.

5. Latham, Michael; McGandy, Robert; McCann, Mary; and Stare, Frederick, *Scope Manual on Nutrition*, Kalamazoo, MI: The Upjohn Company, 1975, 44–48. Hart, Joseph, Subclinical rickets: Unexploited deficiency syndrome, *Nutrition & Healing*, February 1999; 6(2): 5.

6. Travis, J., D-fending the colon, *Science News*, May 18, 2002; 309.

7. Dermer, Gerald, *The Immortal Cell*, Garden City, NY: Avery Publishing Group, 1994, 63.

8. Raloff, Janet, Vitamin boost: From muscle strength to immunity, scientists find new vitamin D benefits, *Science News*, October 9, 2004; 232–233.

9. Raloff, see note 4, 248.

10. Wright, Jonathan, M.D., Warning signs for present or future 'type 2' diabetes: Skin tags, Dupuytren's contracture, and discolorations of lower-leg skin, *Nutrition & Healing*, Phoenix, AZ: Publishers Mgmt. Corp., March 1999; 6(3): 5. Kraft, J., Detection of diabetes mellitus in situ (occult diabetes), *Laboratory Medicine*, February 1975; 10.

11. McDougall, John A., *McDougall's Medicine: A Challenging Second Opinion*, Clinton, NJ: New Win Publishing, Inc., 1985, 206.

12. Kitabchi, Abbas, E., Umpierrez, Guillermo, E., et al, Management of hyperglycemic crises in patients with diabetes, *Diabetes Care* 2001; 24: 131–153.

13. Dahle, Lars O., M.D., et al, The effect of oral magnesium substitution on pregnancy-induced leg cramps, *American Journal of Obstetrics and Gynecology*, July 1995; 173(1): 175–80.

14. Muscle cramps—Check magnesium and sodium, *Cortlandt Forum*, June 1993; 79: 64.

15. Seelig, Mildred, (Mg) treatment or supplementation is often needed when calcium (Ca) intake is increased, *Blaine Journal*, January 1998.

16. Flink, Edmund, Can you spot magnesium deficiency and toxicity? *Modern Medicine*, October 30–November 15, 1979; 48–56.

17. Price, Sylvia A., and Wilson, Lorraine M., *Pathophysiology*, Second Edition, New York: McGraw-Hill, 1978, 746.

18. Chan, P., et al, Randomized, double-blind, placebo-controlled study of the safety and efficacy of vitamin B complex in the treatment of nocturnal leg cramps in elderly patients with hypertension, *Journal of Clinical Pharmacology*, December 1998; 38(12): 1151–1154.

19. Aitchison, W. R., Nocturnal cramps, *New Zealand Medical Journal*, August 14, 1974; 137.

20. Avsar, A. F.; Ozmen S.; and Soylemez F., Vitamin B1 and B6 substitution in pregnancy for leg cramps, *American Journal of Obstetrics and Gynecology*, July 1996; 175(1): 233–234.

21. Ayres, S. Jr, Mihan R., Nocturnal leg cramps (systremma): A progress report on response to vitamin E, *Southern Medical Journal*, November 1974; 67(11): 1308–1312.

22. Yasushi, Matsuzaki, M.D., Ph.D., et al, Is taurine effective for treatment of painful muscle cramps in liver cirrhosis? *American Journal of Gastroenterology*, 1993; 88(9): 1466–1467.

23. Kugelmas, M., Preliminary observation: Oral zinc sulfate replacement is effective in treating muscle cramps in cirrhotic patients, *Journal of the American College of Nutrition*, 2000; 19(1): 13–15.

24. Knowles, F. W., Fluoride and leg cramps, *New Zealand Medical Journal*, January 28, 1981; 60.

25. Tonner, D. R., Schlechte, J. A., Neurologic complications of thyroid and parathyroid disease, *Medical Clinics of North America*, January 1993; 77(1): 251–263.

26. Goldberg, Stephen, *Clinical Neuroanatomy Made Ridiculously Simple*, Miami, FL: Medmaster, Inc., 1997, 26.

27. Hadjivassiliou, M.; Grunewald, R. A.; and Davies-Jones, G. A. B, Gluten sensitivity as a neurological illness, *Journal of Neurology, Neurosurgery, and Psychiatry*, May 2002; 72(5): 560–563.

28. Brown, C. W., *Sprue and Its Treatment*. London: J Bale, Sons, and Danielson, 1908.

29. Cooke, W. T., Thomas-Smith, W., Neurological disorders associated with adult coeliac disease. *Brain*, 1966; 89: 683–722.

30. Lossos, A.; Argov, Z.; Ackerman, Z.; and Abramsky, O., Peripheral neuropathy and folate deficiency as the first sign of crohn's disease, *Journal of Clinical Gastroenterology*, August 1991; 13(4): 442–444.

31. Feldman, E. L., Oxidative stress and diabetic neuropathy: A new understanding of an old problem, *Journal of Clinical Investigation*, February 2003; 111(4): 431–433.

32. Walsh, N., Alpha-lipoic acid for diabetic neuropathy, *Family Practice News*, April 1, 2001; 22.

33. Ziegler, D.; Reljanovic, M.; Mehnert, H.; and Gries, F.A., A-lipoic acid in the treatment of diabetic polyneuropathy in Germany: Current evidence from clinical trials, *Experimental and Clinical Endocrinology & Diabetes*, 1999; 107: 421–430.

34. Traber, Maret G., and Sies, Helmut, Vitamin E in humans: Demand and delivery, *Annual Review of Nutrition*, 1996; 16: 321–347.

35. O'Dell, B. L., et al, Zinc deficiency and peripheral neuropathy in chicks, *Proceedings of the Society for Experimental Biology and Medicine*, 1990; 1994: 1–4.

36. Stracke, H., et al, A Benfotiamine-vitamin B combination in treatment of diabetic polyneuropathy, *Experimental and Clinical Endocrinology and Diabetes*, 1996; 104: 311–316.

37. Paladin, F., Perez, G. R., The haematic thiamine level in the course of alcoholic neuropathy, *European Neurology*, 1987; 26: 129–133.

38. Weir, D. G., Scott, J. M., Brain function in the elderly: Role of vitamin B12 and folate, *British Medical Bulletin*, 1999; 55(3): 669–682.

39. Sima, Anders A. F., et al, Supplemental myo-inositol prevents L-fucose-induced diabetic neuropathy, *Diabetes*, February, 1997; 46: 301–306.

40. Koutsikos, D., et al, Biotin for diabetic peripheral neuropathy, *Biomedicine and Pharmacotherapy*, 1990; 44: 511–514.

41. Horrobin, D. F., n-6 fatty acids and nervous system disorders, *Medical Fatty Acids in Inflammation*, 1998: 65–71.

42. Gaby, Alan, Fish oil for diabetics, *Health & Healing*, October 1997; 4(10): 7–8. Okuda, Y., et al, Long-term effects of eicosapentaenoic acid on diabetic peripheral neuropathy and serum lipids in patients with type II and diabetes mellitus, *Journal of Diabetes and Its Complications*, 1996; 10: 280–287.

43. Sandstead, Harold H., M.D., A brief history of the influence of trace elements on brain function, *Journal of Clinical Nutrition*, February 1986; 43: 293–298.

44. Thomke, F., et al, Increased risk of sensory neuropathy in workers with chlordane after exposure to 2, 3, 7, 8-poly-chlorinated dioxins and furans, *Acta Neurologica Scandinavica*, 1999; 100: 1–5.

45. Sadoh, D. R., et al, Occupational exposure to methyl methacrylate monomer induces generalized neuropathy in a dental technician, *British Dental Journal*, April 24, 1999; 186(8): 380–381.

46. Steenland, Kyle, Chronic neurological effects of organophosphate pesticides: Subclinical damage does occur, but longer follow-up studies are needed, *British Medical Journal*, May 25, 1996; 312: 1312–1313.

47. Oh no, not another cousin of fosamax, and Back in fosamax country..., *John Lee Medical Letter*, December 1998; 4.

48. Eastell, R., Lambert, H., Diet and healthy bones, *Calcified Tissue International*, 2002; 70: 400–404.

49. Gaby, Alan, Aluminum: The ubiquitous poison, *Nutrition & Healing*, October 1997; 4(10): 3–4.

50. Lee, John, and Hopkins, Virginia, *What Your Doctor May Not Tell You About Menopause*, New York: Warner Books, 1996, 183.

51. Lee, 170–183.

52. Wright, Jonathan, Fight—Even prevent osteoporosis with the hidden secrets of this bone-building miracle mineral, *Nutrition & Healing*, February 2003; 10(2): 1. Gaby, Alan R., *Preventing and Reversing Osteoporosis*, Rocklin, CA: Prima Books, 1994, 85–92.

53. Miller, Sigmund S., ed., *Symptoms*, New York: Avon Books, 1978, 485–486.

54. Wright, Jonathan, Lithium, vitamin C and gout, *Nutrition & Healing*, September 1998; 5(9): 7.

55. Wright, Jonathan, Preventing and reversing lithium toxicity and side effects with essential fatty acids, *Nutrition & Healing*, June 1998; 5(6): 11.

56. Giller, Robert, M.D., and Matthews, Kathy, *Natural Prescriptions*, New York: Carol Southern Books, 1994, 161–163.

57. Amand, R. Paul St., M.D., and Marek, Claudia, *What Your Doctor May Not Tell You About Fibromyalgia*, New York: Time Warner, 1999, 43, 71.

58. Werbach, Melvyn, and Moss, Jeffrey, *Textbook of Nutritional Medicine*, Tarzana, CA: Third Line Press, 1999, 400–402.

59. Lutz, E. G., Restless legs, anxiety and caffeinism, *Clinical Psychiatry*, September 1978; 39: 693–698.

60. Roberts, H. J., Spontaneous leg cramps and restless legs due to diabetogenic hyperinsulinism: Observations on 131 patients, *Journal of the American Geriatric Society*, July 1965; 13(7): 602–638.

61. Hornyak, M.; Voderholzer U.; Hohagen F., et al, Magnesium therapy for periodic leg movements–related insomnia and restless legs syndrome: An open pilot study, *Sleep*, 1998; 21(5): 501–505.

62. Murray, Michael, *Encyclopedia of Nutritional Supplements*, Rocklin, CA: Prima Publishing, 1996, 209–213.

63. O'Keefe, S. T., et al., Iron status and restless legs syndrome in the elderly, *Age and Aging*, 1994; 23: 200–203.

64. Morehouse, Lawrence, Early detection of hypokinetic deterioration, *The Art of Predictive Medicine*, ed. Webster Marker and George Congill, Springfield, IL: Charles C. Thomas, 1967, 62.

65. Maxwell, John, *Today Matters*, New York: Warner Faith, 2004, 96.

66. Reuben, David, *The Save Your Life Diet*, New York: Random House, 1975, 75–77.

67. Carpenter, Kenneth J., *Beriberi, White Rice, and Vitamin B*, Berkeley, CA: University of California Press, 2000, *xi*.

68. Raloff, see note 8, 232–233.

Elimination
Chapter 11

1. Reuben, David, *The Save Your Life Diet*, New York: Random House, 1975, *xi*.

2. Reuben, 68.

3. Reuben, 21.

4. Tuckey, E. Hugh, The human need for hydrochloric acid, *National Health Federation Bulletin*, October 1967.

5. Reuben, see note 1, 32.

6. Reuben, 29.

7. Painter, N. S.; Almeida, A. Z.; and Colebourne, K. W., Unprocessed bran in treatment of diverticular disease of the colon, *British Medical Journal,1972*; 2: 137–140.

8. Reuben, see note 1, 72–74.

9. Latham, Michael; McGandy, Robert; McCann, Mary; and Stare, Frederick, *Scope Manual on Nutrition*, Kalamazoo, MI: The Upjohn Company, 1975, 74.

10. Liebman, M., Chai, W. W., Effect of dietary calcium on urinary oxalate excretion after oxalate loads, *American Journal of Clinical Nutrition*, May 1997; 65(5): 1453–1459.

11. Werbach, Melvyn, *Nutritional Influences on Illness*, Second Edition, Tarzana, CA: Third Line Press, 1993, 405.

12. Travis, John, The bacteria in the stone: Extra-tiny microorganisms may lead to kidney stones and other diseases—Includes related information on nanobacteria, *Science News*, Aug 1, 1998; 154(5): 75.

13. Mulhall, Douglas, and Hansen, Katja, *The Calcium Bomb: The Nanobacteria Link to Heart Disease & Cancer*, Cranston, RI: The Writers' Collective, 2005, 94–100, 123–124.

14. Bland, Jeffrey, *Nutraerobics*, San Francisco: Harper and Row, 1983, 46, 229.

15 Michaud, Ellen; Anastas, Lila; and the editors of *Prevention Magazine*, *Listen to Your Body*, Emmaus, PA: Rodale Press, 442.

16. Burkitt, D. P., Western civilization, diet and disease, *Drug Therapy*, January 1974; 51–62.

17. Hoffer, Abram, *Hoffer's Laws of Natural Nutrition*, Ontario, Canada: Quarry Press, 1996, 21.

18. Bland, Jeffrey, *Nutraerobics*, San Francisco: Harper and Row, 1983, 30.

19. Schoenen, Jean., M.D., Ph.D., et al, Effectiveness of high-dose riboflavin in migraine prophylaxis: A randomized controlled trial, *Neurology*, 1998; 50: 466–470.

20. Coimbra C. G., Junqueira V. B., High doses of riboflavin and the elimination of dietary red meat promote the recovery of some motor functions in Parkinson's disease patients. *Brazilian Journal of Medical and Biological Research*, 2003; 36(10): 1409–1417.

21. Gisson, Adam, and Morgenthaler, John, Riboflavin: The dose makes the poison, *Townsend Letter for Doctors and Patients*, June 2003; 135.

22. Wiersum, Jeffery, M.D., Vitamins for migraine, meniere's, *Cortlandt Forum*, February 1991, 97.

Appetite and Digestion
Chapter 12

1. Rensselaer, James Van, Who killed the great gluttons? *Air California Magazine*, October 1979, 47–48.

2. Bryce-Smith, D., and Simpson, R. I. D., Case of anorexia nervosa responding to zinc sulphate, *Lancet* 1984; ii: 350.

3. Schauss, Alexander and Costin, Carolyn, *Zinc and Eating Disorders*, New Canaan, CT: Keats Publishing Co., 1989, 11–22.

4. Ross, Julia, *The Diet Cure*, New York: Viking, 1999, 24.

5. Geiselman, Paula, Sugar infusion can enhance feeding, *Science*, October 29, 1982; 218: 490–491.

6. Stitt, Paul, *Fighting the Food Giants*, Manitowoc, WI: Natural Press, 1981, 135.

7. DesMaisons, Kathleen, *Potatoes Not Prozac*, New York: Simon & Schuster, 1998, 69–70. Blass, E. M.; Fitzgerald, E.; and Kehoe, P., Interactions between sucrose, pain and isolation distress, *Pharmacology, Biochemistry and Behavior*, 1986; 483–89.

8. Budwig, Johanna, *Flax Oil as a True Aid against Arthritis, Heart Infarction, Cancer and Other Diseases*, Vancouver, B.C.: Apple Publishing, 1994, 33.

9. Ross, see note 4, *xvii*.

10. Randolph, Theron, and Moss, Ralph, *An Alternative Approach to Allergies*, New York: Harper and Row, 1990, 27.

11. Mandell, Marshall, and Scanlon, Lynne, *Dr. Mandell's 5-Day Allergy Relief System*, New York: Thomas Y. Crowell, 1979, 108.

12. Tuckey, E. Hugh, The human need for hydrochloric acid, *National Health Federation Bulletin*, October 1967.

13. Cain, Harvey, *Flint's Emergency Treatment and Management*, Sixth Edition, Philadelphia, PN: W. B. Sauders, 1980, 266.

14. Seaman, David, Whole food and nutritional supplementation interactions in the digestive process, In *Clinical Chemistry & Nutrition Guidebook: A Physician's Desk Reference*, edited by Paul Yanick Jr. and Russell Jaffe,

Prepublication for professionals; 463. Nutrients essential for HCL production include methionine, tryptophan, phenlalanine, histidine, B6, acetic acid, pantothenic acid (B5), cysteine, choline, magnesium, potassium, and zinc.

15. Tuckey, see note 12.

16. Ruddell, W. S. J., et al., Gastric juice nitrite: A risk factor for cancer in the hypochlorhydric stomach? *Lancet*, November 13, 1976, 7994.

17. Yanick, Paul, Jr., Assessing the physiological-chemical response, In *Clinical Chemistry & Nutrition Guidebook: A Physician's Desk Reference*, edited by Paul Yanick Jr. and Russell Jaffe, Prepublication for professionals, 392.

18. Wright, Jonathan, *Nutrition & Healing*, September 2001; 8(9): 1.

19. Possible vitamin B6 deficiency uncovered in persons with the Chinese Restaurant Syndrome, *Nutrition Reviews*, January 1982; 40(1): 15–16.

20. Blaylock, Russell, *Health and Nutrition Secrets That Can Save Your Life*, Albuquerque, NM: Health Press, 2002, 171–199.

21. Schwartz, George R., *In Bad Taste: The MSG Syndrome*, New York: Signet Books, 1990, 62.

22. Wright, Ann; King, Janet; Baer, Marion, and Citrol, L., Experimental zinc depletion and altered taste perception for NaCl in young adult males, *American Journal of Clinical Nutrition*, May 1981; 34: 848–852.

23. Pfeiffer, Carl, *Mental and Elemental Nutrients*, New Canaan, CT: Keats Publishing Co., 1975, 227.

24. Hankin, Robert, Dysosmia and dysegeusia after delivery of infant, *Journal of the American Medical Association*, Feb. 27, 1978; 871.

25. Pfeiffer, see note 23, 227.

26. Wright, Jonathan, *Nutrition and Healing*, April 1999; 6(4): 5.

27. Tintera, John, *Hypoadrenocorticism*, Troy, NY: Adrenal Metabolic Research Society of the Hypoglycemia Foundation, 1980, 128.

28. Breneman, J. C., Allergy elimination diet as the most effective gallbladder diet, *Annals of Allergy* 1968; 26: 83.

29. Werbach, Melvyn, *Nutritional Influences on Illness*, Second Edition, Tarzana, CA: Third Line Press, 1993, 296.

30. Gaby, Alan, Vitamin C for gallstone prevention? *Nutrition & Healing*, October 1997; 4(10): 8.

31. Smulian, John, C., M.D., M.P.H., et al, Pica in a rural obstetric population, *Southern Medical Journal*, December, 1995; 88(12): 1236–1240.

32. Schauss, see note 3, 29.

33. Balch, James F., and Balch, Phyllis A., *Prescription for Nutritional Healing*, Garden City, NY: Avery Publishing Group, Inc. 1990, 304.

34. Schauss, Alexander, and Costin, Carolyn, *Zinc and Eating Disorders*, New Canaan, CT: Keats Publishing Co., 1989.

35. Gibson, R. S., Zinc: A critical nutrient in growth and development, *New Zealand Medical Journal*, 1998; 111: 1061.

Brain and Nerves
Chapter 13

1. Blaylock, Russell L., *Excitotoxins*, Santa Fe, New Mexico: Health Press, 1994, 156.

2. Schmidt, Michael, *Smart Fats*, Berkeley, CA: Frog Ltd., 1997, 8.

3. Elizabeth, A. Guillette and others, An anthropological approach to the evaluation of preschool children exposed to pesticides in Mexico, *Environmental Health Perspectives*, June 1998; 106(6): 347–353.

4. Mullenix, Phyllis J.; Denbesten, Pamela; Schunior, Ann; and Kernan, William, Neurotoxicity of sodium fluoride in rats, *Neurotoxicology and Teratology*, 1995; 17(2): 169–177.

5. Tuthill, Robert W. Hair lead levels related to children's classroom attention-deficit behavior, *Archives of Environmental Health*, 1996; 51(3): 214–220.

6. Blaylock, see note 1, 242, (note 201).

7. Leong, C. C. W., Naweed, I. S., Lorscheider, F. L., Retrograde degeneration of neurite membrane structural integrity of nerve growth cones following in vitro exposure to mercury, *Neuroreport*, March 26, 2001; 12(4): 0733–0737. View the video at: http://movies.commons.ucalgary.ca/mercury/. This video can be accessed through a link on the Image Awareness Web Site: www.imageawareness.com.

8. Perlmutter, David, *Brainrecovery.com*, Naples, FL: The Perlmutter Health Center, 2000, 101–105.

9. Gutman, Jimmy and Schettini, Stephen, *Glutathione: Your Body's Most Powerful Healing Agent*, Montreal, Canada: Gutman & Schettini, 1998, 14.

10. Gold, Michael, Plasma and red blood cell thiamine deficiency in patients with dementia of the Alzheimer's type, *Archives of Neurology*, November, 1995; 52: 1081–1085.

11. Blaylock, see note 1, 49.

12. Bernard, Sallie; Enayati, Albert; Binstock, Teresa; Roger, Heidi; Redwood, Lyn; and McGinnis, Woody, *Autism: A Unique Type of Mercury Poisoning*, Cranford, NJ: ARC Research, 2000.

13. Buttar, Rashid, The misdiagnosis of our future generations, U.S. Congressional Sub-Committee Hearing, May 6, 2004.

14. Bernard, S., et al, Autism: A novel form of mercury poisoning, *Medical Hypotheses*, 2001; 56(4): 462–471.

15. Blaylock, Russell, M.D., *Health and Nutrition Secrets That Could Save Your Life*, Albuquerque, NM: Health Press, 2002.

16. Rimland, B., Vitamin C in the prevention and treatment of autism, *Autism Research Review International*, 1998; 12(2): 3. Rimland, Bernard, What is the right 'dosage' for vitamin B6, DMG, and other nutrients useful in autism? *Autism Research Review International*, 1997; 11(4): 3. Autism Research Institute, 4182 Adams Ave., San Diego, CA 92116.

17. Stoll, Andrew, *The Omega-3 Connection*, New York: Simon & Schuster, 2001, 109.

18. Breggin, Peter, *Talking Back to Prozac*, New York: St. Martin's Press, 1994, 96.

19. Hoffer, Abram, and Walker, Morton, *Putting It All Together: The New Orthomolecular Nutrition*, New Canaan, CT: Keats Publishing Co., 1978, 147.

20. Smith, Ronald, S., The macrophage theory of depression, *Medical Hypotheses*, 1991; 35: 298–306.

21. Braly, James and Hoggan, Ron, *Dangerous Grains*, Garden City, NY: Avery Publishing Group, 2002, 192.

22. Christensen, Larry, The role of caffeine and sugar in depression, *Nutrition Report*, March 1991; 9(3): 17, 24.

23. Yudkin, John, *Sweet and Dangerous*, New York: Bantam Books, 1979, 112.

24. Hoffer, see note 19, 101, 150–151.

25. Bland, Jeffrey, *Nutraerobics*, San Francisco: Harper and Row, 1983, 43.

26. Hoffer, see note 19, 38.

27. Mauskop, Alexander and Altura, Burton M., Magnesium for migraine: Rationale for use and therapeutic potential, *CNS Drugs*, March, 1998; 9(3): 185–190. Wright, Jonathan, Migraine headache, *Nutrition & Healing*, May 1995; 2(5): 1.

28. McCarren, T.; Hitzemann, R.; Smith, R., et al, Amelioration of severe migraine by fish oil (omega-3) fatty acids, *American Journal of Clinical Nutrition*, 1985; 41: 874 (Abstract A).

29. Schoenen, J., M.D., Ph.D., et al, Effectiveness of high-dose riboflavin in migraine prophylaxis: A randomized controlled trial, *Neurology*, 1998; 50: 466–470. Wright, Jonathan, Vitamin B2 (riboflavin) and migraine prevention, *Nutrition & Healing*, December 1999; 6(12): 5.

30. Gibb, C. M., et al, Chocolate is a migraine-provoking agent, *Cephalalgia*, 1991; 11: 93–95.

31. Bic, Z., et al, In search of the ideal treatment for migraine headache, *Medical Hypotheses*, 1998; 50: 1–7.

32. Hadjivassiliou, M., et al., Headache and CNS white matter abnormalities associated with gluten sensitivity, *Neurology*, February 13, 2001; 56(3): 385–388.

33. Gabrielle, M., et al., Association between migraine and celiac disease: Results from a case-control and therapeutic study, *American Journal of Gastroenterology*, 2003; 98(3): 626–9.

34. Bruni, O., Galli, F., Guidetti, V., Sleep hygiene and migraine in children and adolescents, *Cephalalgia*, 1999; 19(Suppl 25): 57–59.

35. Wright, Jonathan, Scent of apple relieves migraine, *Nutrition & Healing*, February 1998; 5(2): 7.

36. Gaby, Alan R., Commentary, *Dr. Jonathan V. Wright's Nutrition & Healing*, May 1995; 2(5): 11.

37. Wright, Jonathan, Multiple sclerosis: A revival of hope, *Nutrition and Healing*, October 1999; 6(9): 1-7.

38. Hayes, C. E., Cantorna, M. T., and DeLuca, H. F., Vitamin D and multiple sclerosis, *Proceedings of the Society for Experimental Biology and Medicine*, 1997; 216: 21–27.

39. Cantorna, Margheritia, Vitamin D and autoimmunity: Is vitamin D status an environmental factor affecting autoimmune disease prevalence? *Proceedings of the Society for Experimental Biology and Medicine*, 2000; 223: 230–233.

40. Sicotte, N. L., et al., Treatment of multiple sclerosis with the pregnancy hormone estriol, *Annals of Neurology* 2002; 52: 421–428.

41. Lemon, Henry, Reduced estriol excretion in patients with breast cancer prior to endocrine therapy, *Journal of the American Medical Association*, June 27, 1966; 112–20.

42. Swank, Roy, and Pullen, Mary-Helen, *The Multiple Sclerosis Diet Book*, New York: Doubleday, 1972, 53–57.

43. Smith, R.S., A comprehensive macrophage-T-lymphocyte theory of schizophrenia, *Medical Hypotheses*, 1992; 39: 248–257.

44. Cott, Allan, Controlled fasting treatment for schizophrenia, *Journal of Orthomolecular Psychiatry*, 1974; 3(4): 301–311.

45. Smith, R. S., The GI T-lymphocyte theory of schizophrenia: Some new observations, *Medical Hypotheses*, 1992; 37; 27–30.

46. Osmond, H., and Hoffer, A., Massive niacin treatment in schizophrenia, *Lancet*, Feb. 10, 1962.

47. Hoffer, see note 19, 12–13, 29.

48. Hoffer, Abram, Treatment of schizophrenia, In Williams, Roger and Kalita, Dwight, *A Physician's Handbook on Orthomolecular Medicine*, New York: Pergamon Press, 1977, 84.

49. Rudin, Donald, O., The major psychoses and neuroses as omega-3 essential fatty acid deficiency syndrome: Substrate pellagra, *Biological Psychiatry*, 1981; 16(9): 843.

50. Cheraskin, E.; Ringsdorf, W. M.; and Brecher, Arline, *Psychodietetics*, New York: Bantam Books, 1976, 22.

51. Cheraskin, 89.

52. Pottenger, Francis M., Jr., *Pottenger's Cats*, La Mesa, CA: Price-Pottenger Nutrition Foundation, 1983, 11.

53. Latham, Michael; McGandy, Robert; McCann, Mary; and Stare, Frederick, *Scope Manual on Nutrition*, Kalamazoo, MI: The Upjohn Company, 1975, 43–44.

54. Kalokerinos, Archie, *Every Second Child*, Sydney, Australia: Thomas Nelson, 1974.

55. Franklin, Holland, A possible explanation for SIDS, *The John R. Lee M.D. Medical Letter*, January 2001; 5–6.

56. James, S. J., Cutler, P., et al, Metabolic biomarkers of increased oxidative stress and methylation capacity in children with autism, *American Journal of Clinical Nutrition*, Dec. 2004; 80(6): 1611–1617.

Internal Organs and Conditions
Chapter 14

1. D'Adamo, Peter J., *Eat Right for Your Type*, New York: G. P. Putnam's Sons, 1996. Gaby, Alan, Research review, *Nutrition and Healing*, January 1998; 6(1): 7–8.

2. Yudkin, John, Sugar and disease, *Nature*, Sept. 22, 1972; Vol. 239.

3. Schwartz, Edward, *Endocrines, Organs, and Their Impact*, Maple Valley, WA: Edmar Printing, 1979, 131.

4. Pizzorno, Joseph E., Jr., and Murray, Michael, *Textbook of Natural Medicine*, Vol. I, New York: Churchill Livingstone, 1999, 549.

5. Wright, Jonathan V., Treating weak adrenals, *Nutrition and Healing*, June 1998; 5(6): 1–4.

6. Wright, Jonathan, 4.

7. Schwartz, see note 3, 2.

8. Wright, see note 5, 11.

9. Schwartz, see note 3, 2–3.

10. Jefferies, William, *Safe Uses of Cortisone*, Springfield, IL: Charles C. Thomas, 1981, v–vi.

11. Tintera, John, *Hypoadrenocorticism*, Troy, NY: Adrenal Metabolic Research Society of the Hypoglycemia Foundation, Inc., 1980, 3–8.

12. Hoffer, Abram, *Putting It All together: The New Orthomolecular Nutrition*, New Canaan, CT: Keats Publishing Co., 1996, 44–45.

13. Wright, Jonathan, *Nutrition & Healing*, Nov. 2004; 11(10): 1–3. This newsletter contains an important discussion of the glucose-tolerance-insulin-resistance test (GT-IRT).

14. Hart, Joseph, T., M.D., Subclinical rickets, An unexploited deficiency syndrome, *Int. Journal of Biosocial Research*, 1984; 6(1): 38–43. Also Wright, Jonathan, *Guide to a Nutritionally Oriented Physical Exam*, Phoenix, AZ: Nutrition and Healing, 1999, 3.

15. Plotnikoff, Gregory A., and Quigley, Joanna M., Prevalence of severe hypovitaminosis D in patients with persistent, nonspecific musculoskeletal pain, *Mayo Clinic Proceedings* 2003; 78: 1463–1470.

16. Amand, R. Paul, St., and Marek, Claudia, *What Your Doctor May Not Tell You About Fibromyalgia*, New York: Warner Books, Inc., 1999, 30–38, 47–48, 306, 315.

17. Holick, Michael F., Vitamin D Deficiency: What a Pain It Is, *Mayo Clinic Proceedings* 2003; 78: 1457–1459.

18. Amand, see note 16, 315.

19. Amand, see note 16, 306.

20. Deuster, Patricia and Jaffe, Russell, A novel treatment for fibromyalgia improves clinical outcomes in a community-based study, *Journal of Musculoskeletal Pain*, 1998; 6(2): 133–149.

21. Smith, Ronald, S., The macrophage theory of depression, *Medical Hypotheses*, 1991; 35: 298–306.

22. Cocoa, Arthur F., *The Pulse Test*, New York: Arco Publishing, 1977, 21.

23. Cocoa, 34.

24. Cocoa, 10.

25. Cocoa, 36.

26. Cocoa, 17.

Male and Female Issues
Chapter 15

1. Grant, E. C. G., Hormone replacement therapy and risk of breast cancer, *Journal of the American Medical Association*, May 8, 2002; 287(19): 2360–2361.

2. Charlier, C., Albert A., et al, Breast cancer and serum organochlorine residues, *Occupational and Environmental Medicine*, 2003; 60: 348–351.

3. Zava, D. T., et al, Estrogenic activity of natural and synthetic estrogens in human breast cancer cells in culture, *Environmental Health Perspectives*, April, 1997; 105(Suppl 3): 637–645.

4. Fowke, J. H.; Longcope, C.; and Hebert, J. R., Brassica vegetable consumption shifts estrogen metabolism in healthy postmenopausal women, *Cancer Epidemiology Biomarkers & Prevention*, August 2000; 9: 773–779.

5. Carughi, Arianna, Ph.D., Effect of a flavonoid-rich fruit and vegetable blend on the growth of human breast cancer cells, presentation to the International Society for Free Radical Research, California Chapter 1997 Annual Meeting in Santa Barbara.

6. Sharoni, Y., et al, Effects of lycopene-enriched tomato oleoresin on 7, 12-dimethyl-benz-[a]anthracene-induced rat mammary tumors, *Cancer Detection and Prevention* 1997; 21(2): 118–123.

7. Minton, J. P., et al, Caffeine, cyclic nucleotides, and breast disease, *Surgery*, July, 1979; 86(1): 105–109. Minton J. P., et al, Clinical and biochemical studies on methylxanthine-related fibrocystic breast disease, *Surgery*, August, 1981; 90(2): 299–304.

8. Odenheimer, D. J., et al, Risk factors for benign breast disease: A case-control study of discordant twins, *American Journal of Epidemiology*, 1984; 120(4): 565–571.

9. Boyle, C. A., et al, Caffeine consumption and fibrocystic breast disease: A case-control epidemiologic study, *Journal of the National Cancer Institute*, May, 1984; 72(5): 1015–1019.

10. Rose, D. P., et al, Lowfat diet in fibrocystic disease of the breast with cyclical mastalgia: A feasibility study, *American Journal of Clinical Nutrition*, 1985; 41(4–6(Abstract)):856.

11. Myers, John, Iodine and trace elements in the promotion and maintenance of metabolic excellence, in Myers, John, and Schutte, Karl, *Metabolic Aspects of Health*, Kentfield, CA: Discovery Press, 1979, 288–289.

12. Ghent, W. R., et al, Iodine replacement in fibrocystic disease of the breast, *Canadian Journal of Surgery*, October, 1993; 36(5): 453–460.

13. Ghent, W. R., Choose molecular iodine to treat fibrocystic breast disease, *Modern Medicine*, April 1994; 62: 54, 57. Iodine replacement in fibrocystic disease of the breast, *Canadian Journal of Surgery*, October 1993; 36: 453–460.

14. Krouse, T. B., et al, Age-related changes resembling fibrocystic disease in iodine-blocked rat breasts, *Archives of Pathology & Laboratory Medicine*, November, 1979; 103: 631–634.

15. Ghent, see note 12, 453–460.

16. Lee, John, M.D.; Zava, David; and Hopkins, Virginia, *What Your Doctor May Not Tell You About Breast Cancer*, New York: Time Warner, 2002, 79, 155.

17. Pizzorno, Joseph, and Murray, Michael, *Textbook of Natural Medicine*, Volume 2, 2nd Ed., New York: Churchill Livingston, 1999, 1238.

18. London, R. S., et al., Endocrine parameters and alpha-tocopherol therapy in patients with mammary dysplasia, *Cancer Research* 41(9 Pt 2): 3811–13, 1981.

19. Wright, Jonathan V., and Lenard, Lane, *Maximize Your Vitality & Potency*, Petaluma, CA: Smart Publications, 1999, 153–169, 173–201.

20. Wright, Jonathan, Before you reach for saw palmetto…, *Nutrition & Healing*, October 1998; 5(10): 8.

21. Pasta, pizza and the prostate, *Newsweek*, December 18, 1995; 61.

22. Raloff, Janet, Prostate protection? This is fishy, *Science News*, June 23, 2001; 159: 392. Also, Terry, P, Lichtenstein, P, et al, Fatty fish consumption and risk of prostate cancer, *Lancet*, June 2, 2001; 357: 1764–1766.

23. Hsing, A. W., Chokkalingam A. P., et al, Allium vegetables and risk of prostate cancer: A population-based study, *Journal of the National Cancer Institute*, November 6, 2002; 94(21): 1648–1651.

24. Kristal, A. R., Lampe J. W., Brassica vegetables and prostate cancer risk: A review of the epidemiological evidence, *Nutrition and Cancer*, 2002; 42(1): 1–9.

25. Rogers, Sherry, *Detoxify or Die*, Sarasota, FL: Sand Key Company, 2002, pp. 47–8.26. Nelson, M. A., Reid M., et al, Prostate cancer and selenium, *Urologic Clinics of North America*, 2002; 29: 67–70.

27. Wright, Jonathan, The easiest way to reduce your prostate cancer risk by 41 percent, *Nutrition & Healing*, January 2003; 10(1): 7.

28. Kime, Zane, *Sunlight Could Save Your Life*, Penryn, CA: World Health Publications, 1980, 36–38.

29. Holick, Michael, and Jenkins, Mark, *The UV Advantage*, New York: I Books, 2003, 96–99. Luscombe, C. J., et al, Exposure to ultraviolet radiation: Association with susceptibility and age at presentation with prostate cancer, *Lancet* 358(9282): 641–2.

30. Wilt, T. J., Beta-sitosterol for the treatment of benign prostatic hyperplasia: a systematic review, *BJU International*, June 1999; 83(9): 976–83.

31. Fagelman, E., Lowe F. C., Herbal medications in the treatment of benign prostatic hyperplasia (BPH), *Urologic Clinics of North America*, 2002; 29: 23–29.

32. Awad, A. B.; Fink, C. S.; Williams, H.; Kim, U., In vitro and in vivo (SCID mice) effects of phytosterols on the growth and dissemination of human prostate cancer PC-3 cells, *European Journal of Cancer Prevention*, Dec. 2001; 10(6): 507–13.

33. Awad, A. B.; Chan, K. C.; Downie, A. C.; and Fink, C. S., Peanuts as a source of beta-sitosterol, a sterol with anticancer properties, *Nutrition and Cancer*, 2000; 36(2): 238–41.

34. Kennedy, A. R., The evidence for soybean products as cancer preventative agents, *Journal of Nutrition*, Mar. 1995; 125(3 Suppl): 733S–743S.

35. Meynell, Paul, Role of lipids, *Herald of Health*, 1959.

36. Bland, Jeff, *Improving Genetic Expression in the Prevention of the Diseases of Aging*, Gig Harbor, WA: Healthcomm, 1998, 88.

37. Lithgow, D. M. and Politzer, W. M., Vitamin A in the treatment of menorrhagia, *South African Medical Journal*, 1977; 51: 191.

38. Wright, Jonathan, Vitamin A and heavy menstrual bleeding, *Nutrition and Healing*, January 1999; 6(1): 7.

39. Smith, Charles, M.D., Non-hormonal control of vaso-motor flushing in menopausal patients, *Chicago Medicine*, March 7, 1964; 76: 193-5.

40. Gaby, Alan, Brewer's yeast for premenstrual syndrome, *Nutrition & Healing*, March 1998; 5(3): 7.

41. Holick, Michael, see note 29, 136. Anderson, D. J., et al, Preliminary trial of photic stimulation for premenstrual syndrome, *Journal of Obstetrics and Gynecology*, 1997; 17(1): 76–79.

42. West, Stanley, and Dranov, Paula, *The Hysterectomy Hoax*, New York: Doubleday, 1994.

43. Lee, John, and Hopkins, Virginia, *What Your Doctor May Not Tell You About Menopause*, New York: Warner Books, 1996, 40.

44. Fried, Robert; Merrel, Woodson; and Thornton, James, *The Arginine Solution*, New York: Warner Books, 1999, 5, 152–5, 202–208.

45. Pizzorno, Joseph Jr., and Murray, Michael, *Textbook of Natural Medicine*, Vol. II, Edinburgh: Churchill Livingstone, 1999, 1274–5.

46. Das, Indrajit, et al, Arginine is not responsible for the activation of nitric oxide synthase by garlic, *Journal of Ethnopharmacology*, 1996; 53: 5–9.

Index

Hypothyroid 123

Hysterectomy 164, 241, 251

Ice, craving 142, 180

IGF-1 50

IL-1 215, 221

IL-2 221

Immunization 30–31, 210, 212, 225

Impotence iv, 240, 244, 251–252

INF-α 215

Inositol 43, 162

Insulin 5, 20–21, 24–27, 50–51, 156–157, 167, 227–228, 231–234

Insulin-like growth factor 50

Iodine 95, 99–102, 122, 124, 239, 241–243

IQ 206

Iron 30–31, 78, 83, 127, 137, 141–143, 150, 167–168, 180–181, 200, 248, 250

Ishii, Toshiharu 63

Jaffe, Russell 97, 234

Jefferies, William 230

Jerome, Frank 88

Jonez, Hinton 219

Kajander, Olavi 179

Kalokerinos 224–225

Kauffman, William 83, 109

Kennedy, John 39

Kidney iv, 41, 53, 54, 85, 91, 107, 112–113, 132–136, 147, 162, 165, 178–179, 234–235

Kidney stones iv, 91, 132–135, 147, 165, 178–179, 235

Kissebah, Ahmed 26

Knapp, Arthur 52

Koch, Robert 45

Kunin, Richard 101

Kupffer cells 100

Larson, Eric 25

Latex 111

Lauryl sulfate 78

Lead 29, 105, 113, 162, 208, 211, 218, 234

Lee, John 108, 164, 241, 243

Leg cramps iv, 99, 157, 158, 160, 167–168

Leg, discolored skin iv, 21, 143, 157, 162

Legs, bowed 154, 157, 164

Legs, restless iv, 99, 142, 160, 167–168, 231

Legs, weak 171

Lemon, Henry 175, 200–201, 220

Lesko, Samuel 30

Levine, Norman 143

Levine, Stephen 70

Lhermitte's 96

Libby, Alfred 3, 35

Lichstein, Edgar 63

Lincoln, Abraham 39

Lithgow 248

Lithium 166, 216

Liver, dessicated 56

Liver, enzyme 20

Long Face Syndrome iii, 61, 67–71, 156

Lorscheider, Fritz 209

Louis XIV 187

Lowell, Keith 119

Lumps, breast iv, 101, 123, 239–243

Lupus 107–108, 122, 147

Lutein 48–49

Lycopene 241, 245, 248

Lyme disease 133

Lysine 78–79, 121, 252

Macrophage 215

Macular degeneration iii, 40, 42, 48–51, 58

Magnesium 32, 55, 57, 67–68, 77, 98–99, 119, 131, 132–138, 140, 154, 158–160, 164–168, 171, 175, 178, 179, 180, 184, 195–196, 200, 211–212, 217–218, 221, 232, 234, 250–251

Mandell, Marshall 23, 192

Manganese 124, 214, 242

SSRI 214

Sternlieb, Jack 63

Stiffness iv, 98–99, 128, 134, 139, 145–146, 160, 168–169, 172, 195, 234

Stitt, Paul 22, 190

Stockton, Susan 79, 80

Stoll, Andrew 215

Stomach acid iv, 45–49, 96–97, 118, 124–125, 136, 142, 160, 164–165, 168, 175–176, 181–182, 192–195, 199–201

Stomach acid, self-test iv, 47, 136, 164, 200

Stone, Irwin 3, 35

Stool, bulk and transit time iv, 170, 176–178, 181

Stranges, Saverio 20

Stretch marks iii, 120, 121

Sudden Infant Death Syndrome iv, 72, 224

Sugar 4–5, 10, 14–16, 21–27, 32–34, 37, 40–41, 46, 50–51, 58–62, 66, 71–72, 76, 85, 89–93, 106–115, 119–120, 127, 132, 135, 141, 143, 154, 157–168, 172, 178, 180–181, 189–192, 196–203, 208, 211, 214–218, 224, 228, 230–231, 234–235, 251

Sulforaphane 46, 49, 58

Sulfur 87, 97, 213, 246

Sun 103, 111, 113, 116, 130, 219, 246

Sunscreen 37, 111, 154, 233

Sunlight 27, 37, 41, 93, 96, 105, 114, 154–156, 172, 219–220, 233, 235, 239–240, 244, 246

Swank, Roy 220

Sweating 104, 155, 159, 249

Swelling iii, 53–54, 61, 95, 99, 112, 129, 132, 143, 145–147, 171, 227, 231, 240, 243–244

Syndrome X 20–21, 231

Tartar iii, 77, 90–92, 135, 179, 235

Tea tree oil 111

Temperature, underarm iii, 81, 122, 123

Tetracycline 133–134, 179

Thiamine 56, 112–113, 170–171, 189, 211, 216

Thimerisol 210, 212

Thyroid 22, 37, 71–72, 81, 95, 99–102, 123–124, 127–128, 143, 160, 164–165, 229, 242–243

Tingling 145–146, 159, 161, 195, 218

Tintera, John 89, 197–198, 230

TNF 24, 235

Toe, pain iv, 165, 234–235

Tongue, geographic or fissured iii, 82–83, 98, 109, 114

Tongue, scalloped iii, 89

Tooth decay iii, 15, 50–51, 84–93, 147, 156

Triglycerides, high iv, 66, 231

Trujillo, Nelson 44

Tryptophan 34, 214, 216, 222, 250

Tuckey, Hugh 194

Tumor necrosis factor-alpha 24

Tuthill 208

Tyrosine 34, 89, 122, 143, 229, 242

Ulcers 11, 44–47, 78, 193, 202

Upper body weight gain iii, 21–27, 51, 115, 120, 140, 157, 162

Uric acid 165–166

Urination, frequent iv, 157, 183, 244

Urine, pink iv, 142, 180, 200

Urine, yellow iv, 80, 182–185

Varicose veins iv, 169–178, 181, 185

Vitamin A 42, 50–53, 62, 105–110, 118, 240, 248

Vitamin B12 54, 67, 83, 95–97, 102, 124–125, 141, 160–162

Vitamin B6 55, 71, 78, 93, 121, 127, 136–140, 145–150, 160, 164, 169, 178, 180, 195–197, 212, 214, 216, 222, 234, 250–251

Vitamin C 3, 16, 32, 35–36, 41, 46, 55–56, 64–67, 70, 76–77, 87–89, 106–107, 117, 120–125, 131–132, 142, 157–158, 166–167, 170, 175, 178, 184, 199, 210, 212, 221–229, 231, 234, 240, 250

Vitamin D 27, 36–37, 52, 68, 77, 93, 115, 144, 154–156, 164, 167, 170–171, 210, 218–220, 232–235, 239, 244–246, 248, 250

Vitamin E 64–65, 91–92, 105, 107, 114, 115, 119, 122, 141, 158, 160, 161, 163, 166, 167, 168, 170, 210, 243, 245, 250, 251

Vitiligo iii, 37, 124–125